THE
# WOMEN'S SHARP REVENGE

And from the soul three faculties arise,
The mind, the will, the power; then wherefore shall
A woman have her intellect in vain,
Or not endeavour knowledge to attain?
                    (Rachel Speght, 1621)

# THE
# WOMEN'S SHARP REVENGE

Five Women's Pamphlets from the Renaissance

*edited by Simon Shepherd*

ST. MARTIN'S PRESS   NEW YORK

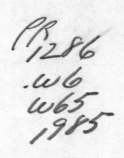

Printed in Great Britan

First published in the United States of America in 1985

ISBN 0–312–88796–5

# Contents

# Foreword

I am a male editor of some female pamphlets, a man muscling in on what women have made. I am aware of the argument that someone needed to bring this writing to light sooner rather than later, but in this patriarchal society I am a man in a controlling position and thus perpetuate part of that society.

I have committed heresy with the text. The trend in modern editing has been to present the original text as authentically as possible. I have made some changes to what the authors wrote in order to make their pamphlets more readable now. Spelling has been modernised ('murder' not 'murther'), but archaic forms have been kept ('scurril' not 'scurrilous'); punctuation has been neatened, reorganised and clarified according to present-day taste – Jacobean sentences were often very long and punctuated mainly with commas; I have retained the Jacobean practice of singular verb and plural noun (and vice versa); where Latin is translated by the authors it is in round brackets, where the translation is mine or taken from Loeb editions it is in square brackets; Greek has been removed from the text (with one exception) and replaced by the authors' or my translations; where pamphlets were printed with errata I have incorporated these and corrected other likely misprints; proper names are corrected to recognised spelling; where authors supply textual references (e.g., to the Bible) I have supplied missing details or corrections – I have not corrected misquotations; God has a capital but the divine 'him' does not (except in one place for emphasis). Some of the allusions are very difficult to trace – the Renaissance used various and often inaccurate histories of the ancient world: I would be grateful for any additional information.

The book is organised as follows: a general introduction airs some of the major issues; each pamphlet is prefaced by a more specific introductory note and is followed by a glossary. All the pamphlets are framed by some short extracts which reflect on the 'nature' and 'place' of women. There is a short bibliography.

My thanks go to Alan Sommerstein, of the Classics Department

7

of Nottingham University, for helping with the Greek. To Maureen Bell for alerting me to the importance of printers, thanks with love.

# Introduction

If some law-courts and most rapists are to be believed, women's clothing is worn specifically to provoke men. This idea, if so it can be called, is part of a long dishonourable tradition in masculine attitudes to women. So vigorous is the tradition that this sort of accusation against women is widely accepted without much question. What is all too frequently questioned is a woman's anger at being thus accused. But the woman's anger has its own tradition, although this tradition, not surprisingly, has been hidden. There is a grim familiarity, even over 350 years, in the words of Ester Sowernam:

> When men complain of beauty and say that 'women's dressings and attire are provocations to wantonness and baits to allure men', it is a direct means to know of what disposition they are. It is a shame for men in censuring of women to condemn themselves.

This quotation is far from untypical of the pamphlets collected here, and is thus a small indication of their importance. So much sense has been buried for so long. There *were* voices of protest in the dim days of Donne and Sidney: little glimmers in the dark ages of patriarchal Renaissance literature. These pamphlets are some women's response to being written about, described, loved, poeticised, catered for. I hope, then, that their republication will extend slightly further our sense of the history of women's writing and assist our understanding of the issues and battles that shaped that history.

The modern reader will not, however, find feminist writing. Broadly, there are two major lines of argument which go to make up the women's case as presented in this collection. The first is a long way from feminism: it consists basically of lists of chaste women, honourable women, courageous women, fruitful mothers, virtuous daughters, pious widows. What links all of these women is that they are acceptable to a male world, acceptable because they have carried out proficiently the tasks allotted to them by a patriarchal society. This line of argument solicits approval from its patriarchal audience for these 'good girls'. The other argument does no such soliciting. Not only does it assert that women as a whole can do things just as well as men, but it analyses how male values and power function in culture and society. It suggests that men have to change and that the sexual power structure is irrational and should be dismantled. Sowernam again:

> if a man abuse a maid and get her with child, no matter is made of it – but as a trick of youth; but it is made so heinous an offence in the maid that she is disparaged and utterly undone by it...forbear to charge women with faults which come from the contagion of masculine serpents.

These pamphlets are far from being the only examples of women's writing from the period 1580–1640. There were a number of aristocratic female poets; there were women who wrote on 'womanly' subjects such as the upbringing of children – what Dorothy Leigh calls *The Mother's Blessing* – and there were women who wrote religious or meditational works, such as Alice Sutcliffe's *Meditations of Man's Mortality* (1634) or Rachel Speght's second work, *Mortality's Memorandum*. The pamphlets collected here, however, have been reprinted because they determine to take issue with some of the ideas popularised by contemporary male writing. As they all say, their specific purpose is to counter male satirical attacks on women. These sorts of supposedly witty assaults on women are common throughout the Renaissance period, and male authors themselves often undertook the defence of women. There are cases, not unexpected, of the same man writing both an attack and a defence of women (Edward Gosynhill did this in 1540), which suggests that the pamphleteers anticipated an audience willing to buy such works. But in the history of what I shall call gender controversy the only women to participate, it seems, are those included here. These women authors are doing something unusual.

It is the authors themselves who insist on the strangeness of women writing. Ester Sowernam apologises for her sex:

> If in this answer I do use more vehement speeches than may seem to correspond the natural disposition of a woman, yet all judicious readers shall confess that I use more mildness than the cause I have in hand provoketh me unto.

Rachel Speght talks of being 'young and the unworthiest of thousands'; Jane Anger refers to herself throughout as a woman. To write this type of pamphlet is to take a step into the frequently

savage world of male satire. It is a much more public world than
that of the female poets (or, indeed, than that of the rare female
dramatist, Lady Elizabeth Cary, author of a 'closet' drama). When
the pamphlet authors talk of their audience, they are frequently
scathing: 'that base and ignoble applause, proceeding from the
giddy-headed plebeians'. To talk of the base, the foolish and the
vulgar is very much in the tradition of the Roman satirists, it has
almost a classical respectability; but I would suggest that the sort of
descriptions employed here *also* proceed from a sense of alienation
from the audience. I shall try to elaborate on this idea of alienation.

There seem to be two particular difficulties about writing specifically for the wider audience of pamphlets and the stage (as
opposed to the more intimate address of poetry). For a start,
women usually received very little formal education. The well
educated women of the period are isolated examples. Our authors
feel that there is a genuine grievance here: it is, for example, well
stated in *The Women's Sharp Revenge* (a rare such moment
admittedly, but good all the same): 'If we be taught to read, they
then confine us within the compass of our mother's tongue, and
that limit we are not suffered to pass.' Women were not, in general,
trained to muster quotations, to analyse grammar, to write for a
public. And if they were trained to do this, they were not widely
encouraged to make use of their new-found skills. So these pamphleteers had to demonstrate their education. They deliberately
display the breadth of their reading, a close knowledge of the Bible
and the classics, an ability to quote in Latin and Greek. All of this
can make the texts difficult going for modern readers but it is proper
to see their style as a gesture, a gesture telling us about intellectual
potential and the equality of ability. The way they write is often a
blend of over-anxious phrase-making and a sense of triumph in the
conquering of literary style. When it works, it produces marvellous
turns of phrase which sparkle with a refreshing directness.

The second difficulty in facing a wider audience is a rather subtler
psychological one. In a world where men were largely thought of as
active and creative, women were frequently limited to a non-
productive role. (Note that here I am talking about received ideas
and theories about gender role in society: in reality, plenty of
women manufactured goods or ran shops or pubs.) The woman
existed supposedly to marry, to give birth, and to keep quiet. Her
marriage prospects were assessed on the basis of her reputation (not
all fathers could afford to tempt suitors with huge dowries). A
woman would not get far in the marriage market if she was *said to
be* a witch or a whore. Notice that it is the woman who is spoken
about; she herself was not meant to be a speaker. The woman who
did speak out, who cursed or yelled or argued with men, was said to
be a scold or a shrew and regarded as little better than a whore. So a
woman's 'value', which in fact meant her social place and, eventual-

ly, her sense of herself, derived from what the 'world' said about her. Her reputation depended rather more upon other people's verbal assessments of her than upon her own capabilities.

If we read over the opinions of the various moralists, playwrights or commentators who had something to say about gender roles we move towards the conclusion that a woman's social and psychological well-being depended somewhat precariously on the verbal approbation of others. Joseph Swetnam advises men about to marry:

> before thou put thy foot out of doors make diligent enquiry of her behaviour (for by the market-folk thou shalt hear how the market goeth): for by enquiry thou shalt hear whether she be wise, virtuous and kind, wearing but her own proper hair and such garments as her friend's estate will afford, or whether she love to keep within the house and to the servants have a watchful eye.

If she attempted to question or refute this judgement of her, she very quickly would be branded a scold and lose her status. Not only was she socially and economically controlled, she was trapped by language, a victim of talk: imprisoned by patriarchal discourse. What follows from this is that a woman's style of life and her sense of herself could be altered whenever what was said about her changed. If she was suddenly the subject of scandal she could become an outcast, rejected not only from the marriage market but from the community at large (witness the case of witches). Hear Joseph Swetnam again:

> it behoveth every woman to have a great regard to her behaviour and to keep herself out of the fire, knowing that a woman of suspected chastity liveth but in a miserable case: for there is but small difference by being naught and being thought naught.

In grasping this, we go some way towards explaining seventeenth-century women's repeated attacks on slander and slanderers. To invent scandal about women or falsely to accuse them may be a male joke but it destroys the life of the woman. On the stage there are female characters who angrily attack the damaging power of slander, but they are unreal women, fictional characters played by boys. Our pamphleteers are answering back as women. They are stepping, very consciously, into a risky and dangerous world:

> you surmised that, inveighing against poor illiterate women, we might fret and bite the lip at you; we might repine to see ourselves baited and tossed in a blanket, but never durst in open view of the vulgar either disclose your blasphemous and deroga-

tive slanders or maintain the untainted purity of our glorious sex. Nay, you'll put gags in our mouths and conjure us all to silence; you will first abuse us, then bind us to the peace.

It is a dangerous world because of the nature of its language; gossip is irresponsible, slander is intangible. And what adds to the difficulty is the ever-present knowledge of not being taken seriously, of being dismissed as a shrew or a scold.

When these female pamphleteers publish they are writing in the medium associated with witty slander and anti-woman jokes. Thus they are caught: they write introductory epistles or poems deliberately addressed to women, but the texts of the pamphlets suggest that they are written with men in mind. This awareness, produced perhaps by writing for what is in many ways a hostile medium and by their alienation – as women – from the world of the satirists, leads these authors to make a simple but important point. All of this satire, all of these poems, are male. The women have identified the gender origins of the culture: it is male-produced. Everything from soggy love poetry to fanatic invective is male-centred. In this world, women are literary objects, the attacked, the adored, the addressed, the done to. When the women attack male love poets it is the selfish insincerity of the men's emotions that they note. A favourite example is that of the male lover undyingly avowing his death for love. This parade of poetic emotion takes no regard of the woman it is addressed to. Male authors invent the psychological and sexual life of the woman for her. As Jane Anger notes:

> For let us look, they will straight affirm that we love: and if then lust pricketh them, they will swear that love stingeth us; which imagination only is sufficient to make them essay the scaling of half a dozen of us in one night, when they will not stick to swear that if they should be denied of their requests death must needs follow.

Woman are the fictions of male writing; the fictions here fight back. And woman is not just the image adored, she is also the abused. Jane Anger again: 'men gloze [talk persuasively] till they have their answers, which are the end of their travail, and then bid modesty adieu and, entertaining rage, fall a-railing on us which never hurt them.' The underside of male flattery is male violence. Here in the middle of the 'golden age' of English letters the sexism of much of that writing is exposed and mocked.

The foundations for a women's critique of culture are laid in these pamphlets. At one level, of course, they are simply effective blows in the battle of satire (Anger is particularly good at producing mocking images of men, Munda at turning to her own use the language of Roman satirists), but we should also see a deeper dimension. In their separate ways, the women attempt to dismantle the sort of writing that oppresses them. Speght calls to her aid a basic training in grammar in order to pull apart her opponent, Swetnam's, prose, and thus his assertions. She is marshalling to the aid of women's interests specifically the general rudiments of Elizabethan education. Munda pushes Speght's detailed work on grammar into a wider arena. She spots the contradictions in the assumed role and image, the discourse, of manliness. She says that the same opponent, Swetnam, attacks scolds, yet Swetnam himself admits that his need to write the pamphlet is like the shrew who can only satisfy herself by talking. From this it follows: 'A man that is accounted a scold hath great discredit; Joseph Swetnam is accounted a scold; *Ergo*, Joseph hath great discredit.' She locates the basic irrationality: a man cannot attack scolds and still justify himself as a male satirist. The only difference in kind between a female scold and a male satirist is gender, and equality of gender is the one thing Swetnam wants to suppress. This suppression leads him into irrational and indefensible positions.

Speght, Sowernam and Munda all use this machinery of the logical syllogism. One effect of this is to demonstrate that they can use effectively logical modes, but its function is also subtler. Many satirical battles tended to fall into the pattern of a steady but single-minded escalation, which consisted of exchanging ever more damaging insults, ever slicker turns of phrase. The structure of this pattern often excludes a re-examination of the fundamental assumptions behind the satirists' arguments. Indeed, many assumptions are shared between antagonists. These women pamphleteers do, however, attempt to explore *how* Swetnam's arguments are shaped. They employ the mechanics of logic to lay bare some of the thinking which underlies his prose. Thus they expose some of the habits of thought about the sexes that more usually remained hidden: 'This antithesis you have found in some author betwixt a warrior and a lover, and you stretch it to show the difference betwixt a man and a woman.'

In Munda, the most obviously 'learned' of the authors, the attack on male writing extends to reflect on the commercialism of that writing. She complains about the improper portrayal of women on stage, just to please an audience. She attacks the abuse of printing, a medium which, she says, should serve higher ends, in the production of satirical writings. There is very much a sense that she has seen the links between male writer and male audience: that they share the same assumptions in a closed and mutually assuring world. Women are the objects talked about in this world while being personally mainly excluded from it – 'poor illiterate women', as Munda says. It is the sense of the exploitation of women for amusement that gives the edge to Munda's references to the 'vulgar' audience – that they provide an unthinking market for the worst misrepresentations of women.

The female authors are adept at dismantling their opponents' logic, correcting their grammar, picking up their mistakes of scholarship. The end this serves is to show how the image of manliness is constructed: Anger tells her readers that men fancy themselves as little game cocks, Munda shows how Swetnam invents attributes he thinks 'proper' to his sex. Masculinity is seen to be partly a product of language. So it should follow that by looking closely at language we can arm ourselves to demolish some of the pretences of masculinity. The problem then is how to make us critical of assumptions that the world (that is, the world run by men) uses without thinking. We need to acquire fresh perspectives on a language which carries the claims and imagery of masculinity.

Several tactics are employed. The first is to repeat phrases until they become nonsensical. Anger uses and re-uses the title of the book she attacks: *His Surfeit in Love*. The careful repetition of that word 'surfeit' prompts us to ask about the attitude it implies. The Swetnam-baiters make endless play with the image of bear-baiting, as we would expect. But they also pick up another useful phrase. Swetnam speaks of himself 'in the rough of my fury' against women. When first used this phrase is printed with 'ruff'. This possibly accidental pun is deliberately reiterated by the women writers. Thus it acquires more significant force for their purposes. The idea of a 'ruff of fury' implies the fury is a piece of dressing-up, a pose. The phrase was so useful to the women because, while Swetnam was claiming to be the sincerely angry male author, he was seen to put on a role. The manly righteousness thus implodes ridiculously.

Puns are useful. Speght has one or two dreadful ones (as/ass; wonderfool); I suspect Munda of a nice one: as printed, the word 'malcontent' is spelt 'malecontent' – a neat bundle of meanings. Puns perform a function similar to repetition – they make us aware of the words we are reading. They break our perhaps uncritical involvement in the argument and force us to notice the choice of language. This is especially useful when countering pamphlets that seek to create an author's voice full of sound and fury. We need to be able to deconstruct that sound and fury.

There is a third way of calling attention to the way language works. An obvious example of this is where Munda quotes what she calls Swetnam's doggerel verse. But what is printed as verse in Swetnam's text is not what Munda quotes. Instead, she has noticed that some of his sentences have internal rhymes. These she has plucked out from various places in the text and cobbled together into a 'poem'. This has two effects. Embedded within the uniform flow of the prose argument, the hackneyed ideas tend to acquire tacit acceptance and escape special scrutiny. But prised loose from their prose and stripped, thus, of their spurious dignity, the ideas are shown to us anew in the shape of a nursery jingle. And they stand revealed as rubbish. Again, by linking together quotations drawn from various parts of the pamphlet Munda demonstrates that there is very little logical development to the argument: Swetnam simply repeats his second-hand ideas. A similar demystifying device is the use of logical syllogisms. As these are arranged on the page, certain phrases are offset, which makes us reconsider those phrases in isolation; and they look pathetic, sitting there shivering in a syllogism.

These are not perhaps unconventional techniques of satire, but the important point is that they are being used in women's interests. I see no reason to suppose that the authors did not know what they were doing with the language of satire. They certainly knew where they stood with regard to literary tradition. Eminent classical authors are arraigned for being anti-female, which might strike the modern reader as a little illiberal, but these women were writing in a world which did not practise the techniques of feminist criticism on traditional texts: there was no room for the benefit of the doubt. And while Sophocles and Euripides are cast out of the window, Hipparchia and Aspasia are brought in. If Hipparchia and Aspasia are unfamiliar names, that surely makes one of the points about the classical tradition. There is a need to establish or bring into the light the largely concealed tradition of female writing – a task begun by these women pamphleteers and continued in the modern antholo- gies of female painters and writers. In a similar way, stories from the Bible about women are given a privileged place. Today we might find the attention to the Bible somewhat excessive, but it was a highly influential book in the Renaissance. Major moral and political arguments were conducted in the language of religion, and it was an important step to be able to demonstrate that the Bible, that repository of law and morality, credits women with the ability to govern and to make laws.

The rejection of traditional classical authors proceeded directly from the writers' involvement with the culture of their own day. But it is symptomatic of a broader way of thinking. Traditional prescriptions for women's role have also to be thrown out. The only weapons that can be employed against tradition, custom, received ideas are logical deduction and the experience of everyday life. Ester Sowernam repeats her claim that she argues by direct proof; the pamphlets contrast quotations from 'authorities' with tales taken from 'daily' life; the words 'experience' or 'daily experience' recur. When Rachel Speght creates an allegory of her intellectual development, she describes how she is not well, she is affected by Ignorance; she asks Thought how to be cured and Thought recommends Experience who is to be found in Age. She eventually approaches Knowledge through Experience. Direct proof and experience are sources of knowledge which may be opposed to the formal, received opinions of the 'authorities' and tradition. The women, pre-eminently the women, are familiar with the clash between the formulae for behaviour and the reality of living.

I am inclined to draw a loose parallel between this early development of women's critique of tradition and contemporary developments in scientific thought. The major movement in scientific practice was to reject Aristotle and the classical authorities which were still largely being taught in the universities (always in the forefront of learning!). In place of traditional explanations for the material world, that world was now newly observed, tested and experimented upon. Rules were formulated on the basis of experiment; the emphasis was on practical demonstration. One of the ideas most frequently attacked was 'custom'. Custom was tradition, the way things had always been done, the dead hand of the past. The author of *Haec Vir* (1620), a pamphlet that set out to defend women's right to wear men's clothes, said 'Custom is an idiot'. New thought had to break with custom.

In their attitudes to the pressure of 'custom' these pamphlets are shaped by the sex of their authors. In a culture where education, and hence progressive thought, are male-dominated less privileged women are left to the precepts of traditional wisdom. The female authors here often think in traditional ways; their lived experience, on the other hand, leads them to reject some of that tradition, that 'custom'. The texts are thus a battle-ground, and we need to read them attentively in order to appreciate just how much constricting thought the authors have thrown off.

To counter traditional beliefs most effectively we have to construct alternative systems of ideas. The women clearly did not like Swetnam's assumptions about women's 'nature'; he quotes Moses:

> He also saith that they were made of the rib of a man, and that their froward nature showeth; for a rib is a crooked thing good for nothing else, and women are crooked by nature, for small occasion will cause them to be angry.

This leaves the women with the problem of defining women's 'nature'. For if women are not, patently not, what males say they are, then what are they? The definition of female 'nature' is argued along two lines: the first and most important is the reconsideration of the story of the creation of woman, to see what God intended; the second involves a reassessment of femaleness in nature. In effect, two questions are woven together here: what is woman's proper social place in the world – that is, what was she made for? – and secondly: what is the difference between male and female? On the one hand social role, on the other natural characteristics: we could employ the modern distinction between socialised gender and biological sex.

To exemplify the distinction we might take two moments of analysis. Here is Sowernam, again laying the stress on the 'real':

> Nature in her vehement motions is not deceived with apparent shows. It is natural, they will say, for the male to follow the female. So it is as natural for the female to be better than the male, as appeareth to be true in observation of hawks: the spar-hawk is of more esteem than the musket; the goshawk more excellent than the tercel; so in falcons the females do excel.

An analysis of femaleness in nature, of biological sex, demonstrates that women should not be socially subjugated. The use of 'natural' evidence strips away assumptions about socialised gender, 'what woman is' socially. It is a way of refuting prescriptions for woman's social place.

To come at the problem in a different way, here is Speght talking about woman's original role in society: 'The other end for which woman was made was to be a companion and helper for man: and if she must be an *helper*, and but an *helper*, then are those husbands to be blamed which lay the whole burden of domestical affairs and maintenance on the shoulders of their wives.' Here the redefinition of woman's role comes from a correct understanding of God's purpose. (Elsewhere Speght too uses analogies from male and female birds to show how husband must help wife – a rather gentler application of the nature analogy than Sowernam's.)

The two ways of looking at the 'nature' of woman come together in the Adam and Eve story. Modern readers may find repeated inspection of this myth rather tedious, but it is a central text in any discussion about God's purpose, nature, society, evil. Above all, it was a text used against women – for example, Swetnam's use of the crooked rib. There is much witty play here on the story of woman's creation from a finer substance than man (he out of mud, she from a rib), and on woman as the last and most perfect of God's works, completing what was left unfinished in man. This undercuts the use patriarchal society makes of the creation story; it feminises the creation myth. Once we acknowledge the women's accounts of Eden we have to start redrawing parts of the literary map. For instance, *Paradise Lost*, written some years later, can be seen to be a text that is much more troubled about Eve than is at first apparent. Milton's more traditional remarks about the process of the Fall exist in a tense, if not contradictory, relationship with his attempts to think through its implications about gender power. The Eden story is particularly effective in producing a positive female perspective and value. Speght tells us

> the final cause or end for which woman was made was to glorify
> God, and to be a collateral companion for man to glorify God, in
> using her body and all the parts, powers and faculties thereof as
> instruments for his honour.

The same point is made by others. What it amounts to is a positive
pleasure in woman's body. This is a vital moment of self-
appreciation and self-respect in a world that took a witty delight in
maligning women's bodies. Swetnam:

> a woman which is fair in show is foul in condition, she is like
> unto a glow-worm which is bright in the hedge and black in the
> hand; in the greenest grass lieth hid the greatest serpents; painted
> pots commonly hold deadly poison; and in the clearest water the
> ugliest toad: and the fairest woman hath some filthiness in her.

Against this it is important to assert that woman's body glorifies
God.

Another aspect of the Adam and Eve story is that, after the Fall,
it is Eve who is blessed in God's promise that she shall bear
children. In this way humankind shall be saved. In Jacobean
society, childbirth was frequently seen as unclean. For the medieval
religious world, the child-bearing capacity of woman was essential-
ly that which made her physically more base than the man – man
did not experience the grubbiness of menstruation or labour pains.
Childbirth is seen only in terms of danger and disease by Joseph
Swetnam:

> the danger of child-bearing must needs be a great terror to a
> woman, which are counted but weak vessels in respect of men:
> and yet it is supposed that there is no disease that a man endureth
> that is one half so grievous or painful as child-bearing is to a
> woman.

In the face of these sorts of beliefs, the assertion that woman
glorifies God in giving birth is a necessary bid for self-respect and
dignity and pride in womanhood: 'Our bodies are fruitful, whereby
the world increaseth; and our care wonderful, by which man is
preserved. From woman sprang man's salvation.'

The creation story also raises questions about society. God
placed all creatures in their respective elements – birds in the air,
and so on. Woman was placed in paradise, an ideal element for
which she was particularly fitted (not being made of mud). We
assume her capacity, then, to share the qualities of that element (this

reasoning is in line with much medieval science too). So then, how does it happen that we find corrupt women; what has happened to their original nature? Sowernam argues that this shows that women are affected by the way they are treated: if you replace Eden with an oppressive household ruled by a cruel man you must expect women to change: 'Men evermore shall this in trial find:/Like to her usage so is woman's mind.' We have now reached a new point. A logical extension of the accepted medieval view that creatures share the characteristics of their 'elements' must mean that the 'essence' of woman is not fixed. Woman is seen to be made by society. This development is clearly radical in implication: discussion centred on the idea of an immutable nature, inherently either good or evil, is replaced by debate about social power and social structure. If women are to change, therefore, society has to change.

Much of the thinking about male and female roles has behind it the plan for a changed society. Here again Adam and Eve are useful. What they offer is the prototype of an equal, mutually dependent relationship. When the female pamphleteers argue that what woman 'is' depends on what man 'is', they suggest that female behaviour is moulded by male in a patriarchal society. So it becomes necessary to write about male behaviour and how it could be improved. At this point, after weathering the Bible and the classics, the modern reader is likely to be even more perturbed. For the social ideals of these pamphlets are based on a respect for well-run marriage and correct manly behaviour. These ideals are, quite properly, being discarded by the more enlightened sectors of late twentieth-century society: here we are at our greatest distance from the pamphlets.

Marriage, in Renaissance discussion, incorporated thoughts about power and sex and social organisation. Thinking about sexual politics was pioneered by people who can be seen as part of that very wide movement we call Puritanism. Here we must ignore the caricatures of Puritans invented by their contemporary enemies. Instead of the Puritan as sexual prude we should rather see the Puritan as sexual libertarian. The more radical Puritan sects advocated marriage without ceremony, by mutual consent in front of one's equals; and similarly divorce by mutual public consent. They experimented with free love, women were encouraged to lead prayers, both sexes debated together on the subjects of religion and morality.

But that was the Puritan radical underground. In the centre, there was still a stress on the equality of men and women. They took seriously the Bible's definition: 'heirs together of the grace of life'. In the eyes of God, it was implied, women were the equals of men. So marriage had to be conducted as an arrangement between equals, with shared work, shared responsibilities and mutual respect. The household cared for the moral life and education of its members. Above all, between husband and wife there ought to be mutual love. These principles are outlined in numerous books about domestic duties, the popularity of which indicates how important and widespread were these ideas. The definition of 'equal' marriage was worked out in a world that practised property marriage, child marriage, institutionalised 'courtly' adultery; where there was a lack of provision or education for women. The well-run household was a centre for the care and education that were not available to witches, whores, unmarried mothers, women who had been picked up and dropped again. The well-run marriage was an image for a well-run society.

There were still male Puritans who insisted that the man was the head. But here, problems arose: if the woman should obey the man, what does she do if the man is not worth obeying? If a husband tells a wife to do ungodly things, should she do them? How much equality should there be? Some male commentators insisted on obedience, come what may, but as we shall see, our pamphleteers dissented from this. What we are left with is the argument that if the marriage is to work, the man's behaviour as much as his wife's has to be legislated for. Hence, in the pamphlets, we encounter an interest in correct manly behaviour.

The definition of the proper man is not a description of a sensual lover or a benevolent father. It is a formula that emphasises the man's moral and social duties as husband. The women authors seem to want to get away from the notion of love and from the language and sentiment of love. Love poetry talks about man's (often spurious) private emotions; it does not speak of how men stand in relation to women; it talks of a man not men. Love language evades specifying social responsibilities; emotive images, self-centred metaphors, the conventions of poetry replace open discussion of the power relations between men and women. Alongside the attack on male poetry writing comes the definition of the proper man. This is an attempt to achieve some clarity in the talk about men and women, in that with the roles clearly specified, women might know where they stand. Jane Anger tells us of the uncertainty of being an object of flattery – violence lies on its underside. To specify rules and roles is to make a world that is intelligible and just. It is not so much love that Ester Sowernam wants but justice: 'the woman was more bound to an upright judge than to a loving husband'. There is a similar stress on proper 'manly virtues' in the Introduction to Mary Wollstonecraft's *Vindication of the Rights of Woman*. It accompanies, likewise, an attack on received man-made descriptions of women: she speaks of educators 'who, considering females rather as women than human creatures, have been more anxious to make them alluring mistresses than affectionate wives and rational mothers' (Penguin edn, p.79).

Unfortunately, the definitions of proper men remained only ideals. The ideals were stated in the pamphlets, but the pamphlets were produced by a <u>male world</u>. This need not have been so, for there were women printers; but these pamphlets were printed by men, and this controlling male presence ends up shaping the whole gender controversy.

We have to think of the Renaissance printer more as we would think of a publisher: they were more than simply technicians. What we see increasingly is a readiness to pick up commercial advantage. Jane Anger's pamphlet seems to have provoked little response. Thirty years later, however, Rachel Speght initiates a minor trend. She herself may have been engineered into answering Swetnam by the printer, but I would have expected the reply to have come sooner if that was the case. Where difficulties really begin is with Sowernam and Munda. Suspicions must arise over their use of obvious pseudonyms, their protests that they have been writing independent answers, and the fact that both were printed by Swetnam's printers. The authors could have been men, encouraged to write for commercial rather than ideological reasons. This is an unpleasant thought, but it must be qualified in two particulars. Most importantly, *if* Sowernam and Munda are male authors they produce texts that radically differ from Swetnam's. It is not simply that they answer him back – this we would expect from an unthinking, simply commercial reply. But they open up his arguments in a way that shows a different set of values, an alternative mode of thinking. *If* they are men, they are men making a positively helpful contribution to the defence of women. And I cannot find a trace of cynicism in their assumed roles. (I shall return to this in more detail in the head-notes to the pamphlets.)

My other qualification to the analysis above is that it is unfair to think of all printers as commercial sharks. For example, two of the male replies to Swetnam, Daniel Tuvil's *Asylum Veneris* and Christopher Newstead's *Defence of Women*, were printed by Edward Griffin, who worked in partnership with his wife Anne. It is they who then printed Rachel Speght's second work, which briefly refers to the Swetnam affair (*Mortality's Memorandum*). They might have been exploiting Speght's name. But a glance at the Stationers' Company Register, where all titles had to be recorded, indicates that the Griffins had a great interest in religious works. Tuvil was a religious writer, *Mortality's Memorandum* is a religious work. (And Newstead's 'reply' was too late – 1620 – to be worth much.) What we seem to have here is the development of a real interest in the religious and doctrinal possibilities opened up by the Swetnam battle.

By contrast, the activities of the printer of *The Women's Sharp Revenge* (hereafter *WSR*) demonstrate the distortions produced by commercially exploitative publishing. *WSR* was supposedly an answer to John Taylor's *Juniper Lecture*, but it is virtually certain that Taylor wrote *WSR* as well (I deal with this in detail in the head-note). The partnership between the printer Okes and Taylor lasted from the 1620s to the 1640s (when *WSR* appeared). They specialised in cliché-ridden satires on up-to-the-minute topics. With the publication of *Juniper* and its sequels they invent a new pamphlet gender controversy. (Taylor seems likely to have read Swetnam and some of the replies, and it was John Okes's father who had originally published Speght.) When Taylor wrote *Juniper* he announced in the text that some women were writing a reply (although he said he had planned one himself). Meanwhile he prepared another text, *Divers Crabtree Lectures*, for the 'women' to answer as well. Okes entered *Crabtree* and *WSR* in the Stationers' Register as titles (to guard against possible competition), but *WSR* was not printed until some months later, at which point an effort was made to spread the controversy wider. A note in *WSR* says it answers *A Bolster Lecture* as well: this work, written by Richard Brathwait, had nothing to do with Taylor's subject matter (it is a compendium of dull stories about aspects of womanliness), but it sounds right for inclusion.

What makes this episode unpleasant is the fact that Taylor's *Juniper* attacks scolds – women who insist on talking out. The 'women' are then offered a chance to reply. But Taylor himself writes this answer. There is thus a two-fold silencing of women: they are attacked as scolds, and their 'reply' is written by a man. The woman is effectively removed from the gender controversy altogether and the male take-over is complete. And indeed is confirmed by history. Swetnam's pamphlet was reprinted steadily up until the eighteenth century. Speght, Munda, Anger were never reprinted. Sowernam was reprinted alongside Swetnam in 1807, as a curio.

I noted earlier that female printers did exist. There were, in fact, the immediate material conditions for all-female production of pamphlets. There were some women authors and a larger number of women printers. But the female printers did not print the work by female writers. Why not? Possibly because the articulate shared consciousness of womanhood was missing. There was no shared objective, no common movement, to draw together the separate female producers. This absence is also notable in the texts themselves: there is no very definite sense of the female alternative, of the self-supporting skills and strength of women. We are left with a handful of texts all limited intellectually and politically by their being produced in an age before feminism, but all nevertheless pre-eminently remarkable for their intellectual bravery and adventure; remarkable, in short, in that they exist.

# Two Short Extracts

The two extracts that follow act as a preface to the pamphlets. The first, from the Homily on Matrimony, gives the Elizabethan establishment's definition of what woman 'is' and should be. Homilies were written to be read out in all parish churches: the populace were exposed to their attitudes at an early age.

But to this prayer must be joined a singular diligence, whereof St Peter giveth his precept, saying, *You husbands, deal with your wives according to knowledge, giving honour to the wife, as unto the weaker vessel, and as unto them that are heirs also of the grace of life, that your prayers be not hindered.* (I Pet.iii.7.) This precept doth peculiarly pertain to the husband: for he ought to be the leader and author of love in cherishing and increasing concord; which then shall take place, if he will use measurableness and not tyranny, and if he yield some things to the woman. For the woman is a weak creature, not endued with like strength and constancy of mind: therefore they be the sooner disquieted, and they be the more prone to all weak affections and disposi- tions of mind, more than men be; and lighter they be and more vain in their fantasies and opinions. These things must be considered of the man, that he be not too stiff; so that he ought to wink at some things, and must gently expound all things, and to forbear.

Howbeit, the common sort of men do judge that such moderation should not become a man: for they say that it is a token of a womanish cowardness; and therefore they think that it is a man's part to fume in anger, to fight with fist and staff. Howbeit, howsoever they imagine, undoubtedly St Peter doth better judge what should be seeming to a man, and what he should most reasonably perform. For he saith reasoning should be used, and not fighting. Yea, he saith more, that the woman ought to have a certain *honour* attributed to her; that is to say, she must be spared and borne with, the rather for that she is *the weaker vessel*, of a frail heart, inconstant, and with a word soon stirred to wrath.

... For thus doth St Peter preach to them; *Ye wives, be ye in subjection to obey your own husbands.* (I Pet.iii.1.) To obey is another thing than to control or command; which yet they may do to their children and to their family; but as for their husbands, them must they obey, and cease from commanding, and perform subjection. For this surely doth nourish concord very much, when the wife is ready at hand at her husband's commandment, when she will apply herself to his will, when she endeavoureth herself to seek his contentation and to do him pleasure, when she will eschew all things that might offend him. For thus will most truly be verified the saying of the poet, 'A good wife by obeying her husband shall bear the rule': so that he shall have a delight and a gladness the sooner at all times to return home to her. But on the contrary part, when the wives be stubborn, froward, and malapert, their husbands are compelled thereby to abhor and flee from their own houses, even as they should have battle with their enemies.

The second extract is taken from a long and detailed legal work called *The Law's Resolutions of Women's Rights*. It was published in 1632 but probably written in the 1580s. It is an extraordinary work which is unfortunately accessible only in its original edition. It offers us an analysis of what happens, not what ought to be and it makes grim reading.

But it seemeth to be very true that there is some kind of castigation which Law permits a husband to use: for if a woman be threatened by her husband to be beaten, mischieved or slain, † Fitzherbert sets down a writ which she may sue out of Chancery to compel him to find surety of honest behaviour toward her, and that he shall neither do nor procure to be done to her (mark I pray you) any bodily damage, otherwise than appertains to the office of a husband for lawful and reasonable correction. See for † this the new *Nat. bre.* fo. 80f. and fo. 238f.

How far that extendeth I cannot tell, but herein the sex feminine is at no very great disadvantage. For first for the lawfulness: if it be in none other regard lawful to beat a man's wife than because the poor wench can sue no other action for it, I pray why may not the wife beat the husband again? What action can he have if she do? Where two tenants in common be on a horse, and one of them will travel and use this horse, he may keep it from his companion a year, two or three and so be even with him. So the actionless woman beaten by her husband hath retaliation left to beat him again, if she dare. (Book III, section 7)

Choose now whether ye will imagine that the widow hath
agreed with him which was her husband's bane or that she hath †
pursued him to death: she remaineth from henceforth a widow, †
giving herself to alms and deeds of charity; and of this good mind
are many of our widows, which purpose constantly to live out
the residue of their days in a devout remembrance of their dear
husbands departed, to whom perhaps they made vows never to
marry again after their deaths. But to what purpose is it for
women to make vows, when men have so many millions of ways
to make them break them? And when sweet words, fair prom- †
ises, tempting, flattering, swearing, lying will not serve to
beguile the poor soul, then with rough handling, violence and
plain strength of arms they are, or have been heretofore, rather
made prisoners to lust's thieves than wives and companions to
faithful honest lovers. So drunken are men with their own lusts,
and the poison of Ovid's false precept, 'Vim licet appellant, vis †
est ea grata puellis', that if the rampier of Laws were not betwixt †
women and their harms, I verily think none of them, being above
twelve years of age and under an hundred, being either fair or
rich, should be able to escape ravishing. (Book III, section 20)

From here until the end of the book there is a discussion of rape and
the law.

## NOTES

PAGE 26
**Fitzherbert**: a Justice of the Court of Common Pleas, author of several legal works.
**Nat. bre.**: presumably *La nouvelle Natura Brevium* (1553), by Fitzherbert.

PAGE 27
**bane**: murderer/ruin.
**widow**: widows were a common target of jokes: they were often depicted as
  voraciously randy; hence the different emphasis of this paragraph gives it its
  force.
**And when sweet** ...: the connection of masculine flattery with masculine violence in
  this sentence is especially recurrent in dramatic characters; it is there at the centre
  of Shakespeare's Claudio in *Much Ado*.
**Vim ... puellis**: Ovid, *Ars Amatoria* i.673: you may call it force: that force is pleasing
  to girls. The word *appellant* should be *appelles*.
**rampier**: rampart, fortified barrier.

# JANE ANGER
## her Protection
## for Women

### To defend them against the

SCANDALOUS REPORTES OF
a late Surfeiting Lover, and all other like
Venerians that complaine so to bee
overcloyed with womens
kindnesse

Written by Ja A. Gent

At London
Printed by Richard Jones, and Thomas
Orwin. 1589.

[Jane Anger's name looks to be fake. But in parts of Berkshire, Cambridge, Cornwall and Essex the surname Anger was common. If we accept that the Christian name could be spelt Jane or Joan, as it is here, we discover a handful of women at the right age at the right time: a Jane Anger and a Joan Anger from Berkshire, two Joan Angers from Essex, a Jane Anger (née Greene) from Lincolnshire and perhaps a Jane Anger from Cornwall. Jane is not one of the Christian names commonly associated with aggressive female types (compare Moll, Meg, Kate, Frank). A pseudonym would, I think, be more elaborate and, at this period, perhaps Italian or Latin-sounding.

It is difficult to say which Jane Anger might be the author, which is unfortunate, since her pamphlet marks the first time that I am aware of that a woman participated in Renaissance gender controversy. Before, it was men who not only attacked but 'defended' women, readily turning their hands to either point of view. How Anger came to be involved is not known, but it seems that she was put up to it by a printer. The name of the man who shared in printing Anger's pamphlet is Thomas Orwin; it is his name that also appears on the work that Anger says she was attacking, *Book: his Surfeit in Love*. This work has unfortunately not survived – it might not even have been printed – but Orwin registered the title with the Stationers' Company (the equivalent of copyrighting it) late in November 1588. Anger wrote her reply, she says, in 1588 and it appeared printed in 1589.

We can guess what *Book: his Surfeit* was like from some of Anger's details. Once we look closely, however, we can spot another text in the background: a work by John Lyly called *Euphues his Censure to Philautus*. (In an essay in 1943 Helen Kahin made this suggestion, although her evidence was slightly vague.) Much of Anger's language is close to *Euphues* (see my notes): yet she never acknowledges this source. So either she deliberately ignored it, or she was unaware that it was her source (in other words, *Book: his Surfeit* could have plagiarised chunks of Lyly).

Although the Lyly piece was published some years before (as part of a larger work, *Euphues the Anatomy of Wit*) it was reprinted separately in September 1587 by Edward White. What may have happened is that the printer Orwin realised the possibilities in the anti-woman text of *Euphues his Censure to Philautus* and deliberately provoked a small controversy. Lyly, published by another printer, remains the unacknowledged source, leaving Orwin free to run his own gender debate (compare the titles: *Euphues his Censure ...*, *Book: his Surfeit ...*, *Anger her Protection ...*). (Orwin could, indeed, have shown Anger the manuscript of *Book: his Surfeit* without ever printing it.)

However Anger's pamphlet came to be printed, what is striking – and I think new – about the text is the way in which it stresses the person of the author. The particular feature of the women's pamphlets (whether the authors were really women or not) is their 'we women' manner: the authors used themselves as subjects, they drew examples from their experience as women; this was the only way they, as 'voices' of women, could challenge authority and received ideas. In men's writing, by contrast, the author tended to efface himself and to write as if objectively: the male author could be 'objective' about the male world.

It is against the following kind of satirical cliché that Jane Anger had to assert her female reality:

Take from them their periwigs, their paintings, their jewels, their rolls, their bolsterings, and thou shalt soon perceive that a woman is the least part of herself. When they be once robbed of their robes, then will they appear so odious, so ugly, so monstrous, that thou wilt rather think them serpents than saints.

Euphues continues:

Moreover, to make thee the more stronger to strive against these sirens, and more subtle to deceive these tame serpents, my counsel is that thou have more strings to thy bow than one ... the mind enamoured on two women is less affected with desire and less infected with despair (Lyly, p. 255).

The classic male-centred text claims to be horrified by women even while it reinforces male social power in a society which actually victimises women: 'It is a world to see how commonly we are blinded with the collusions of women' (who is 'we'?); 'women, when they be most pleasant, pretend most treachery'.

And while, on the one hand, women were forced to tolerate that sort of writing, on the other they were presented with this:

Stella, while now, by honour's cruel might,
  I am from you, light of my life, misled,
  And that fair you, my sun, thus overspread
With absence' veil, I live in sorrow's night;
If this dark place yet show, like candle light,
  Some beauty's piece, as amber-coloured head,
  Milk hands, rose cheeks, or lips more sweet, more red,
Or seeing jets, black, but in blackness bright:
They please, I do confess, they please mine eyes.
          (from Sidney, *Astrophel and Stella*, xci)

Anger has views on both sorts of writing.]

## To the Gentlewomen of England, health

Gentlewomen, though it is to be feared that your settled wits will †
advisedly condemn that which my choleric vein hath rashly set down, and so perchance Anger shall reap anger for not agreeing with diseased persons: yet – if with indifferency of censure you consider of the head of the quarrel – I hope you will rather show †
yourselves defendants of the defender's title than complainants of the plaintiff's wrong. I doubt judgement before trial, which were †
injurious to the law; and I confess that my rashness deserveth no less, which was a fit of my extremity. I will not urge reasons because your wits are sharp and will soon conceive my meaning, [nor] will I be tedious lest I prove too too troublesome, nor †

over-dark in my writing for fear of the name of a riddler. But, in a word, for my presumption I crave pardon because it was Anger that did write it: committing your protection, and myself, to the protection of your selves, and the judgement of the cause to the censures of your just minds, yours ever at commandment,
Ja. A.


† 

## To all Women in general,
### and gentle Reader whatsoever

Fie on the falsehood of men, whose minds go oft a-madding and whose tongues cannot so soon be wagging, but straight they fall a-tattling! Was there ever any so abused, so slandered, so railed upon, or so wickedly handled undeservedly, as are we women? Will the gods permit it, the goddesses stay their punishing judgements, and we ourselves not pursue their undoings for such devilish practices? O Paul's steeple and Charing Cross! A halter hold all such persons. Let the streams of the channels in London streets run so swiftly as they may be able alone to carry them from that sanctuary. Let the stones be as ice, the soles of their shoes as glass, the ways steep like Etna, and every blast a whirlwind puffed out of Boreas his long throat, that these may hasten their passage to the devil's haven. Shall surfeiters rail on our kindness, you stand still and say naught: and shall not Anger stretch the veins of her brains, the strings of her fingers, and the lists of her modesty to answer their surfeitings? Yes truly. And herein I conjure all you to aid and assist me in defence of my willingness, which shall make me rest at your commands. Fare you well.
Your friend,
Ja. A.


# A Protection for
## Women, etc.

The desire that every man hath to show his true vein in writing is unspeakable, and their minds are so carried away with the manner as no care at all is had of the matter. They run so into rhetoric as oftentimes they overrun the bounds of their own wits, and go they know not whither. If they have stretched their invention so hard on a last as it is at a stand, there remains but one help, which is, to write of us women. If they may once encroach so far into our presence as they may but see the lining of our outermost garment, they straight think that Apollo honours them in yielding so good a supply to

refresh their sore over-burdened heads (through studying for
matters to endite of). And therefore, that the god may see how †
thankfully they receive his liberality, their wits whetted and their
brains almost broken with botching his bounty, they fall straight to †
dispraising and slandering our silly sex. But judge what the cause †
should be of this their so great malice towards simple women:
doubtless the weakness of our wits and our honest bashfulness, by
reason whereof they suppose that there is not one amongst us who
can, or dare, reprove their slanders and false reproaches. Their
slanderous tongues are so short, and the time wherein they have
lavished out their words freely hath been so long, that they know
we cannot catch hold of them to pull them out, and they think we
will not write to reprove their lying lips. Which conceits have
already made them cocks and would – should they not be cravened
– make themselves among themselves be thought to be of the game. †
They have been so daintily fed with our good natures that like jades †
(their stomachs are grown so queasy) they surfeit of our kindness. If †
we will not suffer them to smell on our smocks, they will snatch at †
our petticoats: but if our honest natures cannot away with that
uncivil kind of jesting, then we are coy. Yet if we bear with their †
rudeness and be somewhat modestly familiar with them, they will
straight make matter of nothing, blazing abroad that they have †
surfeited with love; and then their wits must be shown in telling the
manner how.

Among the innumerable number of books to that purpose, of late
– unlooked for – the new Surfeit of an old Lover (sent abroad to
warn those which are of his own kind from catching the like disease)
came by chance to my hands: which, because as well women as men †
are desirous of novelties, I willingly read over. Neither did the
ending thereof less please me than the beginning, for I was so
carried away with the conceit of the Gent. as that I was quite out of
the book before I thought I had been in the midst thereof – so pithy
were his sentences, so pure his words and so pleasing his style. The
chief matters therein contained were of two sorts: the one in the
dispraise of man's folly, and the other invective against our sex;
*their* folly proceeding of their own flattery joined with fancy, and
*our* faults are through our folly, with which is some faith.

The bounteous words written over the lascivious King Ninus his †
head, set down in this old Lover his Surfeit to be these 'Demand and
have', do plainly show the flattery of men's false hearts: for
knowing that we women are weak vessels soon overwhelmed, and †
that Bounty bendeth everything to his beck, they take him for their
instrument (too too strong) to essay the pulling down of us so
weak. If we stand fast, they strive; if we totter, though but a little,
they will never leave till they have overturned us. Semiramis †
demanded: and who would not, if courtesy should be so freely
offered? Ninus gave all [of] his kingdom, and that at the last: the

more fool he. And of him this shall be my censure (agreeing with
the verdict of the surfeiting lover, save only that he hath misplaced
and mistaken certain words) in this manner:

> Fools force such flattery – and men of dull conceit:
> Such frenzy oft doth haunt the wise (Nurse Wisdom once
>                                                     rejected);
> Though love be sure and firm yet lust fraught with deceit
> And men's fair words do work great woe, unless they be
>                                                     suspected.
> Then foolish Ninus had but due, if I his judge might be:
> Vile are men's lusts, false are their lips besmeared with flattery.
> Himself and crown he brought to thrall, which passed all the
>                                                     rest;
> His foot-stool match he made his head, and therefore was a
>                                                     beast.
> Then all such beasts such beastly ends I wish the gods to send,
> And worser too if worse may be: like his my censure end.

† The slothful King Sardanapalus with his beastlike and licentious
deeds are so plainly deciphered, and his bad end well-deserved so
truly set down in that *Surfeit*, as both our judgements agree in one.
†     But that Menelaus was served with such sauce it is a wonder. Yet
truly their sex are so like to bulls that it is no marvel though the
gods do metamorphose some of them to give warning to the rest (if
they could think so of it), for some of them will follow the smock as
† Tom Bull will run after a town cow. But lest they should, running,
† slip and break their pates, the gods, provident of their welfare, set a
† pair of tooters on their foreheads, to keep it from the ground; for
doubtless so stood the case with Menelaus – he running abroad as a
† smell-smock got the habit of a cuckold, of whom thus shall go my
verdict:

> The gods most just do justly punish sin
> With those same plagues which men do most forlorn:
> If filthy lust in men to spring begin,
> That monstrous sin he plagueth with the horn.
>     Their wisdom great whereby they men forewarn
>     To shun vile lust, lest they will wear the horn.

> Deceitful men with guile must be repaid,
> And blows for blows who renders not again?
> The man that is of cuckold's lot afraid,
> From lechery he ought for to refrain.
†     Else shall he have the plague he doth forlorn:
>     And ought, perforce constrained, to wear the horn.

The Greek Actaeon's badge did wear, they say,                       †
And worthy too – he loved the smock so well;
That every man may be a bull I pray,
Which loves to follow lust (his game) so well.
    For by that means poor women shall have peace,
    And want these jars: thus doth my censure cease.                 †

The greatest fault that doth remain in us women is that we are too credulous, for could we flatter as they can dissemble, and use our wits well as they can their tongues ill, then never would any of them complain of surfeiting. But if we women be so so perilous cattle as they term us, I marvel that the gods made not Fidelity as well a man †
as they created her a woman – and all the moral virtues of their masculine sex, as of the feminine kind: except their deities knew that there was some sovereignty in us women which could not be in them men. But lest some snatching fellow should catch me before I fall to the ground, and say they will adorn my head with a feather †
(affirming that I roam beyond reason – seeing it is most manifest that the man is the head of the woman, and that therefore we ought †
to be guided by them), I prevent them with this answer. The gods, knowing that the minds of mankind would be aspiring, and having throughly viewed the wonderful virtues wherewith women are enriched, lest they should provoke us to pride and so confound us with Lucifer, they bestowed the supremacy over us to man: that of that coxcomb he might only boast – and therefore for God's sake let †
them keep it. But we return to the *Surfeit*.

Having made a long discourse of the gods' censure concerning love, he leaves them (and I them with him) and comes to the principal object and general foundation of love, which he affirmeth to be grounded on women. And now beginning to search his scroll, wherein are taunts against us, he beginneth and saith that we allure †
their hearts to us. Wherein he saith more truly than he is aware of: for we woo them with our virtues and they wed us with vanities; and men, being of wit sufficient to consider of the virtues which are in us women, are ravished with the delight of those dainties, which allure and draw the senses of them to serve us – whereby they become ravenous hawks, who do not only seize upon us but devour us. Our good toward them is the destruction of ourselves; we being well formed are by them foully deformed. Of our true meaning they make mocks, rewarding our loving follies with disdainful flouts. We are the grief of man, in that we take all the grief from man: we languish when they laugh, we lie sighing when they sit singing, and sit sobbing when they lie slugging and sleeping. *Mulier* †
*est hominis confusio*, because her kind heart cannot so sharply reprove their frantic fits as those mad frenzies deserve. *Aut amat,* †
*aut odit, non est in tertio*: she loveth good things and hateth that which is evil; she loveth justice and hateth iniquity; she loveth truth

and true dealing and hateth lies and falsehood; she loveth man for his virtues and hateth him for his vices. To be short, there is no *medium* between good and bad, and therefore she can be *in nullo*
† *tertio*. Plato his answer to a vicar of fools which asked the question, being, that he knew not whether to place women among those creatures which were reasonable or unreasonable, did as much beautify his divine knowledge as all the books he did write. For, knowing that women are the greatest help that men have, without whose aid and assistance it is as possible for them to live as if they wanted meat, drink, clothing or any other necessary; and knowing also that even then in his age (much more in those ages which should after follow), men were grown to be so unreasonable, as he could not decide whether men or brute beasts were more reasonable.

Their eyes are so curious as, be not all women equal with Venus for beauty, they cannot abide the sight of them; their stomachs so queasy as, do they taste but twice of one dish, they straight surfeit and needs must a new diet be provided for them. We are contrary to men because they are contrary to that which is good. Because they
† are purblind they cannot see into our natures, and we too well – though we had but half an eye – into *their* conditions because they are so bad: our behaviours alter daily because men's virtues decay
† hourly. If Hesiodus had with equity as well looked into the life of man, as he did precisely search out the qualities of us women, he would have said that if a woman trust unto a man it shall fare as well with her as if she had a weight of a thousand pounds tied about her neck and then cast into the bottomless seas.

For by men are we confounded though they by us are sometimes crossed. Our tongues are 'light' because earnest in reproving men's filthy vices, and our good counsel is termed nipping injury in that it accords not with their foolish fancies. Our boldness 'rash' for giving
† noddies nipping answers, our dispositions 'naughty' for not agreeing with their vile minds, and our fury 'dangerous' because it will not bear with their knavish behaviours. If our frowns be so terrible and our anger so deadly, men are too foolish in offering occasions of hatred; which shunned, a terrible death is prevented. There is a continual deadly hatred between the wild boar and tame hounds: I would there were the like betwixt women and men unless
† they amend their manners, for so strength should predominate where now flattery and dissimulation hath the upper hand. The lion rageth when he is hungry, but man raileth when he is glutted. The tiger is robbed of her young ones when she is ranging abroad, but men rob women of their honour undeservedly under their noses. The viper stormeth when his tail is trodden on, and may not we fret when all our body is a foot-stool to their vile lust? Their unreasonable minds which know not what reason is make them nothing better than brute beasts.

But let us grant that Clytemnestra, Ariadne, Delilah and Jezebel †
were spotted with crimes: shall not Nero with others innumerable, †
and therefore unnamable, join hands with them and lead the dance? †
Yet it grieves me that faithful Deianira should be falsely accused of
her husband Hercules' death, seeing she was utterly guiltless (even
of thought) concerning any such crime. For had not the Centaur's
falsehood exceeded the simplicity of her too too credulous heart,
Hercules had not died so cruelly tormented nor the monster's
treason been so unhappily executed. But we must bear with these
faults, and with greater than these; especially seeing that he which
set it down for a maxim was driven into a mad mood through a
surfeit, which made him run quite besides his book and mistake his
case: for where he accused Deianira falsely he would have condem- †
ned Hercules deservedly.                                              †

Marius' daughter, endued with so many excellent virtues, was too †
good either for Metellus or any man living: for though peradventure †
she had some small fault yet doubtless he had detestable crimes. On
the same place where down is on the hen's head, the comb grows on
the cock's pate. If women breed woe to men, they bring care,
poverty, grief and continual fear to women – which if they be not
woes they are worser.

Euthydemus made six kind[s] of women, and I will approve that †
there are so many of men, which be: poor and rich, bad and good,
foul and fair. The great patrimonies that wealthy men leave their
children after their death make them rich: but dice and other
marthrifts, happening into their companies, never leave them till †
they be at the beggar's bush, where I can assure you they become †
poor. Great eaters, being kept at a slender diet, never distemper
their bodies but remain in good case: but afterwards, once turned
forth to liberty's pasture, they graze so greedily as they become
surfeiting jades and always after are good for nothing. There are
men which are snout-fair whose faces look like a cream-pot, and yet †
those not the fair men I speak of; but I mean those whose
conditions are free from knavery, and I term those foul that have
neither civility nor honesty. Of these sorts there are none good,
none rich or fair long. But if we do desire to have them good, we
must always tie them to the manger and diet their greedy paunches,
otherwise they will surfeit. What shall I say? Wealth makes them
lavish, wit knavish, beauty effeminate, poverty deceitful and de-
formity ugly. Therefore of me take this counsel:

Esteem of men as of a broken reed:
Mistrust them still, and then you well shall speed.

I pray you then – if this be true, as it truly cannot be denied –
have not they reason who affirm that a goose standing before a
ravenous fox is in as good case as the woman that trusteth to a man's

fidelity? For as the one is sure to lose his head, so the other is most
certain to be bereaved of her good name, if there be any small cause
† of suspicion. The fellow that took his wife for his cross was an ass,
and so we will leave him: for he loved well to swear on an ale-pot
and because his wife, keeping him from his drunken vein, put his
nose out of his socket, he thereby was brought into a mad mood in
which he did he could not tell what.

†    When provender pricks the jade will winch, but keep him at a
slender ordinary and he will be mild enough. The dictator's son was
† crank as long as his cock was crowing, but proving a craven he made
his master hang down his head.

†    Thales was so married to shameful lust as he cared not a straw for
lawful love, whereby he showed himself to be endued with much
vice and no virtue: for a man doth that oftentimes standing of which
† he repenteth sitting. The Roman could not – as now men cannot –
abide to hear women praised and themselves dispraised, and
† therefore it is best for men to follow Alphonso his rule: let them be
deaf and marry wives that are blind, so shall they not grieve to hear
their wives commended nor their monstrous misdoing shall offend
their wives' eyesight.

†    Tibullus, setting down a rule for women to follow, might have
proportioned this platform for men to rest in. And might have said:
Every honest man ought to shun that which detracteth both health
and safety from his own person, and strive to bridle his slanderous
tongue. Then must he be modest and show his modesty by his
virtuous and civil behaviours; and not display his beastliness
through his wicked and filthy words. For lying lips and deceitful
tongues are abominable before God. It is an easy matter to entreat a
cat to catch a mouse, and more easy to persuade a desperate man to
kill himself. What Nature hath made, Art cannot mar, and (as this
† surfeiting lover saith) that which is bred in the bone will not be
brought out of the flesh. If we clothe ourselves in sackcloth and
† truss up our hair in dish-clouts, Venerians will nevertheless pursue
their pastime. If we hide our breasts, it must be with leather, for no
cloth can keep their long nails out of our bosoms.

   We have 'rolling eyes' and they railing tongues: our eyes cause
them to look lasciviously, and why? because they are given to
lechery. It is an easy matter to find a staff to beat a dog, and a burnt
finger giveth sound counsel. If men would as well embrace counsel
† as they can give it, Socrates' rule would be better followed. But let
Socrates, heaven and earth say what they will, 'man's face is worth a
† glass of dissembling water.' And therefore to conclude with a
proverb: 'Write ever, and yet never write enough of man's falsehood' (I mean those that use it). I would that ancient writers would
as well have busied their heads about deciphering the deceits of their
own sex as they have about setting down our follies; and I would
some would call in question that now which hath ever been

questionless. But sithence all their wits have been bent to write of the contrary, I leave them to a contrary vein, and the surfeiting Lover, who returns to his discourse of love.

Now while this greedy grazer is about his entreaty of love – which nothing belongeth to our matter – let us secretly, ourselves with ourselves, consider how and in what they that are our worst enemies are both inferior unto us and most beholden unto our kindness.

The creation of man and woman at the first (he being formed *in principio* of dross and filthy clay) did so remain until God saw that † in him his workmanship was good, and therefore, by the transformation of the dust which was loathsome unto flesh, it became purified. Then, lacking a help for him, God making woman of man's flesh – that she might be purer than he – doth evidently show how far we women are more excellent than men. Our bodies are fruitful, whereby the world increaseth, and our care wonderful, by † which man is preserved. From woman sprang man's salvation. A woman was the first that believed, and a woman likewise the first that repented of sin. In women is only true fidelity: except in her, † there be [no] constancy, and without her no huswifery. In the time † of their sickness we cannot be wanted, and when they are in health † we for them are most necessary. They are comforted by our means; they nourished by the meats we dress; their bodies freed from diseases by our cleanliness, which otherwise would surfeit unreasonably through their own noisomeness. Without our care they lie in their beds as dogs in litter and go like lousy mackerel † swimming in the heat of summer. They love to go handsomely in their apparel and rejoice in the pride thereof, yet who is the cause of it, but our carefulness to see that everything about them be curious? † Our virginity makes us virtuous, our conditions courteous and our † chastity maketh our trueness of love manifest. They confess we are necessary, but they would have us likewise evil. That they cannot † want us I grant, yet evil I deny (except only in the respect of man † who, hating all good things, is only desirous of that which is ill – through whose desire, in estimation of conceit, we are made ill). But lest some should snarl on me, barking out this reason, that † 'none is good but God, and therefore women are ill', I must yield that in that respect we are ill – and affirm that men are no better, seeing we are so necessary unto them.

It is most certain that if we be ill they are worse: for *Malum malo* † *additum efficit malum peius*; and they that use ill worse than it should be are worse than the ill. And therefore if they will correct *Magnificat*, they must first learn the signification thereof. That we † are liberal they will not deny, sithence that many of them have (*ex* † *confessio*) received more kindness in one day at our hands than they † can repay in a whole year; and some have so glutted themselves with our liberality as they cry 'no more'. But if they shall avow that

women are fools we may safely give them the lie: for myself have
heard some of them confess that we have more wisdom than need is,
and therefore no fools; and they less than they should have, and
therefore fools. It hath been affirmed by some of their sex that to
shun a shower of rain and to know the way to our husband's bed is
† wisdom sufficient for us women; but in this year of '88 men are
grown so fantastical that unless we can make them fools we are
accounted unwise.

And now – seeing I speak to none but to you which are of mine
own sex – give me leave like a scholar to prove our wisdom more
† excellent than theirs, though I never knew what sophistry meant.

There is no wisdom but it comes by grace – this is a principle, and
† *contra principium non est disputandum*: but grace was first given to
a woman, because to Our Lady: which premises conclude that
† women are wise. Now, *primum est optimum*, and therefore women
are wiser than men. That we are more witty, which comes by
nature, it cannot better be proved than that by our answers men are
† often driven to *non plus*; and, if their talk be of worldly affairs, with
our resolutions they must either rest satisfied or prove themselves
fools in the end.

It was my chance to hear a pretty story of two wise men who,
† being cousin german to the town of Gotham, proved themselves as
† very asses as they were fools; and it was this: The stealth of a ring
out of a wise man's chamber afflicted the loser's mind with so
grievous passions as he could take no rest till he went to ask a
friend's counsel how he might recover his loss. Into whose presence
being once entered, his clothes unbuttoned made passage for his
friend's eyesight unto his bosom; who, seeing him in such a taking,
† judging by his looks that some qualm had risen on his stomach the
extremity whereof might make his head to ache, offered him a
† kercher. This distressed man, half besides himself, howled bitterly
that he did mistake his case and, falling into a raving vein, began to
curse the day of his birth and the Destinies for suffering him to live.
His fellow wise man, mistaking this fit, fearing that some devil had
possessed him, began to betake him to his heels; but, being stopped
† from running by his companion, did likewise ban the cause of this
sudden change and the motion that moved the other to enter his
presence. Yet seeing how dangerously he was disturbed, and
knowing that by no means he could shun his company, calling his
wits together (which made him forget his passion), he demanded the
cause of the other's grief; who, taking a stool and a cushion, sat
down and declared that he was undone through the loss of a ring
which was stolen out of his window, further saying: 'Sir, is it not
best for me to go to a wise woman to know of her what is become of
my ring?' The other, answering affirmatively, asked this: if he knew
any? Between whom many wise women reckoned, they both went
together for company, where we will leave them.

Now I pray you, tell me your fancy: were not these men very wise, but especially did they not cunningly display their wisdom by this practice? – sithence that they hope to find that through the wisdom of a woman which was lost by the folly of a man. Well, seeing according to the old proverb 'The wit of a woman is a great matter', let men learn to be wiser or account themselves fools: for they know by practice that we are none.

Now sithence that this overcloyed and surfeiting lover leaveth his love and comes with a fresh assault against us women, let us arm ourselves with patience and see the end of his tongue, which explaineth his surfeit. But it was so lately printed as that I should do the printer injury should I recite but one of them, and therefore, †
referring you to *Book: his Surfeit in Love*, I come to my matter. If to enjoy a woman be to catch the devil by the foot, to obtain the favour of a man is to hold fast his dam by the middle: whereby the one may easily break away and the other cannot go without he carries the man with him.

The properties of the snake and of the eel are the one to sting and the other not to be held: but men's tongues sting against nature and therefore they are unnatural. Let us bear with them as much as may be, and yield to their wills more than is convenient: yet if we cast †
our reckoning at the end of the year we shall find that our losses exceed their gains, which are innumerable. The property of the chameleon is to change himself; but man always remaineth at one stay and is never out of the predicaments of dishonesty and unconstancy. The stinging of the scorpion is cured by the scorpion, whereby it seems that there is some good nature in them. But men never leave stinging till they see the death of honesty. The danger of pricks is shunned by gathering roses glove-fisted; and the stinging of bees prevented through a close hood. But naked dishonesty and bare inconstancy are always plagued through their own folly.

If men's folly be so unreasonable as it will strive against nature it is no matter though she rewards them with crosses contrary to their expectations: for if Tom Fool will presume to ride on Alexander's horse he is not to be pitied though he get a foul knock for his †
labour. But it seems the Gentleman hath had great experience of Italian courtesans, whereby his wisdom is showed. For *Experientia* †
*praestantior arte*: and he that hath Experience to prove his case is in better case than they that have all unexperienced book cases to †
defend their titles.

The smooth speeches of men are nothing unlike the vanishing clouds of the air, which glide by degrees from place to place till they have filled themselves with rain, when, breaking, they spit forth terrible showers. So men gloze till they have their answers, which †
are the end of their travail, and then they bid modesty adieu and, entertaining rage, fall a-railing on us which never hurt them. The rankness of grass causeth suspicion of the serpent's lurking, but his

† lying in the plain path, at the time when woodcocks shoot, maketh the patient passionate through his sting, because no such ill was suspected. When men protest secrecy most solemnly, believe them least, for then surely there is a trick of knavery to be discarded: for in a friar's habit an old fornicator is always clothed.

It is a wonder to see how men can flatter themselves with their own conceits. For let us look, they will straight affirm that we love: and if then lust pricketh them, they will swear that love stingeth us; which imagination only is sufficient to make them essay the scaling of half a dozen of us in one night, when they will not stick to swear that if they should be denied of their requests death must needs follow. Is it any marvel though they surfeit, when they are so greedy? but is it not pity that any of them should perish, which will be so soon killed with unkindness? Yes truly. Well, the onset given,
† if we retire for a vantage they will straight affirm that they have got the victory. Nay, some of them are so carried away with conceit that, shameless, they will blaze abroad among their companions that they have obtained the love of a woman, unto whom they never spake above once, if that. Are not these froward fellows? You must
† bear with them, because they dwell far from lying neighbours; they
† will say *Mentiri non est nostrum* – and yet you shall see true tales
† come from them as wild geese fly under London Bridge. Their fawning is but flattery; their faith falsehood; their fair words allurements to destruction; and their large promises tokens of death, or of evils worse than death. Their singing is a bait to catch us and their playings plagues to torment us; and therefore take heed of them, and take this as an axiom in logic and a maxim in the law:
† *Nulla fides hominibus*. There are three accidents to men which, of all, are most unseparable: lust, deceit and malice. Their glozing tongues, the preface to the execution of their vile minds; and their pens, the bloody executioners of their barbarous manners. A little gall maketh a great deal of sweet sour: and a slanderous tongue poisoneth all the good parts in man.
† Was not the folly of Vulcan worthy of Venus' flouts, when she took him with the manner wooing Briceris? And was it not the flattery of Paris which enticed Helen to falsehood? Yes truly: and the late Surfeiter his remembrance in calling his pen from raging against reason showeth that he is not quite without flattery, for he putteth the fault in his pen when it was his passion that deserved
† reproof. The love of Hipsicrates and Pantheia, the zeal of Artemisia
† and Portia, the affection of Sulpicia and Arria, the true fancy of
† Hipparchia and Prisca, the loving passions of Macrina and of the
† wife of Paudocrus (all manifested in his *Surfeit*) shall condemn the undiscreetness of men's minds; whose hearts delight in naught, save that only which is contrary to good. Is it not a foolish thing to be
† sorry for things unrecoverable? Why then should Sigismunda's
† answer be so descanted upon, seeing her husband was dead and she

thereby free for any man? Of the abundance of the heart the mouth speaketh, which is verified by the railing kind of man's writing. Of all kind of voluptuousness they affirm lechery to be the chiefest, and yet some of them are not ashamed to confess publicly that they have surfeited therewith. It defileth the body and makes it stink – and men use it. I marvel how we women can abide them but that they delude us as, they say, we deceive them with perfumes.

Voluptuousness is a strong beast and hath many instruments to draw to lust: but men are so forward of themselves thereto as they need none to hale them. His court is already so full with them that †
he hath more need to make stronger gates to keep them out than to set them open that they may come in – except he will be pulled out by the ears out of his kingdom. I would the abstinence of King Cyrus, Xenocrates, Caius Gracchus, Pompeius and of Francis †
Sforza, Duke of Milan (recited in *Book: his Surfeit in Love*) might †
be precedents for men to follow, and I warrant you then we should have no surfeiting. I pray God that they may mend: but in the mean time let them be sure that rashness breeds repentance and treacherous hearts tragical ends. False flattery is the messenger of foul folly, and a slanderous tongue the instrument of a dissembling heart.

I have set down unto you which are of mine own sex the subtle dealings of untrue-meaning men: not that you should condemn all men, but to the end that you may take heed of the false hearts of all and still reprove the flattery which remains in all. For as it is reason that the hens should be served first which both lay the eggs and hatch the chickens, so it were unreasonable that the cocks which tread them should be kept clean without meat. As men are valiant so †
are they virtuous; and those that are born honourably cannot bear horrible dissembling hearts. But as there are some which cannot love heartily, so there are many who lust uncessantly; and as many of them will deserve well, so most care not how ill they speed so they may get our company. Wherein they resemble Envy, who will be contented to lose one of his eyes that another might have both his pulled out. And therefore think well of as many as you may, love them that you have cause, hear everything that they say (and afford them nods which make themselves noddies) but believe very little thereof or nothing at all, and hate all those who shall speak anything in the dispraise or to the dishonour of our sex.

Let the luxurious life of Heliogabalus, the intemperate desires of †
Commodus and Proculus, the damnable lust of Chilpericus and †
Xerxes, Boleslaus' violent ravishings, and the unnatural carnal †
appetite of Sigismundus Malateste be examples sufficiently probable †
to persuade you that the hearts of men are most desirous to excel in vice. There were many good laws established by the Romans and other good kings, yet they could not restrain men from lechery; and there are terrible laws allotted in England to the offenders therein, all which will not serve to restrain man.

The Surfeiter's physic is good, could he and his companions follow it: but when the fox preacheth, let the geese take heed – it is
† before an execution. *Fallere fallentem non est fraus*, and to kill that beast whose property is only to slay is no sin: if you will please men you must follow their rule, which is to flatter – for fidelity and they are utter enemies. Things far fetched are excellent and that experience is best which cost most; crowns are costly and that which cost many crowns is well worth 'God thank you' – or else I know who hath spent his labour and cost foolishly. Then if any man giveth such dear counsel gratefully, are not they fools which will refuse his liberality? I know you long to hear what that counsel should be, which was bought at so high a price: wherefore, if you listen, the Surfeiter his pen with my hand shall forthwith show you.

At the end of men's fair promises there is a labyrinth, and therefore ever hereafter stop your ears when they protest friendship lest they come to an end before you are aware – whereby you fall without redemption. The path which leadeth thereunto is man's wit, and the miles' ends are marked with these trees: Folly, Vice, Mischief, Lust, Deceit and Pride. These, to deceive you, shall be clothed in the raiments of Fancy, Virtue, Modesty, Love, True-meaning and Handsomeness. Folly will bid you welcome on your way and tell you his fancy concerning the profit which may come to you by this journey, and direct you to Vice who is more crafty. He, with a company of protestations, will praise the virtues of women, showing how many ways men are beholden unto us; but our backs once turned, he falls a-railing. Then Mischief, he pries into every corner of us, seeing if he can espy a cranny that, getting in his finger into it, he may make it wide enough for his tongue to wag in. Now being come to Lust: he will fall a-railing on lascivious looks, and will ban lechery, and with the collier will say 'the devil take him' though he never means it. Deceit will give you fair words and pick your pockets; nay, he will pluck out your hearts if you be not wary.
† But when you hear one cry out against lawns, drawn-works, periwigs, against the attire of courtesans, and generally of the pride of all women: then know him for a wolf clothed in sheep's raiment and be sure you are fast by the lake of destruction. Therefore take heed of it – which you shall do if you shun men's flattery, the
† forerunner of our undoing. If a jade be galled, will he not winch? And can you find fault with a horse that springeth when he is spurred? The one will stand quietly when his back is healed and the other go well when his smart ceaseth. You must bear with the old Lover his Surfeit because he was diseased when he did write it; and peradventure hereafter, when he shall be well amended, he will repent himself of his slanderous speeches against our sex and curse the dead man which was the cause of it and make a public recantation. For the faltering in his speech at the latter end of his book affirmeth that already he half repenteth of his bargain, and

why? because his melody is past. But believe him not, though he should out-swear you, for although a jade may be still in a stable when his gall back is healed yet he will show himself in his kind † when he is travelling; and man's flattery bites secretly, from which I pray God keep you and me too. Amen.

FINIS

## A Sovereign Salve to Cure the Late Surfeiting Lover

> If once the heat did sore thee beat
>   of foolish love so blind,
> Sometime to sweat, sometime to fret
>   as one bestraught of mind:
>
> If wits were take in such a brake      †
>   that reason was exiled,
> And woe did wake but could not slake,
>   thus love had thee beguiled.
>
> If any wight unto thy sight      †
>   all other did excel,
> Whose beauty bright constrained right
>   thy heart with her to dwell:
>
> If thus thy foe oppressed thee so
>   that back thou could not start,
> But still with woe did surfeit though,
>   yet thankless was thy smart:
>
> If naught but pain in love remain,
>   at length this counsel win:
> That thou refrain this dangerous pain,
>   and come no more therein.
>
> And sith the blast is overpast,
>   it better were certain
> From flesh to fast whilst life doth last,
>   than surfeit so again.

*Vivendo disce.*      Jo. A.     †

## Eiusdem ad Lectorem, de Authore

Though sharp the seed by Anger sown
  we all (almost) confess,

And hard his hap we ay account
   who Anger doth possess:
Yet hapless shalt thou, Reader, reap
   such fruit from Anger's soil,
As may thee please and Anger ease
   from long and weary toil.
Whose pains were took for thy behoof
   to till that cloddy ground,
Where scarce no place free from disgrace
   of female sex was found.
If ought offend which she doth send
   impute it to her mood,
For Anger's rage must that assuage,
   as well is understood.
If to delight ought come in sight
   then deem it for the best,
So you your will may well fulfil
   and she have her request.

FINIS                    Jo. A.


NOTES

PAGE 31
**settled wits**: there is much play on Anger's name – her 'choleric' vein against other people's calmness and balanced judgement; in a way, this makes the name feel genuine.
**head**: main topic or subject.
**doubt**: question, mistrust.
**[nor]**: printed 'ne'.


PAGE 32
**To all Women**: now Anger adopts the style which is to characterise the whole pamphlet.
**A halter**: 'A' printed 'I'; 'halter' has overtones of 'noose' (see title of Sowernam's pamphlet).
**Boreas**: north wind.
**surfeiters**: throughout there is play on the title of *Book: his Surfeit*.
**rail**: verbally attack, scold.
**lists**: limits, bounds.
**manner ... manner**: the balanced phraseology and alliteration mimic a style very fashionable among male writers; in their own way, and for different reasons, the women writers contributed to the movement towards a plain, clear accessible style – rejecting the manner of flattering men.
**last**: model of a foot used by cobblers (*OED* has 19th C. 'stand' meaning the shape of the stretched leather).


PAGE 33
**endite**: write, compose.
**their brains ... bounty**: nice example of stylistic parody being used to depict men as intellectually trapped by their own assumed style.

PAGE 33 CONTINUED

**silly**: simple, innocent; the argument that men feel able to attack women because women will not answer back is picked up by Munda.

**game**: as in game- or fighting-cock: men priding themselves on their pluck, as it were; Lyly uses 'cock of the game' of Curio in *Euphues* ... (p. 247).

**jades**: worn out horses (also used of women).

**stomachs ... queasy**: Euphues says women's cosmetics bring 'queasiness to the stomach' (p. 254).

**smell ... smocks**: a 'smell-smock' was a man who continually sniffed around women, nosing for sex.

**we are coy**: *Euphues*: 'If she be chaste then is she coy' (p. 248).

**blazing**: proclaiming; it is good to have this woman's view of how male writing and speech invent a sexual life for women – and the men are mainly interested in their own style.

**came by chance**: other women are to use this formula – here it looks somewhat suspect, rather overstated; Anger is about to go on and advertise the contents of *Book: his Surfeit*, and its style.

**Ninus**: King of Assyria (d. 1196 BC?), second husband of Semiramis.

**weak vessels**: the often-repeated phrase in all this writing (not without irony) from I Pet. iii.7, quoted in the Homily on Matrimony.

**Semiramis**: legendary builder of Babylon; real name Sammuramat, ruled as regent 810–805 BC.


PAGE 34

**Sardanapalus**: Ashurbanipal, King of Assyria (d. first half of 9th C. BC); used as a literary type of nasty ruler (despite his historical reputation for learning).

**Menelaus**: husband of Helen and cuckolded by Paris (causing the Trojan War).

**Tom Bull**: as in Tom cat, a name signifying maleness.

**pates**: heads.

**tooters**: presumably horns; earliest use (*OED* 1638) as meaning something that projects.

**cuckold**: man whose wife has been supposedly unfaithful.

**forlorn**: destroy, ruin.


PAGE 35

**Actaeon**: spied on the goddess Diana bathing and consequently was turned into a stag and killed by his own hounds; his 'badge': horns.

**want**: lack.

**jars**: disturbances, irritations.

**Fidelity**: most of the moral virtues were traditionally represented as female figures.

**feather**: the badge of a fool.

**head of the woman**: from I Cor.xi.3; the stock idea of male–female relations – Anger, like others, uses it to interrogate the capabilities of the male and hence to question assumptions about maleness.

**coxcomb**: professional fool's cap.

**allure**: *Euphues*: 'allured with their wicked guiles' (p. 248). The 'long discourse' above is not in Lyly.

**Mulier ... confusio**: woman is man's ruin; common idea and phrase in medieval poetry (e.g., Chaucer, *Nun's Priest's Tale*, l. 3164).

**Aut amat ... tertio**: either she loves or she hates: there is no third course; proverbial, more often 'nihil est tertium'.


PAGE 36

**Plato**: possibly a reference to *Republic* v.

**purblind**: partially sighted (original has 'spurblind').

**Hesiodus**: one of the earliest Greek poets; his *Theogŏny* (ll. 600 ff.) claims that

PAGE 36 CONTINUED

women were sent by the gods as an evil to men, his *Works and Days* (ll. 60 ff.) makes a similar debatable point.

**noddies**: fools.

**strength**: Anger, like Sowernam, prefers the clarity of openly aggressive relations between the sexes.


PAGE 37

**Clytemnestra**: wife of Agamemnon; in Aeschylus' play she is made to murder him.

**Ariadne**: helped Theseus with the labyrinth, then escaped from Crete with him; usually seen as the pathetic woman deserted by Theseus, rather than as evil; one story has her commit suicide. This may be a misprint for Arachne (cf. Kyd, *The Spanish Tragedy* III.x.89).

**Delilah**: the treacherous Philistine who betrayed Samson and cut off his hair.

**Jezebel**: wicked domineering wife of Ahab, who insisted on her pagan religion despite Elijah's true faith.

**Nero**: the notorious Roman emperor (ruled 54–68), licentious and murderous, arranged the death of his mother; my favourite entry about him runs: 'vain, egotistic and assertive. Yet his devotion to art was real.'

**lead the dance**: take pride of place.

**Deianira**: wife of Hercules; assaulted by the centaur Nessus; Nessus, killed by Hercules, gave his blood to Deianira as a love potion; when in later years she smeared it on a tunic for Hercules, it turned out to be poisonous.

**have condemned**: original has 'have had condemned'.

**Marius, etc.**: I know of no story of Marius' daughter. Marius (b. 157 BC) was a famous general and seven times consul. The Metelli were a notable Roman family. Plutarch tells a story of Metellus saying that Marius will only be consul when Metellus' son is. (Anger may be recalling a story of a speech made by Quintus Metellus when he spoke of the difficulties of marriage: see Painter, *Palace of Pleasure*, novel 14.)

**Euthydemus**: This may be incorrect. Euthydemus was seen as a type of folly. Simonides made ten kinds of women. Swetnam (p. 36) repeats the six kinds of women.

**marthrifts**: Anger's coinage apparently; someone who spoils thrift.

**beggar's bush**: state of beggary.

**snout-fair**: fair of face.


PAGE 38

**fellow … cross**: Swetnam, interestingly, tells this story (pp. 62–3): a preacher invites whoever will be saved to take up his cross.

**winch**: kick out.

**crank**: high spirited, cocky.

**Thales**: there were two famous Greeks of this name; one was a philosopher (*c.* 640 BC), the other a musician and lyric poet; neither fits this description but Diogenes Laertius (i.33) records the former saying he was glad he was 'born a man and not a woman'.

**Roman**: this could be a reference to Cato the Censor, though it is applicable to many Romans.

**Alphonso**: possibly Alphonso the wise (1221–84), King of Castile, who compiled laws and wrote poetry. This 'rule' has the status of a proverb.

**Tibullus**: Roman poet (?54–18 BC) writing love elegies to a boy and two women; in his *Elegies* III.iv.60 women are accused of being deceivers.

**bred in the bone**: ingrained, as opposed to superficial (of the flesh).

**Venerians**: followers of Venus: licentious men.

**Socrates' rule**: Socrates was most famous for saying 'that he knew nothing except just the fact of his ignorance' (Diogenes Laertius ii.32).

PAGE 38 CONTINUED
**dissembling water:** derived from the proverb 'as false [unstable] as water'.


PAGE 39
**in principio:** in the beginning.
**fruitful:** here is the important stress on the dignity of childbirth (and a female version of the Adam and Eve story).
**first that repented:** Mary Magdalene.
**[no]:** I think this needs to be added.
**wanted:** lacked.
**mackerel:** swim in shoals and spawn in summer.
**curious:** meticulous in appearance.
**conditions:** disposition, particular characteristics.
**necessary, evil:** that 'women are necessary evils' was a Renaissance proverb; it can be traced back to Menander, *Minor Fragments* 651K (Loeb edn): 'Marriage if one will face the truth is an evil but a necessary evil.' But the idea is absorbed into Christian writers: Erasmus has an adage on a similar theme, and Tasso refers us to St Chrysostom.
**want:** lack.
**barking out:** Swetnam picks up this sort of imagery.
**Malum ... peius:** Evil added to evil makes a worse evil. Anger more or less gives this translation.
**Magnificat:** the Virgin Mary's hymn of thanksgiving for being chosen to bear Christ. Anger takes this as divine confirmation of women's virtue.
**sithence:** since.
**ex confessio:** out of their own confession.


PAGE 40
**year of '88:** *Euphues*: 'of late I have been very fantastical' (p. 257). (Also, by the way, Armada year.)
**sophistry:** plausible but deceptive logic, quibbling. Anger is about to give a display of proper logic.
**contra ... disputandum:** against principle there can be no arguing. Close to the proverb 'Contra factum non datur argumentum'.
**primum est optimum:** first is best.
**non plus:** state where they are bewildered (nonplussed), perplexity.
**cousin german:** first cousin.
**Gotham:** proverbial for the folly of its inhabitants.
**stealth:** theft.
**qualm:** fit of sickness.
**kercher:** handkerchief.
**ban:** curse.


PAGE 41
**do the printer injury:** this seems a clear advertisement to the reader to buy *Book: his Surfeit* – the strongest evidence that Anger's pamphlet is set up.
**cast:** calculate.
**Alexander's horse:** notable for its size.
**Italian courtesans:** Euphues also addresses 'the grave matrons and honest maidens of Italy'. It is hard to see how Anger's irony is working here.
**Experientia praestantior arte:** experience (experimental knowledge) is superior to art (theory, mental skill); related to the proverb 'experience is the mother of invention'.
**book cases:** like the cases in a law book (note the deliberate repetition of 'case' – it becomes ridiculous alongside the 'reality' of Experience).
**gloze:** flatter, talk seductively.

PAGE 42

**woodcocks shoot:** fly through woods, i.e. dusk.

**vantage:** retire to a tactically superior position; the military images here can be found in much witty banter between men and women on the stage.

**lying neighbours:** sarcastic – each man always claims that he himself (unlike others) speaks the truth.

**Mentiri ... nostrum:** we are not liars.

**wild geese ... bridge:** an example of their tall stories. (There is also a proverb lurking: about fools going under London Bridge.)

**Nulla ... hominibus:** proverbial: there is no faith or truth in men (*hominibus* should be *hominum*).

**Vulcan:** I cannot trace this story, nor the name Briceris. (I am highly suspicious of most of Anger's classical references.)

**flouts:** mocks and jeers.

**Hipsicrates:** I take this to be Hipsicratea, famous for her love of her husband King Mithridates (d. 63 BC).

**Pantheia:** killed herself after the death of her husband Abradatus (c. 540 BC).

**Artemisia:** (reigned 352–350 BC) showed her love for Mausolus by building a huge monument in his memory.

**Portia:** the wife of Brutus who killed herself (43 BC) by swallowing hot coals.

**Sulpicia:** (end 1st C.) wrote love poetry.

**Arria:** two of this name (d. 42 and 67 respectively). Both wished to die beside their husbands.

**Hipparchia:** (c. 328 BC) despite parental opposition married the philosopher Crates.

**Prisca:** (d. 31) after her husband was put to death she stabbed herself in front of the senate.

**Macrina:** the Younger was elder sister of Basil the Great (b. 327); intellectual, pious, refused all offers of marriage after her fiancé died.

**wife of Paudocrus:** cannot trace (could be misprint for Pandocrus; or Pandoerus/ Pandarus who was mythological).

**Sigismunda:** from Boccaccio's *Decameron*, Day 4, Novel i: Ghismonda (Sigismunda), daughter of Tancred, had been married only a short time when her husband died. She returned to her father's court where she fell in love with a page, Guiscardo. Tancred discovered them having sex together and reproached his daughter. She strongly defended her right to sexual desires.

**descanted:** commented.

PAGE 43

**His court:** i.e., lust's.

**Cyrus:** this Persian king (559–529 BC) controlled his lust for Pantheia because she was another man's wife (the story is in *Euphues*, p. 250).

**Xenocrates:** Diogenes Laertius tells how this Greek philosopher (head of the Academy 339–314 BC) resisted the attempts of Phryne to seduce him (iv.7).

**Caius Gracchus:** (fl. 130 BC) Roman tribune famous for his honour and virtue (Plutarch wrote his life).

**Pompeius:** (106–48 BC) the famous Roman senator and general whose private life was reputed to be very virtuous.

**Francis Sforza:** brought peace and prosperity to Milan, which he captured in 1450.

**tread them:** copulate with them.

**valiant:** the definition here of the proper man, as the solution to a world of sexual deceit and oppression.

**Heliogabalus:** (b. 205) Roman emperor of archetypal decadence. Practised sun worship and, apparently, turned his court into a brothel.

**Commodus:** (161–192) another emperor synonymous with 'the most shameless and beastly debauchery'; sometimes wore Amazon costume.

**Proculus:** 'Proculus Emperor (the story says)/Deflowered one hundred maids in

PAGE 43 CONTINUED

fifteen days' (from John Taylor's poem, *A Common Whore*).

**Chilpericus**: King of the North Franks, 561–584 (his wife Fredegond was apparently ambitious).

**Xerxes**: Persian king (486–465 BC); Plato's *Laws* iii.695 talks of his dissoluteness.

**Boleslaus**: Boleslav, King of Poland (d. 1025).

**Sigismundus Malateste**: of Rimini (1417–68), famously immoral.

**probable**: plausible, reliable.

PAGE 44

**Fallere ... fraus**: it is no crime to deceive the deceiver.

**lawns, drawn-works**: fine linen, ornamented textiles. Compare here *Euphues*: 'Take from them their periwigs' (p. 254).

**galled**: a 'gall' is a swelling or blister on a horse (or a sore) caused by the rubbing of harness; compare *Euphues*: 'I know none will winch except she be galded' (p. 257).

PAGE 45

**in his kind**: according to his real nature.

**brake**: trap, bridle.

**wight**: person.

**Vivendo disce**: learn through living.

**Jo. A.**: Joan was often interchangeable with Jane (if the name was fake I would have expected it to have been consciously regularised, in full).

**Eiusdem ad Lectorem**: from the same to the reader, concerning the author.

# The Swetnam Controversy

Many women are in shape angels but in qualities devils, painted coffins with rotten bones ... Although women are beautiful, showing pity, yet their hearts are black, swelling with mischief, not much unlike unto old trees whose outward leaves are fair and green and yet the body rotten.

Thus the language and the sentiments of Joseph Swetnam's *Arraignment of Lewd, idle, froward and unconstant women*. Printed in 1615 under the pseudonym of Thomas Tel-troth, Swetnam's pamphlet proved a great favourite and was to be reprinted regularly for the next hundred years. It also provoked a response from women.

It is particularly ironic that Swetnam's pamphlet should have proved so popular. Men were (and are) taught to regard themselves as being altogether more intelligent and gifted than women, yet this piece of writing that champions the male cause is, besides being predictably unpleasant, grossly derivative in its language and ideas and loose and repetitive in its expression of them. Oddly enough, one of the texts Swetnam draws on is John Lyly's *Euphues his Censure to Philautus*, the very text that Jane Anger indirectly answered. Swetnam may have been trying deliberately to start a new gender battle; certainly he was a very crude plagiarist. He begins with Lyly's words 'Musing with myself being idle'. Talking of different sorts of women Lyly says 'There is a great difference between the standing puddle and the running stream' and Swetnam echoes him; Lyly talks of a woman 'snatching in jest and keeping in earnest' and Swetnam echoes him, twice. Swetnam repeats the advice to keep two women on the go at once, and repeats and elaborates the idea of stripping off cosmetics and fine attire.

All these notions are quite common in the tradition of anti-woman writing of the period, but Swetnam lifts them specifically from Lyly. Lyly, it might be said in his defence, at least puts his words into the mouth of a fictional character, Euphues; but Swetnam presents them as his own. He is almost cultivating the pose of the woman-hater, a pose so readily assumed by much of the sophisticated 'witty' writing of the period, such as can be found in John Donne's work for example. It was 'witty' to discourse shockingly on the essential evil and moral ugliness of women. Swetnam, unwittily, likes to define women's nature:

> Then who can but say that women sprung from the devil, whose heads, hands and hearts, mind and souls are evil, for women are called the hook of all evil, because men are taken by them as fish is taken with the hook. (p. 15)

There is something almost naive about Swetnam's aping of this manner: his pseudonym is a blatant theft from the famous travel-writer Thomas Coryate, and Swetnam, like Coryate, claims to have travelled for thirty years. (One of his opponents spotted these thefts.) It may be that Swetnam was trying to make a name for himself; woman-hating was fashionable in some quarters; James I's misogyny was notorious. But Swetnam also drew on another source in his literary greed: the Protestant domestic conduct book – those manuals of advice on marital duties and domestic responsibilities that so many Puritans were fond of writing. Having been 'witty' for half his pamphlet, Swetnam then affects moral concern. He advises men not to beat their wives nor to meddle in their wives' work (to observe correct role division); but elsewhere he says 'Eagles eat not men till they are dead but women devour them alive ... they are like eagles which always fly where the carrion is'; he tells jokey stories about widows that hang themselves, and advocates male violence against women. He quotes from the Bible and later advises 'thou must neither chide nor play with thy wife before company: those that play and dally with them before company, they do thereby set other men's teeth on edge and make their wives the less shamefast' (p. 53). All of this, with its pretences and contradictions, makes a nonsense of the Puritan interest in marital equality, and particularly it perverts the central emphasis on mutual love.

I think that it is because of its travesty of domestic advice that Swetnam's book provoked such fury. Witty anti-woman satire could be seen as the product of a specific class group; it was both old-fashioned and irrelevantly literary. Protestant and Puritan ideas about marriage were newer, they had a campaign to fight and they were dealing with the everyday world. Consciousness of these ideas had developed to a point where Swetnam's viciousness could be stopped. James I's decadent court and the attitudes associated with it had by now been around for long enough, sponging off the country, to be met with very definite opposition. Swetnam was no courtier, but his writing reeks of that sort of life-style. When women attacked him in their pamphlets they paid particular attention to his views on marriage and women's social role. Their ideal of marital equality is opposed to his travesty, with its typical blend of violence and sentiment.

We shall see how the women answered, but the battle did not end there. In 1619 a play about Swetnam was performed (so big was the controversy). *Swetnam the Woman-Hater Arraigned by Women* is a fascinating play which draws on the pamphlets written by women (it is possibly the nearest women of the time got to writing a publicly performed play). The sub-plot involves Swetnam being beaten up by women; the main plot is about state politics with parallels with James I (I've tried to analyse it fully in my book *Amazons and Warrior Women*). The play was performed at the Red Bull theatre – a large unfashionable playhouse. While the courtly, expensive theatres were showing plays about virgins in distress, the often grubbier audience at the Red Bull were watching the woman-hater being humiliated. And that humiliation is carried out by women. At first Swetnam is defeated in single combat by a man dressed as a woman (who incidentally has earlier criticised a jury for being composed of men, not women). The man in women's clothes is fairly stage-conventional; he then hands over to a more novel female court who try, and punish Swetnam. These women are anonymous, simply an angry crowd to whom the male hero deliberately defers. It may be the first case of a female mob sympathetically treated on the Jacobean stage.

# A
# MOUZELL FOR MELASTOMUS,

The Cynical Bayter of, and foul
*mouthed Barker against*
*EVAHS SEX*

Or an Apologeticall Answere to
*that Irreligious and Illiterate*
Pamphlet made by *Jo. Sw.* and by him
Intituled, *The Arraignment*
*of Women*

*By Rachel Speght*

PROVERBS 26.5
*Answer a fool according to his foolishnesse, lest*
*he bee wise in his owne conceit*

LONDON
printed by *Nicholas Okes* for *Thomas Archer*, and
are to be sold at his shop in Popes-
head–Palace. 1617.

[Rachel Speght was real. We are told by Ester Sowernam that she was a 'Minister's daughter'. This makes it likely that her father was James Speght, a Yorkshireman who came to London. He was ordained in May 1591 and his first parish was St Mary Magdalene, Milk Street, from 1592. In 1611 he also became responsible for St Clement's, East Cheap. By early May 1637 he was dead, leaving only two extant works, both sermons. We are told that Rachel Speght had 'not yet seen twenty years' when she wrote *A Muzzle* in 1616. In 1621 she published a second work, *Mortality's Memorandum*, which is a verse meditation on death partly in response to her mother's death. This work is dedicated to her god-mother Mary Moundford, wife of Dr Thomas Moundford, who before he came to London was Bursar of King's College, Cambridge.

It seems that early in August 1621, Rachel Speght married William Procter. They are both described as resident in the parish of St Botolph's Aldersgate. It seems likely that Rachel Speght gave up writing for mothering, though not immediately. In February 1626 there was christened Rachel, daughter to William Procter; and in December 1630 a son, William. Both were christened in the same church, and I take it that they were the first two children since they bear their parents' Christian names.

Rachel Speght's pamphlet is learned, especially in scripture. Clearly she had benefited from an educated religious household; there were also links with the more enlightened of the two universities, Cambridge, through her father and her god-mother's husband. Even more importantly, for us, there seems to be a consciousness of femaleness: she dedicates her poem on her mother's death to another woman, her god-mother; she passes on her Christian name to her daughter. Mere hints – but they tie in very nicely with the anger she declares when she hears people attributing the authorship of her first work, *A Muzzle*, to her father. It was partly out of her annoyance with this male obliteration of female writing that she decided to publish her second work (printed by the Griffins, a husband and wife team of printers who had already shown a serious interest in gender controversy). Speght's is a fascinating statement about the woman author's need publicly to claim her rights as an author:

> I know these populous times afford plenty of froward writers and critical readers. Myself hath made up the number of the one too many by one; and, having been touched with the censures of the other (by occasion of my *muzzling Melastomus*), I am now as by a strong motive induced – for my right's sake – to produce and divulge this offspring of my endeavour: to prove [test] them further futurely who have formerly deprived me of my due, imposing my abortive [unfulfilled project/fine vellum/abortion] upon the father of *me* – but not of it. (Epistle Dedicatory, *Mortality's Memorandum*)

(In the allegorical *Dream* which is prefixed to *Mortality's Memorandum* Speght recounts her intellectual autobiography. She searches for Knowledge but the figure of Dissuasion tries to stop her. Dissuasion talks of 'The difficulty of attaining lore [learning],/My time, and sex, with many others more.')

The pamphlet that follows is full of religious references, which Speght

accurately documents. While we know that at least from the 1580s
women led prayers in sectarian meetings and that in the 1640s there were
women preachers, this is the first example I have found of a printed
semi-religious text by a woman. The religious knowledge is necessary
because it allows Speght to examine the role and 'nature' of women in
general. It is only in the second half of the work, separately entitled
*Certain Queries to the Baiter of Women*, that she addresses herself to the
particular controversy.

   Apparently she was much criticised for what she said, but that does
not seem to have deterred her: 'Their variety of verdicts have verified the
adage *quot homines, tot sententiae* [there are as many opinions as there
are men] and made my experience confirm that apothegm which doth
affirm Censure to be inevitable to a public act.']

# To all virtuous ladies honourable or worshipful and to all other of Hevah's sex, fearing God and loving their just reputation, grace and peace through Christ, to eternal glory †

It was the simile of that wise and learned Lactantius, that if fire, †
though but with a small spark kindled, be not at the first quenched
it may work great mischief and damage. So likewise may the
scandals and defamations of the malevolent in time prove pernicious, if they be not nipped in the head at their first appearance. The
consideration of this, right honourable and worshipful ladies, hath
incited me (though young and the unworthiest of thousands) to
encounter with a furious enemy to our sex, lest if his unjust
imputations should continue without answer he might insult and
account himself a victor; and by such a conceit deal as historiographers report the viper to do, who in the winter time doth vomit
forth her poison and in the spring time sucketh the same up again,
which becometh twice as deadly as the former. And this our
pestiferous enemy, by thinking to provide a more deadly poison for
women than already he hath foamed forth, may evaporate, by an †
addition unto his former illiterate pamphlet (entitled *The Arraignment of Women*), a more contagious obtrectation than he hath †
already done and indeed hath threatened to do. Secondly, if it
should have free passage without any answer at all (seeing that
*tacere* is *quasi consentire*), the vulgar ignorant might have believed †
his diabolical infamies to be infallible truths not to be infringed;
whereas now they may plainly perceive them to be but the scum of
heathenish brains, or a building raised without a foundation (at least
from sacred scripture) which the wind of God's truth must needs
cast down to the ground. A third reason why I have ventured to
fling this stone at vaunting Goliath is to comfort the minds of all
Hevah's sex, both rich and poor, learned and unlearned, with this
antidote: that if the fear of God reside in their hearts, maugre all †

adversaries, they are highly esteemed and accounted of in the eyes of their gracious Redeemer, so that they need not fear the darts of † envy or obtrectators. For shame and disgrace, saith Aristotle, is the end of them that shoot such poisoned shafts. Worthy therefore of imitation is that example of Seneca who, when he was told that a certain man did exclaim and rail against him, made this mild answer: † some dogs bark more upon custom than cursedness; and some speak evil of others, not that the defamed deserve it but because through custom and corruption of their hearts they cannot speak well of any. This I allege as a paradigmatical pattern for all women, noble and ignoble, to follow: that they be not inflamed with choler against this our enraged adversary, but patiently consider of him according to the portraiture which he hath drawn of himself – his writings being the very emblem of a monster.

This my brief apology, right honourable and worshipful, did I enterprise not as thinking myself more fit than others to undertake such a task, but as one who, not perceiving any of our sex to enter † the lists of encountering with this our grand enemy among men (I being out of all fear because armed with the truth – which though often blamed yet can never be shamed – and the word of God's † spirit, together with the example of virtue's pupils for a buckler), did no whit dread to combat with our said malevolent adversary. And if in so doing I shall be censured by the judicious to have the victory, and shall have given content unto the wronged, I have both hit the mark whereat I aimed and obtained that prize which I † desired. But if Zoilus shall adjudge me presumptuous in dedicating † this my chirograph unto personages of so high rank (both because of my insufficiency in literature and tenderness in years), I thus apologise for myself: that seeing the Baiter of Women hath opened his mouth against noble as well as ignoble, against the rich as well as the poor, therefore meet it is that they should be joint spectators of this encounter. And withal, in regard of my imperfection both in † learning and age, I need so much the more to impetrate patronage from some of power to shield me from the biting wrongs of † Momus, who oftentimes setteth a rankling tooth into the sides of † truth. Wherefore I, being of Decius his mind who deemed himself safe under the shield of Caesar, have presumed to shelter myself under the wings of you, honourable personages, against the persecuting heat of this fiery and furious dragon: desiring that you would † be pleased not to look so much *ad opus* as *ad animum*. And so, not doubting of the favourable acceptance and censure of all virtuously affected, I rest

your honours' and worships',
humbly at commandment
Rachel Speght.

I f reason had but curbed thy witless will
O r fear of God restrained thy raving quill,
S uch venom foul thou wouldst have blushed to spew,
E xcept that grace have bidden thee adieu:
P rowess disdains to wrestle with the weak
H eathenish affected, care not what they speak.

S educer of the vulgar sort of men,
W as Satan crept into thy filthy pen,
E nflaming thee with such infernal smoke,
T hat (if thou hadst thy will) should women choke?
N efarious fiends thy sense herein deluded,
A nd from thee all humanity excluded.
M onster of men, worthy no other name,
   For that thou didst essay our sex to shame.

                                   Ra[chel] Sp[eght]

## Not unto the veriest Idiot that ever set pen to paper, but to the Cynical Baiter of Women, or Metamorphosed Misogunes, Joseph Swetnam †

From standing water, which soon putrifies, can no good fish be expected; for it produceth no other creatures but those that are venomous or noisome, as snakes, adders and such like. Semblably, no better stream can we look should issue from your idle corrupt brain than that whereto the rough of your fury (to use your own † words) hath moved you to open the sluice. In which excrement of † your raving cogitations you have used such irregularities touching concordance, and observed so disordered a method, as I doubt not to tell you that a very accidence scholar would have quite put you † down in both. You appear herein not unlike that painter who, seriously endeavouring to portray Cupid's bow, forgot the string: for you being greedy to botch up your mingle-mangle invective † against women have not therein observed, in many places, so much as grammar sense. But the emptiest barrel makes the loudest sound, and so we will account of you.

Many propositions have you framed which (as you think) make much against women, but if one would make a logical assumption the conclusion would be flat against your own sex. Your dealing wants so much discretion that I doubt whether to bestow so good a name as the dunce upon you. But minority bids me keep within my bounds, and therefore I only say unto you that your corrupt heart and railing tongue hath made you a fit scribe for the devil.

In that you have termed your virulent foam the 'Bear-baiting of Women' you have plainly displayed your own disposition to be

† cynical, in that there appears no other dog or bull to bait them but yourself. Good had it been for you to have put on that muzzle which St James would have all Christians to wear: 'Speak not evil one of another' (*James* iv.11); and then had you not seemed so like
† the serpent Porphyrus as now you do – which, though full of deadly poison, yet being toothless hurteth none so much as himself. For you, having gone beyond the limits not of humanity alone but of Christianity, have done greater harm unto your own soul than unto women, as may plainly appear. First, in dishonouring of God by palpable blasphemy, wresting and perverting every place of scripture that you have alleged; which by the testimony of St Peter (I *Peter* iii.16) is to the destruction of them that so do. Secondly, it appears by your disparaging of, and opprobrious speeches against, that excellent work of God's hands, which in his great love he perfected for the comfort of man. Thirdly and lastly, by this your hodge-podge of heathenish sentences, similes and examples, you have set forth yourself in your right colours unto the view of the world; and I doubt not but the judicious will account of you
† according to your demerit. As for the vulgar sort, which have no more learning than you have showed in your book, it is likely they will applaud you for your pains.

As for your 'bugbear' or advice unto women, that whatsoever they do think of your work they should conceal it, lest in finding
† fault they bewray their galled backs to the world (in which you allude to that proverb 'Rub a galled horse and he will kick'): unto it I answer by way of apology, that though every galled horse being touched doth kick, yet everyone that kicks is not galled. So that you might as well have said that because burnt folks dread the fire, therefore none fear fire but those that are burnt, as made that illiterate conclusion which you have absurdly inferred.

† In your title leaf you arraign none but lewd, idle, froward and unconstant women, but in the sequel (through defect of memory as it seemeth), forgetting that you had made a distinction of good from bad, condemning all in general you advise men to beware of, and not to match with, any of these six sorts of women, viz. Good and Bad, Fair and Foul, Rich and Poor. But this doctrine of devils St
† Paul, foreseeing would be broached in the latter times, gives warning of (I *Tim.* iv.3).

There also you promise a commendation of wise, virtuous and honest women, whenas, in the subsequent, the worst words and filthiest epithets that you can devise you bestow on them in general, excepting no sort of women. Herein may you be likened unto a man which upon the door of a scurvy house sets this superscription 'Here is a very fair house to be let'; whereas, the door being opened, it is no better than a dog-hole and dark dungeon.

Further, if your own words be true, that you wrote with your hand but not with your heart, then are you an hypocrite in print.

But it is rather to be thought that your pen was the bewrayer of the abundance of your mind, and that this was but a little mortar to daub up again the wall which you intended to break down.

The revenge of your railing work we leave to Him who hath appropriated vengeance unto himself, whose pen-man hath in- †
cluded railers in the catalogue of them that shall not inherit God's kingdom, and yourself unto the mercy of that just judge who is able to save and to destroy.

Your undeserved friend,
Rachel Speght.

### In praise of the Author and her Work

If little David that for Israel's sake
   esteemed neither life nor limb too dear,
In that he did adventure without dread
   to cast at him whom all the host did fear
A stone, which brought Goliath to the ground,
Obtained applause with songs and timbrels' sound: †

Then let another young encombatant
   receive applause and thanks as well as he.
For with an enemy to women-kind
   she hath encountered, as each wight may see; †
And with the fruit of her industrious toil
To this Goliath she hath given the foil.

Admire her much I may, both for her age
   and this her Muzzle for a black-mouthed wight,
But praise her and her work to that desert
   which unto them belongs of equal right
I cannot; only this I say, and end,
She is unto her sex a faithful friend.

Philalethes. †

If he, that for his country doth expose
   himself unto the fury of his foe,
Doth merit praise and due respect of those
   for whom he did that peril undergo:
Then let the author of this Muzzle true
Receive the like, of right it is her due.

For she, to shield her sex from slander's dart
   and from invective obtrectation,
Hath ventured by force of learning's art
   (in which she hath had education)

To combat with him which doth shame his sex
By offering feeble women to perplex.
Philomathes.

† 

Praise is a debt, which doth of due belong
To those that take the path of virtue's trace,
Meting their ways and works by reason's rule,
Having their hearts so lightened with God's grace
   That willingly they would not him offend,
   But holily their lives begin and end.

† 

Of such a pupil unto piety
As is described, I do intend to speak:
A virgin young and of such tender age
As for encounter may be deemed too weak,
   She having not as yet seen twenty years,
   Though in her carriage older she appears.

Her wit and learning in this present work
More praise doth merit than my quill can write;
Her magnanimity deserves applaud
In vent'ring with a fiery foe to fight:
   And now, in fine, what shall I further say?
   But that she bears the triumph quite away.
Favour B.

# A MUZZLE FOR MELASTOMUS,

The Cynical Baiter of, and foul
*mouthed Barker against
Evahs Sex.*

PROVERBS 18.22
*He that findeth a wife findeth a good thing, and
receiveth favour of the Lord.*

If lawful it be to compare the potter with his clay, or the architect
with the edifice: then may I, in some sort, resemble that love of

God towards man in creating woman unto the affectionate care of Abraham for his son Isaac, who that he might not take to wife one of the daughters of the Canaanites did provide him one of his own kindred (*Genesis* xxiv.4).

Almighty God, who is rich in mercy (*Ephes.* ii.4), having made all things of nothing and created man in his own image (*Coloss.* iii.30 [10]) (that is, as the Apostle expounds it, 'In wisdom, righteousness and true holiness;' making him lord over all (*Ephes.* iv. 24)), to avoid that solitary condition that he was then in, having none to commerce or converse withal but dumb creatures, it seemed good unto the Lord that as of every creature he had made male and female, and man only being alone without mate, so likewise to form an help-meet for him. Adam for this cause being cast into a heavy sleep (*Genesis* ii.20), God, extracting a rib from his side, thereof made, or built, woman – showing thereby that man was an unperfect building afore woman was made; and, bringing her unto Adam, united and married them together.

Thus the resplendent love of God toward man appeared, in taking care to provide him an helper before he saw his own want and in providing him such an helper as should be meet for him. Sovereignty had he over all creatures, and they were all serviceable unto him; but yet afore woman was formed there was not a meet help found for Adam (*Genesis* ii.20). Man's worthiness not meriting this great favour at God's hands but His mercy only moving Him thereunto, I may use those words which the Jews uttered when they saw Christ weep for Lazarus: 'Behold how he loved him' (*John* xi.36). Behold, and that with good regard, God's love; yea, his great love which from the beginning he hath borne unto man. Which, as it appears in all things, so next his love in Christ Jesus apparently in this: that for man's sake, that he might not be an unit † when all other creatures were for procreation dual, he created woman to be a solace unto him, to participate of his sorrows, partake of his pleasures and as a good yoke-fellow bear part of his burden (I *Cor.* xi.9). Of the excellency of this structure, I mean of women, whose foundation and original of creation was God's love, do I intend to dilate.

## Of Woman's Excellency, with the causes of her creation, and of the sympathy which ought to be in man and wife each toward other

The work of creation being finished, this approbation thereof was given by God himself, that 'All was very good' (*Genesis* i.31). If All, then woman, who – excepting man – is the most excellent creature under the canopy of heaven. But if it be objected by any:

First, that woman, though created good, yet by giving ear to

Satan's temptations brought death and misery upon all her posterity.

Secondly, that 'Adam was not deceived, but that the woman was deceived and was in the transgression' (I *Tim*. ii.14).

Thirdly, that St Paul saith 'It were good for a man not to touch a woman' (I *Cor*. vii.1).

Fourthly and lastly, that of Solomon, who seems to speak against all of our sex: 'I have found one man of a thousand, but a woman among them all have I not found' (*Eccles*. vii.30) – whereof in it[s] due place.

To the first of these objections I answer: that Satan first assailed the woman because where the hedge is lowest, most easy it is to get

† over, and she being the weaker vessel was with more facility to be seduced – like as a crystal glass sooner receives a crack than a strong stone pot. Yet we shall find the offence of Adam and Eve almost to parallel: for as an ambitious desire of being made like unto God was the motive which caused her to eat, so likewise was it his, as may

† plainly appear by that *ironia*: 'Behold, man is become as one of us' (*Genesis* iii.22) – not that he was so indeed, but hereby his desire to attain a greater perfection than God had given him was reproved. Woman sinned, it is true, by her infidelity in not believing the word of God but giving credit to Satan's fair promises that 'she should not die' (*Genesis* iii.4); but so did the man too. And if Adam had not approved of that deed which Eve had done, and been willing to tread the steps which she had gone, he – being her head – would have reproved her and have made the commandment a bit to restrain him from breaking his maker's injunction. For if a man burn his hand in the fire, the bellows that blowed the fire are not to be blamed, but himself rather for not being careful to avoid the danger. Yet if the bellows had not blowed, the fire had not burnt; no more is woman simply to be condemned for man's transgression. For by the free will, which before his fall he enjoyed, he might have avoided and been free from being burnt or singed with that fire which was kindled by Satan, and blown by Eve. It therefore served not his turn a whit afterwards to say: 'The woman which thou gavest me gave me of the tree, and I did eat' (*Genesis* iii.12). For a penalty was inflicted upon him as well as on the woman, the punishment of her transgression being particular to her own sex and to none but the female kind: but for the sin of man the whole earth was cursed. And he, being better able than the woman to have resisted temptation, because the stronger vessel, was first called to account: to show that to whom much is given, of them much is required; and that he who was the sovereign of all creatures visible should have yielded greatest obedience to God.

True it is (as is already confessed) that woman first sinned, yet find we no mention of spiritual nakedness till man had sinned. Then it is said 'Their eyes were opened' (*Genesis* iii.7), the eyes of their

mind and conscience; and then perceived they themselves naked,
that is, not only bereft of that integrity which they originally had,
but felt the rebellion and disobedience of their members in the †
disordered motions of their now corrupt nature, which made them
for shame to cover their nakedness. Then (and not afore) it is said
that they saw it, as if sin were imperfect and unable to bring a
deprivation of a blessing received, or death on all mankind, till man
(in whom lay the active power of generation) had transgressed. The
offence, therefore, of Adam and Eve is by St Austin thus distin- †
guished: 'the man sinned against God and himself, the woman
against God, herself and her husband'; yet in her giving of the fruit
to eat had she no malicious intent towards him, but did therein
show a desire to make her husband partaker of that happiness which
she thought by their eating they should both have enjoyed. This her
giving Adam of that sauce wherewith Satan had served her, whose
sourness, afore he had eaten, she did not perceive, was that which
made her sin to exceed his. Wherefore, that she might not of him
who ought to honour her (I *Peter* iii.7) be abhorred, the first
promise that was made in Paradise God makes to woman: that by
her seed should the serpent's head be broken (*Genesis* iii.15).
Whereupon Adam calls her Hevah, Life, that as the woman had
been an occasion of his sin so should woman bring forth the Saviour
from sin, which was in the fullness of time accomplished (*Galat.*
iv.4). By which was manifested that he is a Saviour of believing
women no less than of men, that so the blame of sin may not be
imputed to his creature, which is good, but to the will by which Eve
sinned; and yet by Christ's assuming the shape of man was it
declared that his mercy was equivalent to both sexes. So that by
Hevah's blessed seed, as St Paul affirms, it is brought to pass that
'male and female are all one in Christ Jesus' (*Galat.* iii.28).

To the second objection I answer: that the Apostle doth not
hereby exempt man from sin, but only giveth to understand that the
woman was the primary transgressor, and not the man; but that
man was not at all deceived was far from his meaning. For he
afterward expressly saith that as 'in Adam all die, so in Christ shall
all be made alive' (I *Cor.* xv.22).

For the third objection 'It is good for a man not touch a woman':
the Apostle makes it not a positive prohibition but speaks it only
because of the Corinth[ian]s' present necessity (I *Cor.* vii), who
were then persecuted by the enemies of the church. For which
cause, and no other, he saith: 'Art thou loosed from a wife? Seek †
not a wife' – meaning whilst the time of these perturbations should
continue in their heat; 'but if thou art bound, seek not to be loosed;
if thou marriest thou sinnest not, only increasest thy care: for the
married careth for the things of this world. And I wish that you
were without care that ye might cleave fast unto the Lord without
separation: for the time remaineth that they which have wives be as

though they had none, for the persecutors shall deprive you of them either by imprisonment, banishment or death.' So that manifest it is that the Apostle doth not hereby forbid marriage, but only adviseth the Corinth[ian]s to forbear a while till God in mercy should curb † the fury of their adversaries. For (as Eusebius writeth) Paul was afterward married himself, the which is very probable, being that interrogatively he saith: 'Have we not power to lead about a wife being a sister, as well as the rest of the Apostles, and as the brethren † of the Lord, and Cephas?' (I *Cor*. ix.5)

The fourth and last objection is that of Solomon: 'I have found one man among a thousand, but a woman among them all have I not found' (*Eccles*. vii.30). For answer of which, if we look into the story of his life we shall find therein a commentary upon this enigmatical sentence included. For it is there said that Solomon had seven hundred wives and three hundred concubines, which number † connexed make one thousand. These women turning his heart away from being perfect with the Lord his God (I *Kings* xi.3), sufficient cause had he to say that among the said thousand women found he not one upright. He saith not that among a thousand women never any man found one worthy of commendation, but speaks in the first person singularly 'I have not found', meaning in his own experience. For this assertion is to be holden a part of the confession of his former follies and no[t] otherwise, his repentance being the intended drift of *Ecclesiastes*.

Thus having (by God's assistance) removed those stones, whereat some have stumbled, others broken their shins, I will proceed toward the period of my intended task, which is to decipher the excellency of women. Of whose creation I will, for order's sake, observe: first, the efficient cause, which was God; secondly, the material cause, or that whereof she was made; thirdly, the formal cause, or fashion and proportion of her feature; fourthly and lastly, the final cause, the end or purpose for which she was made. To begin with the first:

† The efficient cause of woman's creation was Jehovah the Eternal, † the truth of which is manifest in Moses his narration of the six days' works, where he saith 'God created them male and female' (*Genesis* i.28[27]). And David, exhorting all 'the earth to sing unto the Lord' † (meaning, by a metonymy, 'earth': all creatures that live on the earth, of what nation or sex soever) gives this reason: 'For the Lord hath made us' (*Psalms* c.3). That work then cannot choose but be good, yea very good, which is wrought by so excellent a workman as the Lord: for he, being a glorious Creator, must needs effect a worthy creature. Bitter water cannot proceed from a pleasant sweet fountain, nor bad work from that workman which is perfectly good – and, in propriety, none but he (*Psalms* c.4; *Matthew* xix.7).

Secondly, the material cause, or matter whereof woman was made, was of a refined mould, if I may so speak. For man was created of the dust of the earth (*Genesis* ii.7), but woman was made of a part of man after that he was a living soul. Yet was she not produced from Adam's foot, to be his too low inferior; nor from his head to be his superior; but from his side, near his heart, to be his equal: that where he is lord, she may be lady. And therefore saith God concerning man and woman jointly: 'Let them rule over the fish of the sea, and over the fowls of the heaven, and over every beast that moveth upon the earth' (*Genesis* i.26). By which words he makes their authority equal, and all creatures to be in subjection unto them both. This, being rightly considered, doth teach men to make such account of their wives as Adam did of Eve: 'This is bone of my bone, and flesh of my flesh' (*Genesis* ii.23); as also, that they neither do or wish any more hurt unto them than unto their own bodies. For men ought to love their wives as themselves, because he that loves his wife loves himself (*Ephes.* v.28): and never man hated his own flesh (which the woman is) unless a monster in nature.

Thirdly, the formal cause, fashion and proportion, of woman was excellent. For she was neither like the beasts of the earth, fowls of the air, fishes of the sea, or any other inferior creature; but man was the only object which she did resemble. For as God gave man a lofty countenance that he might look up toward heaven, so did he likewise give unto woman. And as the temperature of man's body is † excellent, so is woman's. For whereas other creatures, by reason of their gross humours, have excrements for their habit – as fowls their † feathers, beasts their hair, fishes their scales – man and woman only have their skin clear and smooth (*Genesis* i.26). And (that more is) in the image of God were they both created; yea, and to be brief, all the parts of their bodies, both external and internal, were correspondent and meet each for other.

Fourthly and lastly, the final cause or end for which woman was made was to glorify God, and to be a collateral companion for man to glorify God, in using her body and all the parts, powers and faculties thereof as instruments for his honour. As with her voice to sound forth his praises, like Miriam and the rest of her company (*Exodus* xv.20); with her tongue not to utter words of strife but to give good counsel unto her husband, the which he must not despise. For Abraham was bidden to give ear to Sarah his wife (*Genesis* xxi.12); Pilate was willed by his wife not to have any hand in the condemning of Christ (*Matthew* xxvii.19) – and a sin it was in him that he listened not to her; Leah and Rachel counselled Jacob to do according to the word of the Lord (*Genesis* xxxi.16); and the Shunamite put her husband in mind of harbouring the prophet Elisha (II *Kings* iv.9). Her hands should be open, according to her ability, in contributing towards God's service and distressed servants, like to that poor widow which cast two mites into the treasury (*Luke* viii), and as Mary Magdalene, Susanna and Joanna, † the wife of Herod's steward, with many other, which of their

substance ministered unto Christ. Her heart should be a receptacle
for God's word, like Mary that treasured up the sayings of Christ in
her heart (*Luke* i.51[45]). Her feet should be swift in going to seek
the Lord in his sanctuary, as Mary Magdalene made haste to seek
Christ at his sepulchre (*John* xx.1). Finally, no power external or
internal ought woman to keep idle, but to employ it in some service
of God, to the glory of her creator and comfort of her own soul.

The other end for which woman was made was to be a companion and helper for man: and if she must be an *helper*, and but an
*helper*, then are those husbands to be blamed which lay the whole
burden of domestical affairs and maintenance on the shoulders of
their wives. For as yoke-fellows they are to sustain part of each
other's cares, griefs and calamities. But as if two oxen be put in one
yoke, the one being bigger than the other, the greater bears most
weight: so the husband, being the stronger vessel, is to bear a
greater burden than his wife. And therefore the Lord said to Adam:
'In the sweat of thy face shalt thou eat thy bread, till thou return to
the dust' (*Genesis* iii.19); and St Paul saith that 'he that provideth
not for his household is worse than an infidel' (I *Tim.* v.8). Nature
hath taught senseless creatures to help one another: as the male
pigeon, when his hen is weary with sitting on her eggs and comes
off from them, supplies her place, that in her absence they may
receive no harm, until such time as she is fully refreshed. Of small
birds, the cock always helps his hen to build her nest; and while she
sits upon her eggs he flies abroad to get meat for her, who cannot
then provide any for herself. The crowing cockerel helps his hen to
defend her chickens from peril, and will endanger himself to save
her and them from harm. Seeing then that these unreasonable
creatures by the instinct of nature bear such affection each to other,
that without any grudge they willingly according to their kind help
† one another, I may reason, *a minore ad maius*, that much more
should man and woman, which are reasonable creatures, be helpers
each to other in all things lawful: they having the law of God to
† guide them, his word to be a lanthorn unto their feet and a light
unto their paths, by which they are excited to a far more mutual
participation of each other's burden than other creatures. So that
neither the wife may say to her husband nor the husband unto his
wife: 'I have no need of thee' (I *Cor.* xii.21), no more than the
members of the body may so say each to other, between whom
there is such a sympathy that if one member suffer all suffer with it.
Therefore though God bade Abraham forsake his country and
kindred, yet he bade him not forsake his wife who, being 'Flesh of
his flesh, and bone of his bone', was to be co-partner with him of
whatsoever did betide him, whether joy or sorrow. Wherefore
Solomon saith 'woe to him that is alone' (*Eccles.* iv.10); for when
thoughts of discomfort, troubles of this world and fear of dangers
do possess him, he wants a companion to lift him up from the pit of

perplexity into which he is fallen (*Eccles.* iv.10). For a good wife,
saith Plautus, is the wealth of the mind and the welfare of the heart: †
and therefore a meet associate for her husband. And 'woman', saith
Paul, 'is the glory of the man' (I *Cor.* xi.7).

Marriage is a merri-age, and this world's Paradise where there is
mutual love. Our blessed Saviour vouchsafed to honour a marriage
with the first miracle that he wrought (*John* ii), unto which miracle
matrimonial estate may not unfitly be resembled. For as Christ
turned water into wine, a far more excellent liquor (which, as the
Psalmist saith, 'Makes glad the heart of man' (*Psalms* civ.15)), so the
single man is by marriage changed from a bachelor to a husband, a
far more excellent title: from a solitary life unto a joyful union and
conjunction with such a creature as God hath made meet for man,
for whom none was meet till she was made. The enjoying of this
great blessing made Pericles more unwilling to part from his wife †
than to die for his country; and Antonius Pius to pour forth that †
pathetical exclamation against death for depriving him of his dearly
beloved wife: 'O cruel hard-hearted death in bereaving me of her
whom I esteemed more than my own life!'. 'A virtuous woman',
saith Solomon, 'is the crown of her husband' (*Proverbs* xii.4); by
which metaphor he showeth both the excellency of such a wife and
what account her husband is to make of her. For a king doth not
trample his crown under his feet, but highly esteems of it, gently
handles it and carefully lays it up as the evidence of his kingdom;
and therefore when David destroyed Rabbah (I *Chron.* xx.2) he †
took off the crown from their king's head. So husbands should not
account their wives as their vassals but as those that are 'heirs
together of the grace of life' (I *Peter* iii.7), and with all lenity and †
mild persuasions set their feet in the right way if they happen to
tread awry, bearing with their infirmities, as Elkanah did with his
wife's barrenness (I *Samuel* i.17).

The kingdom of God is compared unto the marriage of a king's
son (*Matthew* xxii[.2]); John calleth the conjunction of Christ and
his chosen a marriage (*Revelation* xix.7); and not few but many
times doth our blessed Saviour in the canticles set forth his
unspeakable love towards his church under the title of an husband
rejoicing with his wife, and often vouchsafeth to call her his sister
and spouse – by which is showed that with God 'is no respect of
persons,' nations or sexes (*Romans* ii.11). For whosoever, whether
it be man or woman, that doth 'believe in the Lord Jesus, such shall
be saved' (*John* iii.18). And if God's love, even from the beginning,
had not been as great toward woman as to man, then would he not
have preserved from the deluge of the old world as many women as
men. Nor would Christ after his resurrection have appeared unto a
woman first of all other, had it not been to declare thereby that the
benefits of his death and resurrection are as available, by belief, for
women as for men; for he indifferently died for the one sex as well

as the other. Yet a truth ungainsayable is it, that the 'Man is the woman's head' (I *Cor.* xi.3). By which title yet of supremacy no authority hath he given him to domineer, or basely command and employ his wife as a servant; but hereby is he taught the duties which he oweth unto her. For as the head of a man is the imaginer and contriver of projects profitable for the safety of his whole body, so the husband must protect and defend his wife from injuries. For he is her head 'as Christ is the head of his church' (*Ephes.* v.23), which he entirely loveth, and for which he gave his very life (*Job* ii.4) – the dearest thing any man hath in this world. 'Greater love than this hath no man, when he bestoweth his life for his friend' (*John* xv.13), saith our Saviour. This precedent passeth all other patterns, it requireth great benignity and enjoineth an extraordinary affection, for 'men must love their wives even as Christ loved his church' (*Ephes.* v.25). Secondly, as the head doth not jar or contend with the members – which 'being many', as the Apostle saith, 'yet make but one body' (I *Cor.* xii.20) – no more must the husband with the wife, but expelling all bitterness and cruelty he must live with her lovingly and religiously honouring her as the weaker vessel (I *Peter* iii.7). Thirdly and lastly, as he is her head he must, by instruction, bring her to the knowledge of her creator (I *Cor.* xiv.35), that so she may be a fit stone for the Lord's building. Women for this end must have an especial care to set their affections upon such as are able to teach them, that as they 'grow in years they may grow in grace, and in the knowledge of Christ Jesus our Lord' (I [II] *Peter* iii.18).

Thus if men would remember the duties they are to perform in being heads, some would not stand a tip-toe as they do, thinking themselves lords and rulers, and account every omission of performing whatsoever they command – whether lawful or not – to be matter of great disparagement and indignity done them. Whereas they should consider that women are enjoined to submit themselves unto their husbands no otherways than as to the Lord (*Ephes.* v[.22]). So that, from hence, for man ariseth a lesson not to be forgotten, that as the Lord commandeth nothing to be done but that which is right and good, no more must the husband; for if a wife † fulfil the evil command of her husband, she obeys him as a tempter as Sapphira did Ananias (*Acts* v.2). But lest I should seem too partial in praising woman so much as I have (although no more than warrant from scripture doth allow), I add to the premises that I say not all women are virtuous, for then they should be more excellent than men – sith of Adam's sons there was Cain as well as Abel, and † of Noah's Cham as well as Sem. So that of men as of women there are two sorts, namely: good and bad, which in *Matthew* the five and twenty chapter [verse 33] are comprehended under the name of 'sheep' and 'goats'. And if women were not sinful, then should they not need a Saviour: but the Virgin Mary, a pattern of piety, 'rejoiced in God her Saviour' (*Luke* i.47) – *ergo*, she was a sinner. In the *Revelation* the church is called the spouse of Christ; and in *Zechariah* wickedness is called a woman (*Zech.* v.7[–8]), to show that of women there are both godly and ungodly. For Christ would not 'purge his floor' [*Matthew* iii.12] if there were not chaff among the wheat; nor should gold need to be fined if among it there were no dross. But far be it from anyone to condemn the righteous with the wicked (*Genesis* xviii.25), or good women with the bad (as the Baiter of Women doth). For though there are some scabbed sheep in a flock, we must not therefore conclude all the rest to be mangy. And though some men, through excess, abuse God's creatures, we must not imagine that all men are gluttons; the which we may with as good reason do as condemn all women in general for the offences of some particulars. Of the good sort is it that I have in this book spoken, and so would I that all that read it should so understand me. For if otherwise I had done I should have incurred that woe which by the prophet Isaiah is pronounced against them that 'speak well of evil' (*Isaiah* v.20), and should have 'justified the wicked, which thing is abominable to the Lord' (*Proverbs* xvii.15).

## The Epilogue or upshot of the premises

Great was the unthankfulness of Pharaoh's butler upon Joseph, for though he had done him a great pleasure, of which the butler promised requital, yet was he quite forgotten of him (*Genesis* xl.23). But far greater is the ingratitude of those men toward God that dare presume to speak and exclaim against woman, whom God did create for man's comfort. What greater discredit can redound to a workman than to have the man for whom he hath made it say it is naught? Or what greater discourtesy can be offered to one that bestoweth a gift than to have the receiver give out that he cares not for it, for he needs it not? And what greater ingratitude can be showed unto God than the opprobrious speeches and disgraceful invectives which some diabolical natures do frame against women?

Ingratitude is, and always hath been, accounted so odious a vice that Cicero saith: 'If one doubt what name to give a wicked man, let †
him call him an ungrateful person and then he hath said enough'. It was so detested among the Persians as that by a law they provided that such should suffer death as felons which proved unthankful for any gift received. And 'love' (saith the Apostle) 'is the fulfilling of the law' (*Romans* xiii.10). But where ingratitude is harboured, there love is banished. Let men therefore beware of all unthankfulness but especially of the superlative ingratitude, that which is towards God, which is no way more palpably declared than by the condemning of, and railing against, women. Which sin of some men (if to be termed men) no doubt but God will one day avenge, when

they shall plainly perceive that it had been better for them to have been born dumb and lame than to have used their tongues and hands – the one in repugning, the other in writing – against God's handi-work, their own flesh, women I mean: whom God hath made equal with themselves in dignity, both temporally and eternally, if they continue in the faith. Which God for his mercy sake grant they always may, to the glory of their creator and comfort of their own souls, through Christ. Amen.

*To God only wise be glory now and for ever.   Amen.*

## Certain queries to the Baiter of Women.
*With confutation of some part of his diabolical discipline Printed by N.O. for Thomas Archer 1617*

To the Reader

Although, courteous Reader, I am young in years and more defective in knowledge – that little smattering in learning which I have obtained being only the fruit of such vacant hours as I could spare from affairs befitting my sex – yet am I not altogether ignorant
† of that analogy which ought to be used in a literate responsary. But the Bear-baiting of Women unto which I have framed my apologetical answer, being altogether without method, irregular, with-
† out grammatical concordance and a promiscuous mingle-mangle, it would admit no such order to be observed in the answering thereof as a regular responsary requireth.

Wherefore, gentle Reader, favourably consider that as that painter is not to be held unskilful which, having a deformed object, makes the like portraiture, no more am I justly to be blamed for my immethodical Apology: sith any judicious reader may plainly see that the Baiter of Women his pestiferous obtrectation is like a tailor's cushion, that is botched together of shreds. So that, were it not to prevent future infection with that venom which he hath and daily doth sweat out, I would have been loath to have spent time so idly as to answer it at all. But a crooked pot-lid well enough fits a wry-necked pot, an unfashioned shoe a misshapen foot, and an illiterate answer an unlearned religious provocation. His absurdities therein contained are so many that to answer them severally were as frivolous a work as to make a trap for a flea, and as tedious as the
† pursuit of an arrow to an impotent man. Yet to prevent his having occasion to say that I speak of many but can instance none, I have thought it meet to present a few of them to his view (as followeth): that if folly have taken root in him he may seek to extirpate it, and to blush at the sight of that fruit which he hath already brought forth. A fruit I call it (not unfitly I hope) because a crab may so be

termed as well as a good apple. Thus, not doubting of the favour of well affected and of their kind acceptance of my endeavours, of which I desire not applaud but approbation, I rest,

your friend,

Rachel Speght.

## The Preface unto the Subsequent

With edged tools (saith the old proverb) it is ill sporting; but far †
more dangerous, yea damnable, is it to dally with scripture, the two-edged sword of the Eternal (*Hebrews* iv.12): for so to do is a breach of the third commandment, 'and he that fails in one point, is guilty of all' (*James* ii.10). If the magnitude of this sin had been considered by the Baiter of Women, the lamentable yet just reward thereof, as of all other sins without repentance, would – if he had but a servile fear – have restrained him from transgressing herein. But as one devoid of all true fear of God's indignation against wilful sinners (for as ignorance doth somewhat extenuate a fault, so doth knowledge much aggravate it), he hath made the *exordium* of his †
brainsick exhalation against women to be a perverting of a part of †
holy writ. *Ex unguibus leonem*, judge of this lion by his paw: for if †
the fore-foot be monstrous, doubtless the whole body is correspondent thereto. The porch indeed is foul, but he that views the sequel †
(as I have done) shall find a lay-stall of heathenish assertions, similes †
and examples, illiterate composition, irreligious invectives, and (which is worst) impious blasphemies therein included – filthy rubbish, more fit to be heaped up by a pagan than one that beareth the name of a Christian.

But lest it should not only be thought, but also said, that I find fault where none is; or that I do ill to mislike the work and not make the author therewith acquainted (that if he please he may answer for himself): I think it not amiss to propose some few Queries unto the Baiter of Women which I have abstracted out of his infamous book, as himself confesseth it to be in his Epistle to Women.

## Certain queries to the Baiter of Women, with confutation of some part of his diabolical discipline

If it be true, as you affirm (page 2, line 26), that women will not 'give thanks for a good turn':

I demand whether Deborah and Hannah were not women, who both of them sang hymns of thanksgiving unto the Lord? – the one for his mercy in granting her victory over Israel's enemies (*Judges* v.), the other for his favourable giving unto her a son, which she full oft and earnestly had desired (I *Samuel* i.11; ii.1).

And whereas you say (page 4, line 22) that a woman 'that hath a fair face, it is ever matched with a cruel heart, and her heavenly looks with hellish thoughts', you therein show yourself a contradictor of scripture's precedents. For Abigail was a beautiful woman and tender-hearted (I *Samuel* xxv.3, 18); Rebekah was both fair of face and pitiful (*Genesis* xxiv.16, 18). Many examples serving to confute your universal rule might be produced, but these are sufficient to dispel this your cloud of untruth. As for your audacity in judging of women's thoughts, you thereby show yourself an usurper against the king of heaven, the true knowledge of cogitations being appropriate unto him alone (*Matthew* xii.25).

If your assertion that 'a woman is better lost than found, better forsaken than taken' (page 5, line 4) be to be credited, methinks great pity it is that afore you were born there was none so wise as to counsel your father not to meddle with a woman, that he might have escaped those troubles which you affirm that all married men are cumbered with (page 2, line 20). As also, that he might not have
† begotten such a monster in nature *ass* yourself who (like the priest which forgot he was parish clerk) defame and exclaim against women, as though yourself had never had a mother or you never been a child.

You affirm (page 10, line 18) that 'for the love of women David purchased the displeasure of his God'. It had been good that you had cited the place of story where you find it, for I never yet in scripture read that the Almighty was displeased with David for his love to women, but for his lust to Bathsheba, which afterward brought forth his adulterous act and his causing Uriah to be murdered (II *Samuel* xi.).

In saying (page 10, line 25) that 'Job's wife counselled her husband to curse God', you misconster the text; for the true
† construction thereof will show it to be a *sarcasmus* or ironical speech and not an instigation to blasphemy.

(Page 11, line 8) You count it 'wonderful to see the mad feats of women, for she will now be merry, then sad'. But methinks it is far more *wonder-fool* to have one that adventures to make his writing as public as an inn-keeper's sign, which hangs to the view of all passengers, to want grammatical concordance in his said writing: and join together 'women' plural and 'she' singular, *ass* you not only in this place but also in others have done.

Albeit the scripture verifieth that God made woman and brought her to man (*Genesis* ii.22), and that a prudent wife cometh of the Lord (*Proverbs* xix.14): yet have you not feared blasphemously to say 'that women sprung from the devil' (page 15, line 26). But being, as it seems, defective in that whereof you have much need
† (for *mendacem oportet esse memorem*), you suddenly after say that 'women were created by God and formed by nature, and therefore by policy and wisdom to be avoided' (page 16, line 12). An impious

conclusion to infer: that because God created, therefore to be avoided. O intolerable absurdity!

'Men I say may live without women, but women cannot live without men' (page 14, line 18). If any religious author had thus affirmed, I should have wondered that unto Satan's suggestions he had so much subjected himself as to cross the Almighty's providence and care for man's good, who positively said 'It is not good for man to be alone' (*Genesis* ii.18). But being that the sole testimony hereof is your own *dico*, I marvel no whit at the error, †
but heartily wish that unto all the untruths you have uttered in your infamous book you had subscribed your *dico*, that none of them might be adjudged truths. For *mendacis praemium est verbis eius* †
*non adhibere fidem*.

(Page 17, line 5) You affirm that 'Hosea was brought unto idolatry by marrying with a lewd woman' – which is as true as the sea burns. And for proof thereof you cite *Hosea* i, in which chapter is no such matter to be found, it only containing a declaration of the Lord's anger against the idolatrous Jews who had gone a-whoring after other gods, set forth in a parable of an husband and an adulterous wife.

(Page 19) 'Theodora a monstrous strumpet, Lavia, Flora and Lais †
were three notable courtesans.'

'Was not that noble city of Troy sacked and spoiled by the fair Helena?' (page 21) 'Therefore stay not alone in the company of a †
woman, trusting to thy own chastity, except thou be more strong than Samson, more wise than Solomon, or more holy than David – for these and many more have been overcome by the sweet enticements of women' (page 22).

I may as well say Barabbas was a murderer (*Luke* xxiii.19), Joab killed Abner and Amasa (II *Samuel* iii.27; xx.10), and Pharaoh-nechoh slew Josiah (II *Kings* xxiii.29): 'therefore stay not alone in the company of a man, trusting to thy own strength, except thou be stronger than Josiah and more valiant than Abner and Amasa – for these and many more have been murdered by men'. The form of argumentation is your own, the which if you dislike blame yourself for proposing such a pattern, and blush at your own folly *quod te* †
*posse non facile credo*. For it is an old saying, how true I know not, that blushing is a sign of grace.

(Page 31, line 15) 'If God had not made women only to be a plague to men, he would never have called them necessary evils.' Albeit I have not read Seton or Ramus, nor so much as seen (though †
heard of) Aristotle's *Organon*, yet by that I have seen and read in †
compass of my apprehension I will adventure to frame an argument or two, to show what danger for this your blasphemy you are in.

To fasten a lie upon God is blasphemy: but the Baiter of Women fastens a lie upon God: *ergo*, the Baiter is a blasphemer.

*The Proposition, I trow, none will gainsay; the assumption I thus prove*:

Whosoever affirms God to have called women necessary evils fastens a lie upon God: for from the beginning of *Genesis* to the end of the *Revelation* is no such instance to be found. But the Baiter affirms God so to have called women: *ergo*, the Baiter fastens a lie upon God.

*The reward according to Law Divine due unto the Baiter of Women*:

Whosoever blasphemeth God ought by his law to die: the Baiter of Women hath blasphemed God: *ergo*, he ought to die the death.

*The Proposition is upon record* (*Levit.* xxiv.14, 16).

*The Assumption is formally proved.*

'If thou marryest a still and a quiet woman, that will seem to thee that thou ridest but an ambling horse to hell; but if with one that is froward and unquiet; then thou wert as good ride a trotting horse to the devil.' (page 35, line 13)

† If this your affirmation be true, then seems it that hell is the period of all men's travels and the centre of their circumference. A man can but have either a good wife or a bad: and if he have the former, you say he doth but seem to amble to hell; if the latter, he were as good trot to the devil. But if married men ride, how travel bachelors? Surely, by your rule, they must go on foot, because they
† want wives – which (inclusively) you say are like horses to carry their husbands to hell. Wherefore, in my mind, it was not without mature consideration that you married in time, because it would be too irksome for you to travel so tedious a journey on foot.

'Now the fire is kindled, let us burn this other faggot' (page 38, line 4).

Beware of making too great a fire, lest the surplusage of that fire's effect which you intended for others singe yourself.

† 'She will make thee wear an ox feather in thy cap' (page 44, line 4).

If oxen have feathers, their hairs more fitly may be so termed than their horns.

(Page 50, line 28) 'There is no joy nor pleasure in this world which may be compared to marriage, for if the husband be poor and in adversity then he bears but the one half of the grief; and furthermore, his wife will comfort him with all the comfortable means she can devise.'

(Page 51, line 16) 'Many are the joys and sweet pleasures in marriage, as in our children,' etc.

(Page 34, line 5) 'There are many troubles comes galloping at the heels of a woman. If thou wert a servant or in bondage afore, yet when thou marriest thy toil is never the nearer ended; but even then, and not before, thou changest thy golden life which thou didst lead before (in respect of the married) for a drop of honey, which quickly turns to be as bitter as wormwood.'

(Page 53, line 19) 'The husband ought (in sign of love) to impart his secrets and counsel unto his wife, for many have found much comfort and profit by taking their wives' counsel; and if thou impart any ill hap to thy wife, she lighteneth thy grief either by comforting thee lovingly or else in bearing a part thereof patiently.'

(Page 41, line 12) 'If thou unfoldest anything of secret to a woman, the more thou chargest her to keep it close, the more she will seem, as it were, with child till she have revealed it.'

It was the saying of a judicious writer, that whoso makes the fruit of his cogitations extant to the view of all men should have his work to be as a well-tuned instrument, in all places according and agreeing – the which I am sure yours doth not. For how reconcile you those dissonant places above cited? or how make you a consonant diapason of those discords wanting harmony? †

(Page 34, line 19) You counsel all men to 'shun idleness', and yet the first words of your Epistle to Women are these: 'musing with myself being idle'. Herein you appear not unlike unto a fencer † which teacheth another how to defend himself from enemies' blows, and suffers himself to be stricken without resistance. For you warn others to eschew that dangerous vice wherewith (by your own confession) yourself is stained.

(Page 57, line 5) 'If thou like not my reasons to expel love, then thou mayst try Ovid's Art, for he counsels those that feel this † horrible heat to cool their flames with herbs which are cold of nature, as rue, etc.'

Albeit you doubt not but by some to be reputed for a good archer, yet here you shot wide from the truth in saying, without contradiction of Ovid's error, that rue is of a cold nature. For most physicians (if not all), both ancient and modern, hold it to be hot and dry in the third degree; and experience will tell the user thereof that the temperature is hot, not cold. And though the sense of tasting, without further trial, doth repel this error, I doubt not but in citing this prescription you have verified the opinion of that philosopher which said that 'there are some who think they speak † wisest, and write most judiciously, when they understand not themselves'.

But, *ut opus ad finem perducam*, sith I have trod my utmost † intended step – though left one path ungone, I mean the *Bear-baiting of Widows* unviewed. In that I am ignorant of their † dispositions (accounting it a folly for me to talk of Robin Hood, as † many do, that never shot in his bow), I leave the speculation (with approbation of their *Bear-baiting*) to those that regard neither affability nor humanity. And wishing unto every such Misogunes a Tyburn tiffany for curation of his swollen neck, which only † through a cynical inclination will not endure the yoke of lawful matrimony, I bid farewell.

† F ret, fume, or frump at me who will, I care not;
I will thrust forth thy sting to hurt and spare not.
N ow that the task I undertook is ended
I dread not any harm to me intended,
S ith justly none therein I have offended.

## NOTES

PAGE 57
**Melastomus**: name derived from Greek, meaning 'black mouth', i.e. slanderer.

PAGE 59
**Hevah**: Eve (spelled thus in the Geneva Bible, much used by English Protestants).
**Lactantius**: L. Caelius Firminianus (*c*. 240–320), resident of North Africa, Christian convert. The saying can be traced to Quintus Curtius, *De Rebus Gestis Alexandri Magni* vi.3.11; Swetnam and Lyly use it without identifying it – Speght is being scholarly.
**evaporate**: give vent to.
**obtrectation**: slander, calumny.
**tacere ... consentire**: to keep quiet is as if to consent.
**maugre**: in spite of.

PAGE 60
**Aristotle**: possibly a reference to *Ethics* IV.ix.6.
**cursedness**: bad temper, peevishness.
**lists**: barriers enclosing space for tilting.
**buckler**: shield.
**Zoilus**: a Cynic philosopher (4th C. BC), notorious for his bitter attacks, hence a name for any bitter critic.
**chirograph**: a formally written document.
**impetrate**: entreat, request.
**Momus**: personification of fault-finding.
**Decius**: the name is associated with military bravery; in Livy, *Ab Urbe Condita* viii.9, the consul Decius Mus (*c*. 340 BC) appeals to the gods and achieves victory in battle but loses his own life. This sentiment may be found in other dedications, e.g. W. Cuningham, *The Cosmographical Glass* (1559), asking Leicester that his book 'be defended as Tucer was under the shield of mighty Ajax'.
**ad ... animum**: not at the work but its spirit.

PAGE 61
**Misogunes**: Misogynos, from misogynist.
**rough of your fury**: this joke runs through all the pamphlets, from Swetnam's 'rough of my fury': 'rough' becomes a pun on 'ruff'.
**excrement**: (waste) product.
**accidence scholar**: one learned in the rules of grammar.
**mingle-mangle**: confused mess.

PAGE 62
**cynical**: a pun on the original Greek meaning – dog-like.
**serpent Porphyrus**: famous for the inability cited.
**the vulgar sort**: Munda also attacks 'low' taste and education; a sentiment also to be found in classical writers (for instance, Lactantius).
**bewray**: reveal.

PAGE 62 CONTINUED
**galled:** sore, as a horse's back rubbed by harness.
**froward:** peevish, perverse.
**St Paul:** all the Bible references are Speght's, unless otherwise indicated (here it should be to verse 1).


PAGE 63
**pen-man:** the Bible has several moments that seem to condemn 'railers' (e.g., I Cor. v.11 advises the good man not to keep company with 'railers', drunkards, extortioners, etc.).
**timbrels:** tambourines.
**wight:** person.
**Philalethes:** loving truth.


PAGE 64
**Philomathes:** loving learning.
**Meting:** measuring.


PAGE 65
**apparently:** the redeeming grace of Jesus is 'apparent', or fore-shadowed in several places in the Old Testament.


PAGE 66
**weaker vessel:** famous phrase from I Peter iii.7 which is used in the Homily on Matrimony and recurs throughout the period (often used in plays by female characters who are patently not weak).
**ironia:** irony; technical term which Puttenham, the poetic theorist, glosses as the 'dry mock'.


PAGE 67
**members:** parts of the body.
**St Austin:** St Augustine (Adam and Eve are discussed in *City of God* XIV, though the exact quotation is not there).
**Art thou loosed:** this is all loosely quoted from I Cor. vii. 27–33.


PAGE 68
**Eusebius:** (260–340) Bishop of Caesarea, famous as a church historian; the reference is to *Ecclesiastical History* iii.30.
**Cephas:** rock, stone (name given to Paul).
**connexed:** joined, totalled.
**efficient cause:** the theory of causes here comes from Aristotle (esp. *Physics* ii. 3,7): 'efficient cause' – the force or agency by which something is produced or created; 'material cause': the matter from which it is produced; 'formal cause': the essence (as opposed to material aspects) of the thing produced; 'final cause': the purpose for which it was produced.
**Moses:** taken to be the author of Genesis.
**metonymy:** an attribute of something which represents the whole thing itself.


PAGE 69
**temperature:** temperament, which is created by a particular combination of *humours*, the four main fluids which compose the body (blood, choler, melancholy, phlegm) according to medieval science.
**excrements:** superfluous (or waste) matter.
**Susanna:** (mentioned in Luke viii.2–3) she announced the resurrection.
**Joanna:** (Luke viii.1–3) her husband, Chuza, was healed by Jesus.

PAGE 70
**a minore ad maius:** from the smaller to the greater.
**lanthorn:** lantern.


PAGE 71
**Plautus:** (?254–184 BC) Roman dramatist; the saying could loosely derive from *Amphitryo* ll.839 ff.
**Pericles:** Athenian ruler (495–429 BC), whose second marriage to the scholarly Aspasia was famous for its affection.
**Antonius Pius:** Antoninus Pius, Roman emperor (86–161), famous for his integrity, married to Faustina.
**David:** in fact Joab did the destroying; David removed the crown.
**heirs together:** the phrase is quoted in the Homily on Matrimony.


PAGE 72
**evil command:** most writers on marriage and sex relations assumed that the woman should obey her husband; they met difficulties where the husband was irresponsible, blasphemous, drunken or downright violent and there was much controversy over whether he should then be obeyed. The conservative theorists complacently suggested, of course, that the woman should accept the assaults and trust in heaven. To take seriously the idea of spiritual equality was to advocate disobedience in these cases and separation, which some writers suggested.
**Cham:** or Ham committed the grievous crime of seeing his father Noah naked and drunk.
**Sem:** was the eldest son.


PAGE 73
**Cicero:** possibly a reference to Cicero, *Ad Atticum* viii.4.


PAGE 74
**responsary:** used of church responses, but here of literary debate.
**promiscuous:** confused, haphazard.
**impotent:** physically weak.


PAGE 75
**edged tools:** from the proverb, 'Children and fools must not play with edged tools.'
**exordium:** introduction.
**exhalation:** blowing out, puffing.
**Ex unguibus leonem:** proverbial phrase which Speght translates (omitting the Latin *aestimare:* judge).
**porch:** image for the opening of Swetnam's pamphlet (he talks of being 'one of your parish' and being placed in 'the body of the church').
**lay stall:** stalls in the nave for laity (as opposed to clergy).


PAGE 76
**ass:** in the original there are several dreadful puns like this (including 'whereasse').
**priest ... parish clerk:** proverbial – to act hypocritically or deny one's origins.
**sarcasmus:** a common 16th and early 17th C. version of sarcasm.
**mendacem ... memorem:** proverbial – a liar should have a good memory.


PAGE 77
**dico:** author's opinion, personal statement.
**mendacis ... fidem:** it is best not to believe the words of a liar.
**Theodora:** famous courtesan of Constantinople, married the Emperor Justinian in 525. (But this is Swetnam's mistake for Theodote – see Munda p. 156.)
**Lavia:** another mistake of Swetnam's for Lamia, who seduced Demetrius of

PAGE 77 CONTINUED
Macedonia on Cyprus.

**Flora and Lais:** two successful high-class prostitutes. Flora, of Rome, is more or less mythic. Lais of Corinth flourished *c.* 360 BC. The story of Lamia, Flora and Lais is in Painter, *Palace of Pleasure,* novel 79.

**Helena:** the abduction of Helen by Paris from her husband Menelaus is taken to have been the cause of the Trojan War.

**quod ... credo:** which I think you cannot easily do.

**Seton:** (1498?–1567) his *Dialectica* was a standard treatise on logic; hounded for his Catholicism.

**Ramus:** (1515–1572) French humanist, later a Calvinist; important as an opponent of Aristotelian thought, stressing the use of deduction as scientific method.

**Organon:** the title for all of Aristotle's writings on logic and the rules of thinking.

PAGE 78
**travels:** spelt 'travails' in the original.
**want:** lack.
**ox feather:** the horn (a sign of cuckoldry).

PAGE 79
**diapason:** concord, harmony.
**fencer:** it seems that Swetnam ran a fencing school in Bristol (he published a work on fencing in 1617, printed by N. Okes, Speght's printer).
**Ovid's Art:** the influential *Ars Amatoria, the Art of Love.*
**philosopher:** this sounds like Socrates talking to Euthydemus (Xenophon, *Memorabilia* IV.ii.esp. 25–30).
**ut ... perducam:** so I may bring the work to an end.
**Bear-baiting of Widows:** Swetnam's last chapter.
**Robin Hood:** a proverb about bragging and false assertion.
**Tyburn tiffany:** a hangman's noose (from Tyburn – famous site of gallows near the present Marble Arch).
**curation:** cure.

PAGE 80
**frump:** jeer, taunt.

# Ester hath hang'd †

## Haman:

or

# AN ANSWERE TO

## a lewd Pamphlet, entituled

### *The Arraignment of Women*

## With the arraignment of lewd, idle

### froward, and unconstant men, and

### HUSBANDS

---

*Divided into two Parts*

## The first proveth the dignity and worthinesse

*of Women, out of divine Testimonies*

## The second shewing the estimation of the Fœ-

### minine Sexe, in ancient and Pagan times; all which

is acknowledged by men themselves in their
daily actions

---

## Written by Ester Sowernam, neither Maide, †

### Wife nor Widdowe, yet really all, and there-

fore experienced to defend all

---

JOHN 8.7.
*He that is without sinne among you, let him first cast a stone at her*

---

*Neque enim lex iusticior vlla* †

*——Quam necis Artificem arte perire sua*

---

LONDON
Printed for Nicholas Bourne, and are to be sold at his shop
at the entrance of the Royall Exchange. 1617

[Ester Sowernam's name, like that of Constantia Munda, is clearly a pseudonym. Esther was a biblical heroine who defended her nation, as this Ester defends her sex. And *Sower*nam is a pun on *Sweet*nam. This is the first suspicious detail; next is the author's insistence on her work's novelty. Sowernam says that 'she' was preparing a reply to Swetnam before she heard that Speght had written; she then says she is critical of Speght's answer. What follows, by implication, is that her pamphlet has something new to say in this developing battle. Viewed cynically, this could be seen to be a man taking advantage of Speght's precedent and rushing out a pamphlet in the guise of a woman.

If 'Ester Sowernam' does conceal a man, however, I would suggest that it in no way invalidates the arguments put forward in the pamphlet. There seems to be no trace of mockery or parody of women in the writing; the cynicism is directed towards men. And if Sowernam was a man, it was a very well kept secret. In her *Dream* prefixed to *Mortality's Memorandum*, Speght describes the events of the Swetnam controversy and she gives a stanza to Ester Sowernam:

> But, as it seems, my mood out-ran my might;
> Which when a self-conceited creature saw,
> She passed her censure on my weak exploit
> And gave the beast a harder bone to gnaw.
> *Haman* she hangs; 'tis past, he cannot shun it:
> For *Ester*, in the pretertense, hath done it.

Speght gives no hint that she thinks Sowernam is male; indeed, given her annoyance at being criticised it would probably have been convenient to have revealed that the 'self-conceited creature' was a man. News travelled easily and quickly in London. It could be surprising if Speght, who was so interested in the problems of women authors, had not known whether Sowernam were a man. (Munda also thinks Sowernam is female.)

Where we may be able to detect the hand of a man is in the publication. The 1616 and 1617 reprints of Swetnam's work were printed by Thomas Snodham to be distributed by Thomas Archer. It was Snodham who, early in 1617, printed Sowernam's pamphlet, but for a different distributor (Snodham possibly venturing on his own?). It could be that he arranged for Sowernam to answer Swetnam: she tells us that a gentleman brought her a copy of Swetnam's work at the start of the Michaelmas Term (9 October). Certainly someone seems to have rushed her pamphlet out before she was quite ready for it, since she tells us in the preface to the second part that she is planning a third part, which never appears. Instead it is replaced by a poem cobbled together from the existing contents of the pamphlet and signed by Joan Sharp. It says nothing new; its author's name is probably a pseudonym. I would suggest that the poem is nothing more than a make-weight appended to an otherwise unfinished pamphlet in order to make it suitable for publication. It is easy to see the reason for Snodham's haste: on 14 November 1616 it was revealed that the original distributor, Archer, already had his hands on an answer to Swetnam (Speght's pamphlet). This must have coincided with the moment Sowernam mentions, when someone brought her news that Speght had written an answer. Sowernam had already written some of her pamphlet. This I take to be the first part, which is mainly religious in argument. After the delay, in which she read Speght's pamphlet, she wrote a second part which is much more overtly satirical in tone and contains the imaginary trial of Swetnam. She says she will write a third part when she returns next term (Michaelmas Term ended on 28 November). But she did not get the chance. On 4 January 1617 Snodham claimed her pamphlet was ready for printing – and that is the last we hear of her, but not of him.

A mystery remains. The mention of Michaelmas Term and the apology for writing seem to be literary convention. But if they are real information, what is she doing coming to London for the legal terms? What business does she have? Again what is interesting is her religious knowledge, which seems to range over the various different Bibles (all of them having different doctrinal positions). I cannot work out the 'story' behind this. Which leaves us only with her own words in the pamphlet.]

### To all right honourable, noble and worthy ladies, gentlewomen and others virtuously disposed of the feminine sex

Right honourable, and all others of our sex, upon my repair to London this last Michaelmas Term – being at supper amongst † friends, where the number of each sex were equal – as nothing is more usual for table talk, there fell out a discourse concerning women, some defending, others objecting against our sex. Upon which occasion there happened a mention of a pamphlet entitled *The Arraignment of Women*, which I was desirous to see. The next day a gentleman brought me the book which, when I had super-ficially run over, I found the discourse as far off from performing what the title promised as I found it scandalous and blasphemous. For where the author pretended to write against lewd, idle and unconstant women, he doth most impudently rage and rail general-ly against all the whole sex of women. Whereupon I, in defence of our sex, began an answer to that shameful pamphlet. In which, after I had spent some small time, word was brought me that an Apology for women was already undertaken, and ready for the press, by a Minister's daughter. Upon this news I stayed my pen, being as glad † to be eased of my intended labour, as I did expect some fitting performance of what was undertaken. At last the maiden's book was brought me, which, when I had likewise run over, I did observe that whereas the maid doth many times excuse her tenderness of years, I found it to be true in the slenderness of her answer: for the undertaking to defend women doth rather charge and condemn women, as in the ensuing discourse shall appear. So that whereas I expected to be eased of what I began, I do now find myself double charged, as well to make reply to the one as to add supply to the other.

In this my Apology, right honourable, right worshipful and all others of our sex, I do in the first part of it plainly and resolutely deliver the worthiness and worth of women, both in respect of their creation as in the work of redemption. Next I do show in examples out of both the Testaments what blessed and happy choice hath been made of women, as gracious instruments to derive God's blessings and benefits to mankind.

In my second part I do deliver of what estimate women have been valued in all ancient and modern times, which I prove by authorities, customs and daily experiences. Lastly, I do answer all material objections which have or can be alleged against our sex; in which also I do arraign such kind of men which correspond the humour and disposition of the author: lewd, idle, furious and beastly disposed persons.

† This being performed, I doubt not but such as heretofore have been so forward and lavish against women will hereafter pull in their horns, and have as little desire, and less cause, so scandalously and slanderously to write against us than formerly they have.

The ends for which I undertook this enterprise are these. First, to set out the glory of Almighty God in so blessed a work of his creation. Secondly, to encourage all noble, honourable and worthy women to express in their course of life and actions that they are the same creatures which they were designed to be by their creator, and by their redeemer; and to parallel those women whose virtuous examples are collected briefly out of the Old and New Testament. Lastly, I write for the shame and confusion of such as degenerate from womanhood and disappoint the ends of creation and redemption.

There can be no greater encouragement to true nobility than to know and stand upon the honour of nobility; nor any greater confusion and shame than for nobility to dismount and abase itself to ignoble and degenerate courses.

You are women: in creation noble, in redemption gracious, in use most blessed; be not forgetful of yourselves, nor unthankful to that Author from whom you receive all.


## To All Worthy and Hopeful young Youths of Great Britain; But Respectively to the best † disposed and worthy Apprentices of London


Hopeful and gallant youths of Great Britain and this so famous a city: there hath been lately published a pamphlet entitled *The Arraignment of lewd, idle, froward and inconstant women*. This patched and misshapen hotch-potch is so directed that, if Socrates did laugh but once to see an ass eat thistles, he would surely laugh twice to see an idle frantic direct his misshapen labours to giddy-headed young men. He would say, as he did when the ass did eat

thistles, 'like lips, like lettuce'; so a frantic writer doth aptly choose †
giddy favourites.

The author of the *Arraignment* and myself, in our labours, do altogether disagree. He raileth without cause, I defend upon direct proof; he saith women are the worst of all creatures, I prove them blessed above all creatures; he writeth that men should abhor them for their bad conditions, I prove that men should honour them for their best dispositions; he saith women are the causes of men's overthrow, I prove if there be any offence in a woman men were the beginners. Now, in that it is far more womanlike to maintain a right than it is manlike to offer a wrong, I conceived that I could not err in my choice if I did direct a labour well-intended to worthy young youths which are well-disposed.

When you have passed your minority or served your apprenticeships under the government of others, when you begin the world for yourselves, the chiefest thing you look for is a good wife.

The world is a large field, and it is full of brambles, briars and weeds. If there be any more tormenting, more scratting or more †
poisonable weed than other, the author hath collected them in his loathsome pamphlet, and doth utter them to his giddy company.

Now myself presuming upon your worthy and honest dispositions, I have entered into the garden of Paradise and there have gathered the choicest flowers which that garden may afford, and those I offer to you.

If you believe our adversary, no woman is good, howsoever she be used; if you consider what I have written, no woman is bad except she be abused.

If you believe him that women are so bad creatures, what a dangerous and miserable life is marriage?

If you examine my proofs to know directly what women are, you shall then find there is no delight more exceeding than to be joined in marriage with a Paradisian creature. Who, as she cometh out of the garden, so shall you find her a flower of delight, answerable to the country from whence she cometh.

There can be no love betwixt man and wife but where there is a respective estimate the one towards the other. How could you love – nay, how would you loathe such a monster to whom Joseph Swetnam pointeth?

Whereas, in view of what I have described, how can you but regardfully love with the uttermost strain of affection so incomparable a jewel?

Some will perhaps say I am a woman and therefore write more for women than they do deserve. To whom I answer: if they misdoubt of what I speak, let them impeach my credit in any one particular. In that which I write, Eve was a good woman before she met with the serpent; her daughters are good virgins, if they meet with good tutors.

You, my worthy youths, are the hope of manhood: the principal point of manhood is to defend, and what more manlike defence than to defend the just reputation of a woman? I know that you, the apprentices of this city, are as forward to maintain the good as you are vehement to put down the bad.

That which is worst I leave to our adversary, but what is excellently best, that I commend to you. Do you find the gold, I do here deliver you the jewel: a rich stock to begin the world withal, if you be good husbands to use it for your best advantage.

Let not the title of this book in some point distaste you, in that † men are arraigned – for you are quit by nonage. None are here arraigned but such old fornicators as came with full mouth and open † cry to Jesus, and brought a woman to him taken in adultery, who when our Saviour stooped down and wrote on the ground, they all fled away. Joseph Swetnam saith 'A man may find pearls in dust' (page 47). But if they who fled had seen any pearls they would rather have stayed to have had share, than to fly and to leave the woman alone: they found some foul reckoning against themselves in our Saviour's writing, as they shall do who are here arraigned. And if they dare do like as our Saviour bade the woman's accusers, 'He that is without sin throw the first stone at her': so let them rail against women, who never tempted any woman to be bad. Yet this is an hard case. If a man rail against a woman, and know no lewdness by any, he shall prove himself a compound fool. If he rail at women, who in his own experienced trial had made many bad, he † shall show himself a decompounded K (I do not mean Knight). The best way is, he that knoweth none bad, let him speak well of all; he who hath made more bad than he ever intended to make good, let him hold his peace lest he shame himself. Farewell.

Ester Sowernam.

## An Answer to the First Chapter of the Arraignment of Women

### CHAP[TER] I

If the author of this *Arraignment* had performed his discourse either answerable to the title, or the arguments of the chapters, he had been so far off from being answered by me that I should have commended so good a labour, which is employed to give vice just reproof and virtue honourable report. But at the very first entrance of his discourse, in the very first page, he discovereth himself neither to have truth in his promise nor religious performance. If in this answer I do use more vehement speeches than may seem to correspond the natural disposition of a woman, yet all judicious readers shall confess that I use more mildness than the cause I have in hand provoketh me unto.

I am not only provoked by this author to defend women, but I am more violently urged to defend divine Majesty, in the work of his creation. In which respect I say with St Jerome: 'Meam injuriam † patienter sustinui, impietatem contra deum ferre non potui' (*Epist. ad Ciprianum*). For as St Chrysostom saith, 'injurias Dei dissimu- † lare impium est' (*Sup. Math.*).

If either Julian the Apostata or Lucian the Atheist should † undertake the like work, could the one devise to write more blasphemously or the other to scoff and flout at the divine creation of woman more profanely, than this irreligious author doth?

Homer doth report in his *Iliad* that there was at the siege of Troy † a Grecian, called Thersites, whose wit was so blockish he was not worthy to speak: yet his disposition was so precipitate he could not hold his tongue. Joseph Swetnam in all record of histories cannot be so likely paralleled as with this Thersites. What his composition of † body is I know not, but for his disposition otherwise, in this pamphlet, I know he is as monstrous as the work is misshapen, which shall plainly appear in the examination of the first page only.

The argument of the first chapter is to show 'to what use women † were made'; it also showeth 'That most of them degenerate from the use they were framed unto', etc.

Now, to show to what use woman was made, he beginneth thus: 'At the first beginning a woman was made to be an helper to man; and so they are indeed, for they help to consume and spend,' etc. This is all the use and all the end which the author setteth down in all his discourse for the creation of woman. Mark a ridiculous jest in this: spending and consuming of that which man painfully getteth is by this author the use for which women were made. And yet (saith he in the argument) 'most of them degenerate from the use they were framed unto'. Woman was made to spend and consume at the first: but women do degenerate from this use: *ergo*, Midas doth † contradict himself. Beside this egregious folly, he runneth into horrible blasphemy. Was the end of God's creation in woman to spend and consume? Is 'helper' to be taken in that sense, to help to spend, etc.? Is spending and consuming 'helping'?

He runneth on, and saith: 'They were made of a rib, and that their froward and crooked nature doth declare, for a rib is a crooked thing,' etc.

Woman was made of a crooked rib, so she is crooked of conditions. Joseph Swetnam was made as from Adam of clay and dust, so he is of a dirty and muddy disposition. The inferences are both alike in either: woman is no more crooked in respect of the one, but he is blasphemous in respect of the other. Did woman receive her soul and disposition from the rib, or, as it is said in

*Genesis*, 'God did breathe in them the spirit of life'? Admit that this author's doctrine be true, that woman receiveth her froward and crooked disposition from the rib, woman may then conclude upon

† that axiom in philosophy, *Quicquid efficit tale, illud est magis tale*: that which giveth quality to a thing, doth more abound in that quality – as fire which heateth is itself more hot. The sun which giveth light is of itself more light: so, if woman received her crookedness from the rib, and consequently from the man, how doth man excel in crookedness, who hath more of those crooked ribs? See how this vain, furious and idle author furnisheth woman with an argument against himself and others of his sex.

The author, having desperately begun, doth more rashly and impudently run on in blasphemy, which he doth evidently show in the inference upon his former speeches. And therefore (saith he) 'Ever since they have been a woe unto man, and follow the line of the first leader'. Now let the Christian reader please to consider how dishonestly this author dealeth, who, undertaking a particular, prosecuteth and persecuteth a general: under the cloak and colour of lewd, idle and froward women to rage and rail against all women in general.

Now, having examined what collections Joseph Swetnam had wrested out of scriptures to dishonour and abuse all women, I am resolved, before I answer further particulars made by him against our sex, to collect and note out of scriptures: first, what incomparable and most excellent prerogatives God hath bestowed upon women, in honour of them and their creation; secondly, what choice God hath made of women, in using them as instruments to work his most gracious and glorious designs for the general benefit

† of mankind, both during the law of nature and of Moses; thirdly, what excellent and divine graces have been bestowed upon our sex, in the law of grace and the work of redemption; with a conclusion, that to manifest the worthiness of women they have been chosen to perform and publish the most happy and joyful benefits which ever came to mankind.

## CHAPTER II

*What incomparable and excellent prerogatives God hath bestowed upon Women in their first Creation*

† In this ensuing chapter I determine briefly to observe (not curiously to discourse at large) the singular benefits and graces bestowed upon women. In regard of which it is first to be considered: that the Almighty God in the world's frame, in his divine wisdom, designed to himself a main end to which he ordained all the works of his creation; in which he, being a most excellent work-master, did so create his works that every succeeding work was ever more

excellent than what was formerly created. He wrought by degrees, providing in all for that which was and should be the end.

It appeareth, by that sovereignty which God gave to Adam over all the creatures of sea and land, that man was the end of God's creation: whereupon it doth necessarily, without all exception, follow that Adam, being the last work, is therefore the most excellent work of creation. Yet Adam was not so absolutely perfect but that, in the sight of God, he wanted an helper. Whereupon God created the woman, his last work, as to supply and make absolute that imperfect building which was unperfected in man, as all divines do hold, till the happy creation of the woman. Now of what estimate that creature is and ought to be, which is the last work, upon whom the Almighty set up his last rest – whom he made to add perfection to the end of all creation – I leave rather to be acknowledged by others than resolved by myself.

It is further to be considered, as the maid in her *Muzzle for* † *Melastomus* hath observed, that God intended to honour woman in † a more excellent degree in that he created her out of a subject refined, as out of a quintessence. For the rib is in substance more † solid, in place as most near, so in estimate most dear, to man's heart: which doth presage that as she was made for an helper, so to be an helper to stay – to settle all joy, all contents, all delights, to and in man's heart, as hereafter shall be showed.

That delight, solace and pleasure, which shall come to man by woman, is prognosticated by that place wherein woman was created: for she was framed in Paradise, a place of all delight and pleasure. Every element hath his creatures, every creature doth † correspond the temper and the inclination of that element wherein it † hath and took his first and principal *esse* or being. So that woman neither can or may degenerate in her disposition from that natural inclination of the place in which she was first framed: she is a Paradisian, that is, a delightful creature, born in so delightful a country.

When woman was created God brought her unto Adam, and then did solemnise that most auspicious marriage betwixt them with the greatest majesty and magnificence that heaven or earth might afford. God was the father which gave so rich a jewel; God was the priest which tied so inseparable a knot. God was the steward which provided all the pleasures, all the dainties, all the blessings which his divine wisdom might afford, in so delightful a place.

The woman was married to Adam as with a most sure and inseparable band; so with a most affectionate and dutiful love Adam † was enjoined to receive his wife, as is noted in the bible printed 1595. †

There is no love (always excepting the transcending love) which is so highly honoured, so graciously rewarded, so straightly command-ded, or which being broken is so severely punished, as the love and

duty which children owe to their parents. Yet this love, albeit never
so respective, is dispensed withal in respect of that love which a man
† is bound to bear to his wife. 'For this cause', saith Adam (as from
the mouth of God), 'shall a man leave father and mother, and cleave
only to his wife.' The word 'cleave' is uttered in the Hebrew with a
more significant emphasis than any other language may express –
such a cleaving and joining together which admitteth no separation.
It may be necessarily observed that that gift of the woman was most
singularly excellent, which was to be accepted and entertained with
so inestimable a love, and made inseparable by giving and taking the
ring of love, which should be endless.

Now, the woman taking view of the garden, she was assaulted
with a serpent of the masculine gender; who, maliciously envying
the happiness in which man was at this time, like a mischievous
† politician he practised, by supplanting of the woman, to turn him
out of all. For which end he most craftily and cunningly attempted
the woman: and telleth her that therefore they were forbidden to eat
of the fruit, which grew in the midst of the garden, that in eating
they should not be like unto God. Whereupon the woman
accepted, tasted and gave to her husband. In accepting the serpent's
offer, there was no sin: for there was no sin till the fruit was eaten.
Now, albeit I have undertaken the defence of women, and may in
that respect be favoured in taking all advantages I may to defend my
sex.

There are many pregnant places in the scripture which might be
alleged to extenuate the sin of the woman in respect of the sin of
Adam: it is said (*Ecclesiasticus* xxv[.24]) 'Sin had his beginning in
woman'; *ergo*, his fullness in man.

St Paul saith (*Romans* v[.12]): 'By one man's sin death came into
the world', without mention of the woman. The same St Paul
writeth to the *Corinthians* [xv.22], to whom he affirmeth 'that all
die in Adam', in which the fullness and effects of sin are charged
upon Adam alone: not but that woman had her part in the tragedy,
but not in so high a degree as the man.

When Adam had eaten, and sin was now in fullness, he beginneth
to multiply sin upon sin. First he flieth from the sight of God; next,
being called to account, he excuseth his sin; and doth expostulate (as
it were) with Almighty God, and telleth him 'That woman which
thou gavest me, gave me, and I did eat': as who should say, if *thou*
hadst not given the cause, *I* had not been guilty of the effect –
making (herein) God the author of his fall.

Now what is become of that love which Adam was bound to bear
towards his wife? He chargeth her with all the burden: so he may
† discharge himself, he careth little how he clog her.

God having examined the offenders, and having heard the
uttermost they could allege for themselves, he pronounceth sentence of death upon them as a punishment in justice due and

deserved. Justice he administered to Adam. Albeit the woman doth taste of justice, yet mercy is reserved for her; and of all the works of mercy which mankind may hope for the greatest, the most blessed and the most joyful is promised to woman.

Woman supplanted by tasting of fruit, she is punished in bringing forth her own fruit. Yet what by fruit she lost, by fruit she shall recover.

What more gracious a gift could the Almighty promise to woman than to bring forth the fruit in which all nations shall be blessed? So that as woman was a means to lose Paradise, she is, by this, made a means to recover heaven. Adam could not upbraid her for so great a loss but he was to honour her more for a greater recovery. All the punishments inflicted upon women are encountered with most gracious blessings and benefits; she hath not so great cause of dolour in one respect as she hath infinite cause of joy in another. She is commanded to obey her husband: the cause is, the more to increase her glory. Obedience is better than sacrifice (I *Samuel* xii[.15]): for nothing is more acceptable before God than to obey. Women are much bound to God, to have so acceptable a virtue enjoined them for their penance.

Amongst the curses and punishments heaped upon the serpent, what greater joy could she hear, or what greater honour could be done unto her, than to hear from the voice of God these words: 'I will put enmity betwixt the woman and thee, betwixt thy seed and her seed', and that her seed should break the serpent's head? This must perforce be an exceeding joy for the woman, to hear and to be assured that her fruit should revenge her wrong.

After the fall and after they were all arraigned and censured, and that now Adam saw his wife's dowry and what blessings God hath bestowed upon her: he being now a bondslave to death and hell, struck dead in regard of himself – yet he comforts himself: he taketh heart from grace, he engageth his hope upon that promise which was made to the woman. Out of this most comfortable and blessed hope he now calleth his wife by a name, in whose effects not only he but all mankind should most blessedly share. He calleth her Eve, which is, the mother of the living. Which is suitable as well in respect of the promise made to her and her seed as in respect of those employments for which in her creation she and all women are designed: to be helpers, comforters, joys and delights, and in true use and government they ever have been and ever will be (as hereafter shall be showed), maugre the shameful, blasphemous and profane speech of Joseph Swetnam (page 31, beginning line 15) as followeth:

'If God had not made them only to be a plague to a man, he would never have called them necessary evils.'

Out of what scripture, out of what record, can he prove these impious and impudent speeches? They are only feigned and framed

out of his own idle, giddy, furious and frantic imaginations. If he
† had cited Euripides for his author, he had had some colour, for that
profane poet in *Medea* useth these speeches: 'Quod si deorum
aliquis mulierem formavit, opificem se malorum sciat, maximum et
hominibus inimicum'. (If any of the gods framed woman, let him
know he was the worker of that which is naught, and what is most
hurtful to men.) Thus a pagan writeth profanely, but for a Christian
to say that God calleth women 'necessary evils' is most intolerable
and shameful to be written and published.


# CHAPTER III

### *What choice God hath made of women to be instruments to derive his benefits to mankind*

Abraham, being in danger, was blessed and preserved in respect of
† Sara (*Genesis* xx).

Rebecca by God's providence was the means to bring the blessing
of Isaac to fall upon Jacob (*Genesis* xxvii).

The Egyptian mid-wives were a means to preserve the male
children of the Israelites from the murder intended by Pharaoh
(*Exodus* i).

Moses was preserved by the daughter of Pharaoh (*Exodus* ii).

The messengers sent by Duke Joshua to view the Land of
Promise were harboured and freed from danger by a woman
(*Joshua* ii.6).

When the children of Israel had been twenty years oppressed by
Jabin, King of Canaan: Deborah and Jael, two women, the one
won the battle, the other slew the general (*Judges* iv).

When Abimelech had murdered seventy of his brethren, he was
punished and slain by a woman at the siege of Thebes (*Judges* ix).
† Michal adventured the hazard of her father's displeasure to
preserve her husband David (I *Kings* xix).

Abigail by incomparable wisdom withheld David from shedding
of innocent blood (I *Kings* xv).

The city of Abdela, being in danger, was preserved by a wise
woman of that city (II *Kings* xx).

In the great famine of Samaria, the widow of Sarepta was chosen
to preserve Elias and Elias to preserve her (III *Kings* xvii).

The like provision did the woman, a Shunammite, make for
Elizeus and Elizeus for the woman (IV *Kings* iv).

When the blood-royal of Judah had been all murdered, Joas,
afterwards king, was preserved by a woman (IV *Kings* xi).
† What was that noble adventure so blessedly performed by Judith
in cutting off the head of Holofernes? (*Judith*)

With what wisdom did Queen Hester preserve her people and
caused their enemies to be hanged? (*Hester*)

What a chaste mirror was Susanna, who rather hazarded her life †
than offend against God? (*Susanna*)

Never was greater magnanimity showed by a woman than by that
mother which saw her seven children tormented most cruelly, yet
she encouraged them to the death (II *Machabees* vii).

## CHAPTER IV

### *What excellent blessings and graces have been bestowed upon women in the Law of Grace*

The first which cometh in this place to be mentioned is that blessed
mother and mirror of all womanhood, the Virgin Mary, who was
magnified in the birth of Jesus, glorified by angels, chosen by the
Almighty to bear in her womb the Saviour of mankind.

With what a faithful salutation did Elizabeth, St John Baptist['s]
mother, entertain the Virgin upon her repair unto her? (*Luke* i)

Anna the old prophetess did miraculously demonstrate our
Saviour (*Luke* ii).

The woman which had the issue of blood (*Matthew* ix.15[20]);
the woman of Canaan; (*John* iv) the Samaritan woman; Martha (the †
xi of *John*): all these and sundry others are saved, healed and have
their sins forgiven, in respect of their true and lively faith.

What faith, what zeal, what devotion did Mary Magdalene show
toward Jesus, in prostrating herself at the feet of Jesus, anointing
them with precious ointment, washing them with tears and drying
them with the hair of her head? (*Luke* vii)

With what bounty and devotion did the Maries, the wife of
Herod's steward, did Joanna, with other women, contribute of
their goods to Jesus? (*Luke* viii)

How charitable was that poor widow, whose two mites our
Saviour valued at a greater estimate than any gift of any other
whatsoever? (*Luke* ii.2)

In all dangers, troubles and extremities which fell to our Saviour,
when all men fled from him, living or dead, women never forsook
him.

I should be over-tedious to repeat every example of most zealous,
faithful and devout women which I might in the New Testament,
whose faith and devotion was consented by our Saviour to be
without compare.

I will conclude for women that they have been chosen both to set
out God's glory, and for the benefit of all mankind, in more
glorious and gracious employments than men have been.

The first promise of a Messias to come was made to a woman; the
birth and bearing of that promised Messias was performed by a
woman.

The triumphant resurrection, with the conquest over death and

† hell, was first published and proclaimed by a woman.

I might hereunto add those wives, widows and virgins who flourished in the primitive church and all succeeding ages sithence; who in all virtues have excelled, and honoured both their sex in general and themselves in particular; who in their martyrdoms, in their confession of Jesus, and in all Christian and divine virtues have in no respect been inferior unto men.

† Thus out of the second and third chapters of *Genesis* and out of the Old and New Testaments, I have observed in proof of the worthiness of our sex: first, that woman was the last work of creation (I dare not say the best); she was created out of the chosen and best refined substance; she was created in a more worthy country; she was married by a most holy priest; she was given by a most gracious father; her husband was enjoined to a most inseparable and affectionate care over her; the first promise of salvation was made to a woman; there is inseparable hatred and enmity put
† betwixt the woman and the serpent; her first name, Eva, doth presage the nature and disposition of all women, not only in respect of their bearing but further, for the life and delight of heart and soul to all mankind.

I have further showed the most gracious, blessed and rarest benefits, in all respects, bestowed upon women – all plainly and directly out of scriptures.

All which doth demonstrate the blasphemous impudency of the author of the *Arraignment*, who would or durst write so basely and shamefully, in so general a manner, against our so worthy and honoured a sex.

## To the Courteous and Friendly Reader

Gentle Reader, in my first Part I have (what I might) strictly observed a religious regard not to intermingle anything unfitting the gravity of so respective an argument.

Now that I am come to this second Part, I am determined to solace myself with a little liberty. What advantages I did forbear to take in the former I mean to make use of in this second. Joseph Swetnam hath been long unanswered, which had been performed sooner if I had heard of his book before this last term – or if the report of the maiden's answer had not stayed me. I have not so amply and absolutely discharged myself in this Apology as I would have done if either my leisure had been such as I could have wished, or the time more favourable that I might have stayed. What my repair into the country enforceth me to leave rather begun than finished I mean, by God's grace, to make perfect the next term. In the mean time, gentle Reader, I bid thee kindly farewell.

Ester Sowernam.

## CHAPTER IV                                              †

*At what estimate women were valued in ancient and former times*

Plato, in his books *De Legibus*, estimateth of women: which do †
equal men in all respects, only in body they are weaker but in wit
and disposition of mind nothing inferior, if not superior. Whereupon he doth, in his so absolute a commonweal, admit them to †
government of kingdoms and commonweals, if they be either born †
thereunto by nature or seated in government by election.

It is apparent that, in the prime of antiquity, women were valued
at highest estimate in that all those most inestimable and incomparable benefits, which might either honour or preserve mankind, are all
generally attributed to the invention of women – as may appear in
these few examples following.

When *meum et tuum* (mine and thine), when right and wrong
were decided by wars, and their weapons then were the furniture of
nature – as fists, teeth, stones, stakes or what came next to hand – a
lady of an heroical disposition, called Bellona, did first invent a †
more manlike and honourable weapon for war, which was the
sword, with other armour correspondent; for which she was at first
(and so ever since) honoured as the goddess of war.

When at the first the finest manchet and best bread in use was of †
acorns, by the singular and practical wit of a lady called Ceres the †
sowing of corn and tillage was invented.

The invention of the seven liberal sciences, of all arts, of all
learning hath been generally with one consent ascribed to the
invention of Jupiter's daughters, the nine muses, whose mother was †
a royal lady, Mnemosum.                                    †

Carmentis, a lady, first invented letters and the use of them by †
reading and writing.

The royal and most delightful exercise of hunting was first found
out and practised by Diana, who thereupon is celebrated for the †
goddess of hunting.

The three graces, which add a decorum and yield favour to †
persons, actions and speeches, are three ladies, Aglaia, Thalia and
Euphrosyne.

The heroical exercises of Olympus were first found and put in
practice by Palestra, a woman.                             †

The whole world being divided into three parts in more ancient †
times, every division to this day keepeth the name in honour of a
woman.

The feminine sex is exceedingly honoured by poets in their
writings. They have gods as well for good things as for bad; but
they have no women goddesses but in things which are especially
good. They have Bacchus for a drunken god but no drunken †
goddess. They have Priapus the lustful god of gardens but no †
garden goddesses, except of late in the garden-alleys. They will †

object here unto me Venus: she indeed is the goddess of love, but it
† is her blind son which is the god of lust. Poor lady, she hath but her
† jointure in the manor of love; Cupid is lord of all the rest, he hath
† the royalty. She may not strike a deer but she must employ her son,
that saucy boy.

For pride, they held it so far from women that they found out
† Nemesis or Rhamnusia to punish and revenge pride, but none to
infect with pride.

They have Pluto the god of hell, but no proper goddess of hell
† but Proserpina, whom Pluto forcibly took from Mount Etna and
carried her away, and made her queen of hell; yet she doth not
remain in hell but one half of the year, by a decree from Jupiter.

If I should recite and set down all the honourable records and
monuments for and of women, I might write more books than I
have yet written lines. I will leave and pass over the famous
testimonies of foreign kingdoms and commonwealths in honour of
our sex; and I will only mention some few examples of our own
country and kingdom, which have been incomparably benefited
and honoured by women.

Amongst the old Britons, our first ancestors, the valiant
† Boadicea: that defended the liberty of her country against the
strength of the Romans when they were at the greatest, and made
them feel that a woman could conquer them who had conquered
almost all the men of the then known world.

† The devout Helen: who – besides that she was the mother of that
religious and great Constantine (who first seated Christian religion
in the imperial throne) and in that respect may be styled the mother
of religion – is still more honoured for her singular piety and charity
towards him and his members who died for us upon the cross, than
for her care and industry in finding out the wood of that cross on
which he died.

† In the time of the Danes, chaste Emma, whose innocency carried
her naked feet over the fire-hot ploughshares unfelt; with the
† Saxons, Queen Elfgive the holy widow and the king's daughter
† Edith, a virgin saint: both greater conquerors than Alexander the
Great that men so much boast of, who could not conquer himself.

† Since the Normans, the heroical virtues of Eleanor, wife to
Edward the first: who when her husband in the Holy Land was
wounded with a poisoned arrow, of which there was no hope of
† recovery from the chirurgeons, she sucked the poison into her own
body to free him: together curing that mortal wound and making
her own fame immortal; so that I think this one act of hers may
equal all the acts that her great husband did in those wars besides.

† Philip, wife to Edward the third: no less to be honoured for being
the mother of so many brave children than of so many good deeds,
which worthily got her the title of 'good'.

† Margaret the wise, wife to Henry the sixth: who, if her husband's

fortune, valour and foresight had been answerable to hers, had left the crown of England to their own son and not to a stranger.

The other Margaret, of Richmond, mother to Henry the seventh: † from whose breasts he may seem to have derived as well his virtues as his life, in respect of her heroical prudence and piety; whereof, besides other monuments, both the universities are still witnesses.

Besides this, it was by the blessed means of Elizabeth, wife to † Henry the seventh, that the bloody wars betwixt the houses of York and Lancaster were ended, and the red rose and the white united, etc.

It was by the means of the most renowned Queen (the happy † mother of our dread sovereign) that the two kingdoms, once mortal foes, are now so blessedly conjoined.

And that I may name no more (since in one only were comprised all the qualities and endowments that could make a person eminent), Elizabeth our late sovereign: not only the glory of our sex but a pattern for the best men to imitate, of whom I will say no † more but that while she lived she was the mirror of the world, so then known to be, and so still remembered, and ever will be.

Daily experience and the common course of nature doth tell us that women were by men in those times highly valued, and in worth by men themselves preferred and held better than themselves.

I will not say that women are better than men, but I will say men are not so wise as I would wish them to be, to woo us in such fashion as they do; except they should hold and account of us as their betters.

What travail, what charge, what study do not men undertake to gain our good-will, love and liking? What vehement suits do they make unto us? With what solemn vows and protestations do they solicit us? They write, they speak, they send, to make known what entire affection they bear unto us: that they are so deeply engaged in love, except we do compassion them with our love and favour they are men utterly cast away. One he will starve himself, another will hang, another drown, another stab, another will exile himself from kindred and country – except they may obtain our loves. What? will they say that we are baser than themselves? Then they wrong themselves exceedingly to prefer such vehement suits to creatures inferior to themselves. Suitors do ever in their suits confess a more worthiness in the persons to whom they sue. These kind of suits are from nature, which cannot deceive them: nature doth tell them what women are and custom doth approve what nature doth direct. Aristotle saith 'Omnia appetent bonum' (everything by nature doth † seek after that which is good). Nature then doth carry men with violence to seek and sue after women. They will answer and seek to elude this maxim with a distinction: that *bonum* is duplex – *aut verum, aut apparens*, that goodness or the thing which is good is either truly good or but apparently good. So they may say women

are but apparently good. But the heathen orator, and the divine
† philosopher too, affirm if we follow the true direction of nature we
shall never be deceived. Nature in her vehement motions is not
deceived with apparent shows. It is natural, they will say, for the
male to follow the female. So it is as natural for the female to be
better than the male, as appeareth to be true in observation of
† hawks: the spar-hawk is of more esteem than the musket; the
goshawk more excellent than the tercel; so in falcons the females do
excel. The like men are bound to acknowledge women – the rather
in respect of their own credit and honour. To what obsequious duty
and service do men bind themselves to obtain a favour from their
devoted mistress? – which if he may obtain he thinketh himself to
be much honoured, and puts in place of most noted view that the
world may take note. He weareth in his hat or on his breast or upon
his arm the glove, the scarf or ring of his mistress. If these were not
relics from saintly creatures, men would not sacrifice so much
devotion unto them.

Amongst divers causes which proceed from nature and custom
why men are so earnest suitors to women, I have observed one
† which by practice is daily confessed. Plato saith that honesty is of
that worthiness that men are greatly inflamed with the love of it;
and as they do admire it, so they study how to obtain it. It is
apparent young men which are unmarried, and called bachelors,
they may have a disposition or may serve an apprenticeship to
† honesty, but they are never free-men, nor ever called honest men,
† till they be married: for that is the portion which they get by their
wives. When they are once married, they are forthwith placed in the
rank of honest men. If question be asked, what is such a man? – it is
presently resolved, he is an honest man. And the reason presently
added, for he hath a wife: she is the sure sign and seal of honesty. It
is usual amongst old and grave fathers, if they have a son given to
spending and company-keeping who is of a wild and riotous
disposition, such a father shall presently be counselled: 'help your
son to a good wife, marry him, marry him – that is the only way to
bring him to good order, to tame him, to bring him to be an honest
man'. The ancient fathers do herein acknowledge a greater worthiness in women than in men: the hope which they have, of an
untowardly son, to reclaim him, is all engaged upon the woman.

In no one thing men do acknowledge a more excellent perfection
in women than in the estimate of the offences which a woman doth
commit; the worthiness of the person doth make the sin more
markable. What an hateful thing is it to see a woman overcome with
drink? – whenas in men it is noted for a sign of good fellowship.
And, whosoever doth observe it, for one woman which doth make
a custom of drunkenness, you shall find an hundred men. It is
abhorred in women, and therefore they avoid it; it is laughed at and
made but as a jest amongst men, and therefore so many do practise

it. Likewise, if a man abuse a maid and get her with child, no matter
is made of it – but as a trick of youth; but it is made so heinous an
offence in the maid that she is disparaged and utterly undone by it.
So in all offences, those which men commit are made light and as
nothing, slighted over; but those which women do commit, those
are made grievous and shameful – and not without just cause. For
where God hath put hatred betwixt the woman and the serpent, it is
a foul shame in a woman to curry favour with the devil, to stain her
womanhood with any of his damnable qualities, that she will shake
hands where God hath planted hate.

Joseph Swetnam in his pamphlet aggravateth the offences of
women in the highest degree – not only exceeding but drawing men
into all mischief. If I do grant that women degenerating from the
true end of womanhood prove the greatest offenders, yet in
granting that I do thereby prove that women in their creation are
the most excellent creatures. For corruption, *boni pessima*: the best  †
thing corrupted proveth the worst; as for example, the most
glorious creature in heaven is by his fall the most damned devil in
hell. All the elements in their purity are most precious, in their
infection and abuse most dangerous. So the like in women: in their
most excellent purity of nature, what creature more gracious! but in
their fall from God and all goodness, what creature more mischievous? Which the devil knowing, he doth more assault woman
than man, because his gain is greater by the fall of one woman than
of twenty men. Let there be a fair maid, wife or woman in country,
town or city: she shall want no resort of serpents nor any variety of
tempter; let there be, in like sort, a beautiful or personable man: he
may sit long enough before a woman will solicit him. For where the
devil hath good acquaintance, he is sure of entertainment there
without resistance. The serpent at first tempted woman: he dare
assault her no more in that shape: now he employeth men to supply
his part. And so they do: for as the serpent began with Eve to
delight her taste, so do his instruments draw to wine and banquet-
ing. The next, the serpent enticed her by pride and told her she
should be like to God, so do his instruments: first, they will extol
her beauty, what a paragon she is in their eyes; next, they will
promise her such maintenance as the best woman in the parish or  †
country shall not have better. What care they if they make a
thousand oaths and commit ten thousand perjuries, so they may
deceive a woman? When they have done all and gotten their
purpose, then they discover all the woman's shame and employ
such an author as this (to whose Arraignment I do make haste) to
rail upon her and the whole sex.

## CHAPTER V

*The Arraignment of Joseph Swetnam who was the Author of the
Arraignment of Women; and under his person, the Arraignment
of all idle, frantic, froward and lewd men*

Joseph Swetnam having written his rash, idle, furious and shameful
discourse against women, it was at last delivered into my hands.
Presently I did acquaint some of our sex with the accident, with
whom I did advise what course we should take with him. It was
concluded that, his unworthiness being much like to that of
Thersites whom I have formerly mentioned, we would not answer
† him either with Achilles' fist or Stafford law; neither pluck him in
† pieces as the Thracian women did Orpheus for his intemperate
railing against women: but, as he had arraigned women at the bar of
fame and report, we resolved at the same bar where he did us the
wrong to arraign him – that thereby we might defend our assured
right. And withal (respecting ourselves) we resolved to favour him
so far in his trial that the world might take notice there was no
partial or indirect dealing, but that he had as much favour as he
could desire, and far more than he did or could deserve.

So that we brought him before two judgesses, Reason and
† Experience, who being both in place, no man can suspect them with
any indirect proceedings. For albeit Reason of itself may be blinded
by passion, yet when she is joined with Experience she is known to
be absolute and without compare. As for Experience, she is known
of herself to be admirable excellent in her courses, she knoweth how
to use every man in her practice: she will whip the fool to learn him
more wit; she will punish the knave to practise more honesty; she
will curb in the prodigal and teach him to be wary; she will trip up
the heels of such as are rash and giddy, and bid them hereafter look
before they leap. To be short, there is not in all the world, for all
estates, degrees, qualities and conditions of men, so singular a
mistress or so fit to be a judgess as she. Only one property she hath
above all the rest: no man cometh before her but she maketh him
ashamed, and she will call and prove almost every man a fool,
especially such who are wise in their own conceits.

For his jury, albeit we knew them to be of his dearest and nearest
inward familiar friends, in whose company he was ever and did
spend upon them all that he could get or devise to get: yet we did
† challenge no one of them but were well pleased that his five senses
and the seven deadly sins should stand for his jury.

The party which did give evidence against him we knew to be a
† sure card, and one which would not fail in proof of anything, and
such proof which should be without all exception: Conscience is a
sure witness.

So all things being accordingly provided, the prisoner was
brought to the bar, where he was called and bid hold up his hand;

which he did, but a false hand God he knows; his indictment was read, which was this which followeth.

## CHAPTER VI

### *Joseph Swetnam his Indictment*

Joseph Swetnam, thou art indicted by the name of Joseph Swetnam of Bedlammore, in the County of Onopoly. For that thou the † twentieth day of December in the year etc. didst most wickedly, blasphemously, falsely and scandalously publish a lewd pamphlet, entitled the *Arraignment of Women*. In which, albeit thou didst honestly pretend to arraign lewd, idle, froward and unconstant women, yet contrary to thy pretended promise thou didst rashly and maliciously rail and rage against all women generally; writing and publishing most blasphemously that women by their creator were made for 'helpers', for 'helpers' (thou sayst) 'to spend and consume that which man painfully getteth'. Furthermore, thou dost write 'That being made of a rib, which was crooked, they are therefore crooked and froward in conditions, and that woman was no sooner made but her heart was set upon mischief'; which thou dost derive to all the sex generally, in these words: 'And therefore ever since they have been a woe unto man, and follow the line of their first leader.' Further than all this, thou dost affirm an impudent lie upon Almighty God, in saying that God calleth them 'necessary evils, and that therefore they were created to be a plague unto man'. Thou writest also: 'That women are proud, lascivious, froward, cursed, unconstant, idle, impudent, shameless, and that they deck and dress themselves to tempt and allure men to lewdness', with much and many more foul, intemperate and scandalous speeches, etc.

When Joseph Swetnam was asked what he said to his indictment: 'Guilty or not guilty', he pleaded the general issue: 'not guilty'; † being asked how he would be tried, he stood mute, for Conscience did so confront him that he knew upon trial there was no way but one. Whereupon he thought it much better to put himself upon our mercy than to hazard the trial of his own jury.

Whereupon we did consider if we should have urged him to be pressed, the disadvantage had been ours. For then his favourites would have said, as some did say, that Joseph Swetnam did not stand mute as misdoubting the proof of what he had written: but seeing the judgesses, the jury, the accuser, and all others, most of them of the feminine gender, he sus[pected], the question by us † being made general, that they would rather condemn him to please a general – although in particular respect of himself he knew they would favour him. And besides, that he held it a strange course that the self and the same persons should be judges and accusers.

Whereupon we resolved to grant him longer time to advise with himself whether he would put himself to trial or, upon better deliberation, to recall his errors.

But that the world might be satisfied in respect of the wrongs done unto us, and to maintain our honourable reputation, it was concluded that myself should deliver before the judges to all the assembly speeches to these effects following.


## CHAPTER VII

### *The Answer to all objections which are material made against Women*

Right honourable and worshipful, and you of all degrees: it hath ever been a common custom amongst idle and humorous poets, pamphleteers and rhymers, out of passionate discontents – or having little otherwise to employ themselves about – to write some bitter satire-pamphlet or rhyme against women. In which argument, he who could devise anything more bitterly or spitefully against our sex hath never wanted the liking, allowance and
† applause of giddy-headed people. Amongst the rabble of scurril writers, this prisoner now present hath acted his part. Whom albeit women could more willingly let pass than bring him to trial, and, as ever heretofore, rather condemn such authors than deign them any
† answer, yet – seeing his book so commonly bought up, which argueth a general applause – we are therefore enforced to make answer in defence of ourselves, who are by such an author so extremely wronged in public view.

You all see he will not put himself upon trial. If we should let it so pass, our silence might implead us for guilty; so would his pamphlet
† be received with a greater current and credit than formerly it hath been. So that as well in respect of our sex, as for a general satisfaction to the world, I will take this course with our prisoner: I will at this present examine all the objections which are most material which our adversary hath vomited out against woman, and not only what he hath objected but what other authors of more import than Joseph Swetnam have charged upon women. Alas,
† seely man, he objecteth nothing but what he hath stolen out of
† English writers, as *Euphues*, the *Palace of Pleasure*, with the like, which are as easily answered as vainly objected. He never read the vehement and professed enemies against our sex, as, for Grecians,
† Euripides, Menander, Simonides, Sophocles, with the like; amongst
† Latin writers, Juvenal, Plautus, etc.

But of all that ever I read, I did never observe such general scurrility in any as in this adversary, which you shall find I will make as manifest as the sun to shine at mid-day.

It is the main end that our adversary aimeth at in all his discourse to prove and say that women are bad. If he should offer this upon particulars, no one would deny it: but to lavish generally against all women, who can endure it? You might, Mr. Swetnam, with some show of honesty have said some women are bad, both by custom and company; but you cannot avoid the brand both of blasphemy and dishonesty, to say of women generally they are all naught – both in their creation and by nature – and to ground your inferences upon scriptures.

I let pass your objections in your first page, because they are formerly answered; only, whereas you say 'woman was no sooner made, but her heart was set upon mischief', if you had then said 'she had no sooner eaten of the fruit, but her heart was set upon mischief', you had had some colour for your speeches: not in † respect of the woman's disposition, but in consideration both of her first tutor and her second instructor. For whereas scripture doth say 'Woman was supplanted by a serpent', Joseph Swetnam doth say 'she was supplanted by the devil, which appeared to her in the shape of a beautiful young man'. Men are much beholding to this author, who will seem to insinuate that the devil would in so friendly and familiar a manner put on the shape of man when he first began to practise mischief. The devil might make bold of them whom he knew in time would prove his familiar friends. Hereupon it may be imagined it cometh to pass that painters and picture-makers, when they would represent the devil, they set him out in the deformed shape of a man: because under that shape he began first to act the part of a devil – and I doubt he never changed his suit sithence. Here † it is to be observed, that which is worst is expressed by the shape of a man; but what is the most glorious creature is represented in the beauty of a woman, as angels. Woman at the first might easily learn mischief: where or how should she learn goodness? Her first school-master was abundant in mischief, and her first husband did exceed in bad examples. First, by his examples he taught her how to fly from God; next how to excuse her sin; then how to cample and † contest with God and to say, as Adam did, 'thou art the cause, for the woman whom thou gavest me was the cause I did eat'. What Adam did at the first, bad husbands practise with their wives ever sithence – I mean in bad examples. It was no good example in Adam, who having received his wife from the gift of God – and bound to her in so inseparable a bond of love, that forthwith he, being taken tardy, would presently accuse his wife and put her in all the danger. But the woman was more bound to an upright judge than to a loving husband: it would not serve Adam's turn to charge her, thereby to free himself. It was an hard and strange course that he who should have been her defender is now become her greatest accuser. I may here say with St Paul 'by one man's sin, death' etc.: so by the contagion of original sin in Adam, all men are infected with his diseases. And look what examples he gave his wife at the first: the like examples and practices do all men show to women ever sithence. Let me speak freely, for I will speak nothing but truly, neither shall my words exceed my proof.

In your first and second page, you allege David and Solomon for exclaiming bitterly against women; and that Solomon saith: 'Women, like as wine, do make men drunk with their devices'. What of all this?

† Joseph Swetnam, a man which hath reason, will never object that unto his adversary which, when it cometh to examination, will disadvantage himself. Your meaning is, in the disgrace of women to exalt men: but is this any commendation to men, that they have been and are over-reached by women? Can you glory of their holiness, whom by women prove sinful? Or in their wisdom, whom women make fools? Or in their strength, whom women overcome? Can you excuse that fall which is given by the weaker? Or colour that foil which is taken from women? Is holiness, wisdom and strength so slightly seated in your masculine gender as to be stained, blemished and subdued by women?

But now, I pray you let us examine how these virtues in men so potent came by women to be so impotent. Do you mean in comparative degree that women are more holy, more wise, more strong than men? If you should grant this, you had small cause to write against them. But you will not admit this. What is or are the causes then why men are so overtaken by women? You set down the causes in your fourth page; there you say: 'They are dangerous for men to deal withal, for their faces are lures, their beauties baits, their looks are nets and their words are charms', and all to bring
† men to ruin. *Incidit in Scyllam qui vult vitare Charibdim*, whilst he seeketh to avoid one mischief he falleth into another. It were more credit for men to yield our sex to be more holy, wise and strong, than to excuse themselves by the reasons alleged: for by this men are proved to have as little wit as they are charged to exceed in wickedness. Are external and dumb shows such potent baits, nets,
† lures, charms, to bring men to ruin? Why? Wild asses, dotterels and woodcocks are not so easily entangled and taken! Are men so idle, vain and weak as you seem to make them? Let me now see how you can free these men from dishonest minds, who are overtaken thus with beauty, etc. How can beauty hurt? How can it be a cause of a man's ruin of itself? What, do women forcibly draw? – why, men are more strong! Are they so eloquent to persuade? – why, men too wise. Are they mischievous to entice? – men are more holy. How then are women causes to bring men to ruin? Direct causes they cannot be in any respect: if they be causes, they are but
† accidental causes. (A 'cause' as philosophers say: *causa sine qua non.*) A remote cause: which cause is seldom alleged for cause, but where want of wit would say somewhat and a guilty conscience would excuse itself by anything.

Philosophers say *nemo leditur nisi a seipso* (no man is hurt but the cause is in himself). The prodigal person amongst the Grecians is called Asotos, as a destroyer, an undoer of himself. When an heart † fraughted with sin doth prodigally lavish out a lascivious look out of a wanton eye, when it doth surfeit upon the sight, who is Asotos? Who is guilty of this lascivious disease but himself? *Volenti non fit injuria*: he who is wounded with his own consent hath small cause to complain of another's wrong. Might not a man as easily – and more honestly – when he seeth a fair woman which doth make the best use that she can to set out her beauty, rather glorify God in so beautiful a work than infect his soul with so lascivious a thought? And for the woman, who having a jewel given her from so dear a friend: is she not to be commended rather that, in the estimate which she showeth, she will as carefully and as curiously as she may † set out what she hath received from Almighty God – than to be censured that she doth it to allure wanton and lascivious looks?

The difference is in the minds: things which are called *Adiaphora* † (things indifferent), whose qualities have their name from the uses, are commonly so censured and so used as the mind is inclined which doth pass his verdict. A man and a woman talk in the fields together: an honest mind will imagine of their talk answerable to his own disposition, whereas an evil disposed mind will censure according to his lewd inclination. When men complain of beauty and say that 'women's dressings and attire are provocations to wantonness and baits to allure men', it is a direct means to know of what disposition they are. It is a shame for men in censuring of women to condemn themselves: but a common inn cannot be without a common sign. It is a common sign to know a lecher by complaining upon the cause and occasion of his surfeit: who had known his disease but by his own complaint? It is extreme folly to complain of another when the root of all resteth within himself. Purge an infected heart and turn away a lascivious eye, and then neither their dressings nor their beauty can any ways hurt you.

Do not men exceed in apparel and therein set themselves out to the view? Shall women betray themselves and make it known that they are either so bad in their disposition, or so wanton in their thoughts, or so weak in their government as to complain that they are tempted and allured by men? Should women make themselves more vain than youngest children, to fall in love with babies? † Women are so far off from being in any sort provoked to love upon the view of men's apparel and setting forth themselves, that no one thing can more draw them from love than their vanity in apparel. Women make difference betwixt colours and conditions, betwixt a fair show and a foul substance. It shows a levity in man to furnish himself more with trim colours than manlike qualities; beside that, how can we love at whom we laugh? We see him gallant it at the court one day and brave it in the counter the next day; we see him †

wear that on his back one week which we hear is in the broker's
† shop the next. Furthermore, we see divers wear apparel and colours
made of a lordship, lined with farms and granges, embroidered with
all the plate, gold and wealth their friends and fathers left them. Are
these motives to love or to laughter? Will or dare a woman trust to
their love for one month who will turn her off the next? This is the
surfeit which women take by brave apparel. They rather suspect his
worth, than wish his love who doth most exceed in bravery. So,
Mr. Swetnam, do you and all yours forbear to censure of the
dressings and attires of women for any such lewd intent as you
imagine. Bad minds are discovered by bad thoughts and hearts. Do
not say and rail at women to be the cause of men's overthrow, when
the original root and cause is in yourselves.

If you be so affected that you cannot look but you must
forthwith be infected, I do marvel, Joseph Swetnam, you set down
no remedies for that torment of love, as you call it. You bid men
shun and avoid it, but those be common and ordinary rules and
instructions: yet not so ordinary as able to restrain the extraordinary humours of your giddy company. I will do you and your
friends a kindness if you be so scorched with the flames of love.
† Diogenes did long since discover the sovereign salve for such a
wound. The receipt is no great charge, yourself may be the
apothecary. It is comprehended in three words: first, try with
† (time); next with (hunger); if both these fail, the third is sure, (a
halter). This was Diogenes' antidote against that venomous infection. There are more milder remedies which you may put in
practice: if your hearts be so fleshly or your eyes so tender that you
dare trust neither of them, then trust to your reason to turn your
† eyes away, or trust to your heels, as Joseph did, to carry all away.

After you have railed against women you bring in a fable of a
contention betwixt the wind and the sun, and you apply the moral
to women – whenas it hath a far other relation. For it ever hath been
applied to men, to instruct them in the government of woman: for I
pray you, who is to govern or who are to be governed? You should
† seem to come from the Sauromatians whose wives were their
masters. But I will set you down both the fable and the moral, as it
† was written in English verse long sithence.

> The sun and wind at variance did fall,
> Whose force was greatest in the open field.
> A traveller they choose to deal withal:
> Who makes him first unto their force to yield
>     To cast off cloak, they that agreement make
>     The honour of the victory must take.
>
> The wind began and did increase, each blast
> With raging beat upon the silly man;

The more it blew, the more he grasped fast
And kept his cloak, let wind do what it can.
    When all in vain the wind his worst had done,
    It ceased, and left a trial to the sun.

The sun begins his beams for to display,
And by degrees in heat for to increase;
The traveller, then warm, doth make a stay,
And by degrees his cloak he doth release.
    At length is forced both coat and cloak to yield,
    So gives the sun the honour of the field.

Who by extremes doth seek to work his will,
By raging humours thinking so to gain,
May like the wind augment his tempest still
But at the length he finds his fury vain:
    For all he gets by playing frantic parts,
    He hardeneth more the mild and gentle hearts.

Like as all plants, when at the first they spring,
Are tender, and soft-barked on every side;
But as they grow, continual storms do bring
Those are more hard which Northern blasts abide.
    What's toward the Southern tenderer we find,
    And that more hard which feels the Northern wind.

Nature his course most carefully doth bend,
From violence to seek itself to arm;
Where raging blasts the trees would break and rend,
There nature strives to keep her plants from harm:
    Where violence is unto nature strange,
    Continual custom there doth nature change.

So 'tis with women, who by nature mild,
If they on froward crabbed husbands light,
Continual rage by custom makes them wild:
For crooked natures alter gentle quite.
    Men evermore shall this in trial find:
    Like to her usage so is woman's mind.                    †

As of themselves, let men of others judge;
What man will yield to be compelled by rage?
At crabbedness and cursedness hearts do grudge,
And to resist, themselves they more engage.
    Forbear the wind, shine with the sun awhile;
    Though she be angry, she will forthwith smile.

This is the true application of the moral. As for that crookedness and frowardness with which you charge women, look from whence they have it. For of themselves and their own disposition it doth not proceed, which is proved directly by your own testimony. For in your 46 page, line 15[16], you say: 'A young woman of tender years is flexible, obedient and subject to do anything, according to the will and pleasure of her husband'. How cometh it then that this gentle and mild disposition is afterwards altered? Yourself doth give the true reason, for you give a great charge not to marry a widow. But why? Because, say you in the same page, 'A widow is framed to

† the conditions of another man'. Why then, if a woman have froward conditions, they be none of her own, she was framed to them. Is not our adversary ashamed of himself to rail against women for those faults which do all come from men? Doth not he

† most grievously charge men to learn their wives bad and corrupt behaviour? For he saith plainly: 'Thou must unlearn a widow, and make her forget and forego her former corrupt and disordered behaviour'. Thou must unlearn her; *ergo*, what fault she hath she learned: her corruptness cometh not from her own disposition but from her husband's destruction.

Is it not a wonder that your pamphlets are so dispersed? Are they not wise men to cast away time and money upon a book which cutteth their own throats? 'Tis pity but that men should reward you

† for your writing (if it be but as the Roman Sertorius did the idle poet: he gave him a reward, but not for his writing – but because he should never write more). As for women, they laugh that men have no more able a champion. This author cometh to bait women or, as he foolishly saith, the 'Bear-baiting of Women', and he bringeth but

† a mongrel cur who doth his kind to brawl and bark, but cannot bite. The mild and flexible disposition of a woman is in philosophy proved in the composition of her body, for it is a maxim: *Mores animi sequntur temperaturam corporis* (the disposition of the mind is answerable to the temper of the body). A woman in the temperature of her body is tender, soft and beautiful, so doth her disposition in mind correspond accordingly: she is mild, yielding and virtuous. What disposition accidentally happeneth unto her is by the contagion of a froward husband, as Joseph Swetnam affirmeth.

And experience proveth. It is a shame for a man to complain of a froward woman – in many respects all concerning himself. It is a shame he hath no more government over the weaker vessel. It is a shame he hath hardened her tender sides and gentle heart with his boisterous and Northern blasts. It is a shame for a man to publish and proclaim household secrets – which is a common practice amongst men, especially drunkards, lechers and prodigal spend-thrifts. These when they come home drunk, or are called in question for their riotous misdemeanours, they presently show

themselves the right children of Adam. They will excuse themselves
by their wives and say that their unquietness and frowardness at
home is the cause that they run abroad: an excuse more fitter for a
beast than a man. If thou wert a man thou wouldst take away the
cause which urgeth a woman to grief and discontent, and not by thy
frowardness increase her distemperature. Forbear thy drinking, thy †
luxurious riot, thy gaming and spending, and thou shalt have thy
wife give thee as little cause at home as thou givest her great cause of
disquiet abroad. Men which are men, if they chance to be matched
with froward wives – either of their own making or others' marring
– they would make a benefit of the discommodity: either try his
skill to make her mild or exercise his patience to endure her
cursedness; for all crosses are inflicted either for punishment of sins
or for exercise of virtues. But humorous men will sooner mar a †
thousand women than out of an hundred make one good.

   And this shall appear in the imputation which our adversary
chargeth upon our sex: to be lascivious, wanton and lustful. He
saith: 'Women tempt, allure and provoke men.' How rare a thing is
it for women to prostitute and offer themselves? How common a
practice is it for men to seek and solicit women to lewdness? What
charge do they spare? What travail do they bestow? What vows,
oaths and protestations do they spend to make them dishonest?
They hire panders, they write letters, they seal them with damna-
tions and execrations to assure them of love when the end proves
but lust. They know the flexible disposition of women, and the
sooner to overreach them some will pretend they are so plunged in
love that, except they obtain their desire, they will seem to drown,
hang, stab, poison or banish themselves from friends and country.
What motives are these to tender dispositions? Some will pretend
marriage, another offer continual maintenance; but when they have
obtained their purpose, what shall a woman find? – just that which
is her everlasting shame and grief: she hath made herself the
unhappy subject to a lustful body and the shameful stall of a †
lascivious tongue. Men may with foul shame charge woman with
this sin which she had never committed, if she had not trusted; nor †
had ever trusted, if she had not been deceived with vows, oaths and
protestations. To bring a woman to offend in one sin, how many
damnable sins do they commit? I appeal to their own consciences.
The lewd disposition of sundry men doth appear in this: if a woman
or maid will yield unto lewdness, what shall they want? – but if they †
would live in honesty, what help shall they have? How much will
they make of the lewd? how base account of the honest? How many
pounds will they spend in bawdy houses? but when will they
bestow a penny upon an honest maid or woman, except it be to
corrupt them?

   Our adversary bringeth many examples of men which have been
overthrown by women. It is answered before: the fault is their own.

But I would have him, or anyone living, to show any woman that offended in this sin of lust, but that she was first solicited by a man.

Helen was the cause of Troy's burning: first, Paris did solicit her; next, how many knaves and fools of the male kind had Troy, which to maintain whoredom would bring their city to confusion?

When you bring in examples of lewd women and of men which have been stained by women, you show yourself both frantic and a profane irreligious fool to mention Judith, for cutting off Holofernes' head, in that rank.

You challenge women for untamed and unbridled tongues: there was never woman was ever noted for so shameless, so brutish, so beastly a scold as you prove yourself in this base and odious pamphlet. You blaspheme God, you rail at his creation, you abuse and slander his creatures; and what immodest or impudent scurrility is it which you do not express in this lewd and lying pamphlet?

Hitherto I have so answered all your objections against women that, as I have not defended the wickedness of any, so I have set down the true state of the question. As Eve did not offend without the temptation of a serpent, so women do seldom offend but it is by provocation of men. Let not your impudency, nor your consorts' dishonesty, charge our sex hereafter with those sins of which you yourselves were the first procurers. I have, in my discourse, touched you, and all yours, to the quick. I have taxed you with bitter speeches; you will, perhaps, say I am a railing scold. In this objection, Joseph Swetnam, I will teach you both wit and honesty. The difference betwixt a railing scold and an honest accuser is this: the first rageth upon passionate fury without bringing cause or proof, the other bringeth direct proof for what she allegeth. You charge women with clamorous words, and bring no proof; I charge you with blasphemy, with impudency, scurrility, foolery and the like. I show just and direct proof for what I say. It is not my desire to speak so much; it is your desert to provoke me upon just cause so far. It is no railing to call a crow black, or a wolf a ravenor, or a drunkard a beast; the report of the truth is never to be blamed: the deserver of such a report deserveth the shame.

Now, for this time, to draw to an end. Let me ask according to † the question of Cassian, *cui bono?* – what have you gotten by publishing your pamphlet? Good I know you can get none. You have, perhaps, pleased the humours of some giddy, idle, conceited persons. But you have dyed yourself in the colours of shame, lying, slandering, blasphemy, ignorance and the like.

The shortness of time and the weight of business call me away, and urge me to leave off thus abruptly; but assure yourself, where I † leave now I will by God's grace supply the next term, to your small content. You have exceeded in your fury against widows, whose defence you shall hear of at the time aforesaid. In the mean space, recollect your wits; write out of deliberation, not out of fury; write

out of advice, not out of idleness: forbear to charge women with
faults which come from the contagion of masculine serpents.

## CHAPTER VIII                    ÷

*A Defence of Women against the Author of the Arraignment of*
*Women*

An idle companion was raging of late,
Who in fury 'gainst women expresseth his hate:
He writeth a book, an *Arraignment* he calleth,
In which against women he currishly bawleth.
He deserveth no answer but in ballad or rhyme
Upon idle fantastics who would cast away time:
Any answer may serve an impudent liar,
Any mangy scabbed horse doth fit a scaled squire.                    †
In the ruff of his fury, for so himself saith,                    †
The blasphemous companion he shamefully playeth.
The woman for an helper God did make, he doth say,
But to 'help to consume and spend all away'.
Thus at God's creation to flout and to jest,
Who but an atheist would so play the beast?
The scriptures do prove that when Adam did fall,
And to death and damnation was thereby a thrall,
Then woman was an helper, for by her blessed seed
From Hell and damnation all mankind was freed.
He saith women are froward, which the rib doth declare,
For like as the rib so they crooked are:
The rib was her subject for body we find,
But from God came her soul and dispose of her mind.
Let no man think much if women compare
That in their creation they much better are:
More blessings therein to women do fall
Than unto mankind have been given at all.
Women were the last work, and therefore the best,
For what was the end excelleth the rest.
For woman's more honour, it was so assigned,
She was made of the rib of mettle refined;                    †
The country doth also the woman more grace,
For Paradise is far the more excellent place.
Yet women are mischievous this author doth say,
But scriptures to that directly say nay:
God said 'twixt the woman and serpent for ever
Strong hatred he would put, to be qualified never'.
The woman being hateful to the serpent's condition,
How excellent is she in her disposition?
The serpent with men in their works may agree,

But the serpent with women – that never may be.
If you ask how it happens some women prove naught:
By men turned to serpents they are over-wrought.
What the serpent began, men follow that still:
They tempt what they may to make women do ill.
They will tempt and provoke and follow us long;
They deceive us with oaths and a flattering tongue.
To make a poor maiden or woman a whore,
They care not how much they spend of their store.
But where is there a man that will anything give
That woman or maid may with honesty live?
If they yield to lewd counsel they nothing shall want;
But for to be honest – then all things are scant.
It proves a bad nature in men doth remain,
To make women lewd their purses they strain.
For a woman that's honest they care not a whit:
They'll say she is honest because she lacks wit.
† They'll call women whores, but their stakes they might save –
There can be no whore but there must be a knave.
They say that our dressings and that our attire
Are causes to move them unto lustful fire.
Of all things which are, we evermore find
Such thoughts do arise as are like to the mind:
† Men's thoughts being wicked they wrack on us thus –
That scandal is taken, not given by us.
If their sight be so weak and their frailty be such,
Why do they then gaze at our beauty so much?
Pluck away those ill roots whence sin doth arise;
Amend wicked thoughts, or pluck out the eyes.
The humours of men – see how froward they be;
We know not to please them in any degree:
For if we go plain, we are sluts, they do say;
They doubt of our honesty if we go gay;
† If we be honest and merry, giglots they take us;
If modest and sober, then proud they do make us;
Be we housewifely, quick, then a shrew he doth keep;
If patient and mild, then he scorneth a sheep.
What can we devise to do or to say,
But men do wrest all things the contrary way.
'Tis not so uncertain to follow the wind
As to seek to please men of so humorous mind.
Their humours are giddy and never long lasting;
We know not to please them – neither full nor yet fasting.
Either we do too little or they do too much:
They strain our poor wits, their humours are such.
They say women are proud: wherein made they trial?
They moved some lewd suit, and had the denial:
To be crossed in such suits men cannot abide,

And thereupon we are entitled with pride.
They say we are cursed and froward by kind:
Our mildness is changed where raging we find.
A good Jack, says the proverb, doth make a good Jill;                †
A cursed froward husband doth change woman's will.
They use us (they say) as necessary evils:
We have it from them – for they are our devils.
When they are in their rages and humorous fits,
They put us poor women half out of our wits.
Of all naughty women name one if you can:
If she proved bad it came by a man.
Fair Helen forsook her husband of Greece:
A man called Paris betrayed that piece.                †
Medea did rage and did shamefully murder:                †
A Jason was cause which her mischief did further.
A Cressid was false and changed her love:                †
Diomedes her heart by constraint did remove.
In all like examples the world sure may see:
Where women prove bad, there men are not free.                †
But in those offences they have the most share,
Women would be good, if serpents would spare.
Let women and maids, whatsoever they be,
Come follow my counsel, be warned by me.
Trust not men's suits, their love proveth lust;
Both hearts, tongues and pens do all prove unjust.
How fair they will speak and write in their love,
But put them to trial – how false do they prove?
They love hot at first, when the love is a stranger,
But they will not be tied to rack and to manger.
What love call you that, when men are a-wooing
And seek nothing else but shame and undoing?
As women in their faults I do not commend,
So wish I all men their lewd suits they would end.
Let women alone and seek not their shame,
You shall have no cause then women to blame.
'Tis like that this author against such doth bawl,
Who by his temptations have gotten a fall.
For he who of women so wickedly deemeth
Hath made them dishonest, it probably seemeth.
He hath been a traveller, it may be well so,
By his tales and reports as much we do know.
He promiseth some poison 'gainst women to thrust:
He doth it for physic or else he would burst.
Thus I bid him farewell till next we do meet:                †
And then as cause moveth, so shall we greet.

Joan Sharp

FINIS

NOTES

(NB I have omitted most of the marginal notes, which simply summarise points in the argument.)

PAGE 85
**Ester**: Esther attained a position of eminence in the court of Xerxes I, King of Persia, and was thus able to save her Jewish people from the attacks of the Vizier Haman.

**neither Maide**: based on Swetnam, p. 27 – he addresses 'unmarried wantons' that 'you have thus unluckily made yourselves neither maidens, widows nor wives'. Sowernam provocatively writes as an 'unmarried wanton'.

**Neque enim ... perire sua**: For there is no law more just ... than that the creator of a piece of violence should perish by his own art. Based on Ovid, *Ars Amatoria* i.655–6.

PAGE 87
**Michaelmas Term**: most business and social life in London followed the legal terms; those who resided outside London in the summer would come back to town.

**Minister's daughter**: see headnote on Speght.

PAGE 88
**forward**: bold.

**Apprentices**: the interest of this dedication is that the city apprentices were often the targets of satirists who fancied themselves more genteel and chic than craftsmen and shop-keepers; it thus becomes a sort of alignment. During the traditional Shrove Tuesday apprentice celebration in 1617, the apprentices wrecked a theatre as well as brothels (both haunts, in this part of the town, of the wealthy).

PAGE 89
**like ... lettuce**: in fact an alleged saying of M. Crassus (originating in Jerome); it is a proverbial saying – like has met like.

**scratting**: scratching.

PAGE 90
**quit**: acquitted.

**nonage**: under-age, minority.

**woman ... adultery**: the story in John viii.3.

**decompounded**: an intensification of compounded – further compounded.

**K**: uncertain – could have associations of folly, from 'kay-footed/handed': left-footed/handed, or 'kae': jackdaw. An interesting sidelight: Coryate wrote under the name Thomas Telltroth, which Swetnam borrowed. On the title page of Coryate's most famous work, *Coriat's Crudities*, there is an annotated illustration – the section marked 'k' is a portrait of Telltroth. Sowernam may be making this complex link, though it's a long shot.

PAGE 91
**St Jerome**: Eusebius Hieronymus (342–420), biblical scholar: the text quoted here is from letter 150 'To a Cyprian priest, on Psalm 89': I patiently bore my injury, impiety against God I could not bear.

**St Chrysostom**: Bishop of Constantinople (347–407), an ascetic famous for his personal holiness, his preaching and exegesis of the Bible. The text referred to here is one of a series of homilies on biblical texts, here the Gospel according to St Matthew: it is impious to conceal injuries towards God.

**Julian the Apostata**: (332–363) a Roman emperor who tried to re-establish pagan worship and to promote heathen religion rather than Christianity.

PAGE 91 CONTINUED

**Lucian the Atheist**: Lucian of Samosata (115–200), a satirist who attacked, amongst other things, popular religious ideas.

**Iliad**: printed '*Iliads*'.

**Thersites**: notable for his ugliness and foul speech (see, for example, Shakespeare's portrayal of the character in *Troilus and Cressida*).

**first chapter**: I have decided against inserting additional page references to Swetnam – Sowernam is sufficiently clear; the quotations are not always totally accurate, but the sense is unchanged.

**Midas**: the king who turned things to gold; here chosen as an example of foolishness – Midas was given ass's ears for adjudicating against the god Apollo in a contest (gods, like the police, have to win).

PAGE 92

**Quicquid ... tale**: Sowernam adequately translates most of the Latin she uses (for this see Aristotle, *Categories* viii.9–10).

**law of nature, etc.**: Moses' law differs from the law of nature in that it is written legislation; the law of grace is the new doctrine of forgiveness instituted by Christ (part of the basic distinction between the Old and New Testaments); the English Catholic Bible, printed at Douai in 1609, has a useful note: 'As here we see example [in Adam's gifts to God] in the law of nature: and the same was ordained by written precept in the law of Moses: the prophets also foretold that external sacrifice should be offered in the law of grace and new Testament, to wit the same which Christ instituted' (notes to Gen. iv, p.15).

**curiously**: elaborately, ornately, even pedantically.

PAGE 93

**the maid**: the acknowledgement of Speght is proper since the argument here follows hers quite closely.

**quintessence**: highly purified; most perfect embodiment.

**element**: the idea here is a commonplace of medieval natural philosophy (God put creatures in their elements – birds in air, etc.).

**temper**: is the distinctive quality and **inclination** the general characteristic of the surrounding element.

**band**: bond (interchangeable with 'band' in 17th C.).

**bible printed 1595**: the Geneva Bible (a reprint of Tomson's 1587 edition), much used by English Puritans; the note to Gen. ii.24 reads: 'So that marriage requireth a greater duty of us toward our wives, than otherwise we are bound to show to our parents' (an interesting reflection on patriarchy).

PAGE 94

**For this cause**: Gen. ii.24 (Geneva trans.); what is fascinating is that Sowernam does not always use the Geneva Bible – choice of text was usually dictated by doctrinal position (the Bishops' Bible was Anglican, Douai was Catholic).

**politician**: crafty dealer, sharp practiser.

**clog**: burden.

PAGE 96

**Euripides**: Greek dramatist (*c.* 485–406 BC); Medea killed Creon, his daughter and her own children; the quotation is closest to *Medea*, 573–75.

**Sara**: all the Bible spellings in this section are as in Bishops' and Douai Bibles, with the exception of **Abdela**, only spelt thus in Douai.

**Michal**: Sowernam's reference here is unusual, in that in the Authorised Version and Geneva Bibles this is called I Samuel. In the Catholic Douai Bible, the text makes a point over the naming of this book: 'The First Book of Samuel, which we call the First of Kings'. What is interesting is to find here an author who might be

PAGE 96 CONTINUED

openly using a Catholic Bible. Again Douai, unlike Authorised and Geneva, has Elias for Elijah and Eliseus for Elisha – although so does the Anglican establishment's Bible, the so-called Bishops' Bible. Choice of Bible is significant for our guesses at an author's doctrinal position.

**Judith**: this story is in the Apocrypha; the Jewish city of Bethunia was besieged by Nebuchadnezzar's general Holofernes; Judith saved her people by getting Holofernes drunk and then beheading him – a story properly popular with women artists of the Renaissance.

PAGE 97

**Susanna**: another Apocrypha story; two elders lusted after her and blackmailed her by threatening that if she did not allow them to have sex with her they would charge her publicly with adultery. She refused, and went to court; she won her case on a second trial.

**woman of Canaan**: from Matt. xv.22.

PAGE 98

**resurrection ... a woman**: Mary Magdalene.

**second and third chapters**: these are concerned with the 'law of nature'.

**Eva**: Douai has 'Eve', Bishops' has 'Heva', Geneva has 'Hevah' (Gen. iii.20).

PAGE 99

**Chapter IV**: the original has two Chapters IV – evidence of writing or printing in parts?

**De Legibus**: *Laws* – the last and longest of Plato's dialogues, concerned with the best constitution for a city; in many places he asserts the equality of men and women, and advocates equal physical and intellectual training (Book vi).

**absolute**: perfect.

**born ... nature**: Spenser adds divine selection when he justifies the presence on the throne of a woman – Elizabeth I. The argument for women here is largely drawn from Plato's *Republic* v.

**Bellona**: early Roman war goddess.

**manchet**: the best wheat bread.

**Ceres**: classical corn goddess.

**nine muses**: the deities of poetry, literature, music, dance and other intellectual and artistic activities.

**Mnemosum**: Mnemosyne, generally associated with memory.

**Carmentis**: or Carmenta, a mythical prophetess who first taught writing.

**Diana**: a strange goddess combining hunting and chastity with fertility.

**graces**: personifications of social grace and beauty.

**Palestra**: the Latin name given to a gymnasium or place for wrestling, etc.

**world**: Asia, Africa, Europa – represented as female figures (see, eg., Ripa's *Iconologia* (1611)).

**Bacchus**: divinity not just associated with drink but also with ecstatic and orgiastic religion.

**Priapus**: a fertility god whose symbol was the phallus, later made respectable as a god of gardens (bushes in general, not just gooseberry bushes).

**garden goddesses**: presumably refers to a developing taste for garden statuary.

PAGE 100

**god of lust**: Cupid was the son of Venus.

**jointure**: the woman's share of the property which will provide for her as a widow, as opposed to the overall control – the 'royalty'.

**deer**: pun on 'dear'.

**Nemesis or Rhamnusia**: the best known shrine to Nemesis was at Rhamnus in

PAGE 100 CONTINUED
  Attica; she represented (divine) retribution.
**Proserpina**: the daughter of Demeter/Ceres, carried off by Pluto, King of the underworld; a compromise settlement involved her spending half the year above and half below the earth (summer and winter).
**Boadicea**: or Bonduca, or more correctly Boudicca (d.62); Queen of the Iceni (East Anglians) who led them in revolt against Roman rule. Behind this, as behind other references, lies some 17th C. political rhetoric: Britons versus Romans, Jews versus Babylon or Egypt were all ways of talking about a righteous minority in the hands of a corrupt government.
**Helen**: St Helena (255–330), famous for supposedly discovering the cross on which Christ was crucified while visiting the Holy Land. (It should also be recorded that she was abandoned by her husband when it became politically expedient to do so.) Medieval legend claimed she was a native of England.
**Emma**: daughter of Richard II of Normandy, married Aethelred in 1002, mother of Edward the Confessor.
**Elfgive**: Aelfgifu, wife of Eadwig (fl. 956); sometimes confused with her mother, Aethelgifu.
**Edith**: Eadgyth (962?–984); her mother was a nun who refused to marry King Eadgar, her father.
**Alexander**: (356–323 BC) famous for being unable to control his own inner passions, although (or because?) he was a world conqueror.
**Eleanor**: of Castile, went with husband on crusade in 1270 (he was wounded at Acre).
**chirurgeons**: surgeons.
**Philip**: (1314?–69) mother of John of Gaunt and the Black Prince, among others; went to the siege of Calais with her husband.
**Margaret**: of Anjou (1430–82), caught up in the factional battles of the Wars of the Roses; her husband went mad in 1453 and she briefly acted as regent.

PAGE 101
**Margaret, of Richmond**: the devout Margaret Beaufort (1443–1509), who left Lady Margaret foundations to Oxbridge; founded St John's College, Cambridge.
**Elizabeth**: (1465–1503), daughter of Edward IV; Henry married her after winning Bosworth.
**renowned Queen**: Mary Queen of Scots (1542–87). It is unusual to find tributes to her.
**pattern for ... men**: the opposition to James I's rule used the image of Elizabeth I as an example of what a monarch should be (although she in her turn had been criticised).
**Aristotle**: this is the general idea of *Ethics* (especially I.i–ii) and *Politics* (see the summary in Diogenes Laertius v.30).

PAGE 102
**divine philosopher**: St Aquinas, working with William of Moerbecke, prepared the most influential Latin translation and exposition of Aristotle; **heathen orator**: Cicero, *De Officiis* I.xxviii: 'If we follow nature as our guide, we shall never go astray.'
**spar-hawk**: sparrow hawk, used in hunting but mentioned here because the female is a larger bird than the male (the musket); the same applies with the goshawk and the smaller male tercel.
**honesty**: here means chastity of life, and the sentiment, especially applied to Sparta, is common in Plato (see *Republic* ix; see also *Laws* iv.721B).
**freemen**: after serving the apprenticeship, the apprentice becomes the freeman of a company.
**portion**: dowry.

PAGE 103
**boni pessima**: Sowernam explains this. Recorded in the 1630s as a proverb: the corruption of the best is worst.
**maintenance**: livelihood, subsistence.


PAGE 104
**Achilles' fist**: in Homer's *Iliad* ii.212 ff. it is Odysseus who silences Thersites: Achilles is the famous killer of Hector and lover of Patroclus.
**Stafford law**: club law (pun on staff); *OED* quotes Breton, 1599; 'Stafford law, martial law, killing or hanging'.
**Orpheus**: legendary poet and lyre-player from Thrace, torn apart by maenads – women possessed by religious and drunken frenzy.
**Experience**: Sowernam, Speght and Anger lay stress on the value of experience, of practical testing and proving. In its own small way this ties in with the major drive of enlightened Renaissance science which battled against modes of thinking that relied on tradition and scholarly hand-downs. For women specifically the practical daily experience was the only way of expressing some of the injustices which traditional ideas about women's place manage to conceal.
**challenge**: question, find fault with.
**sure card**: reliable way of achieving something.


PAGE 105
**Bedlammore**: name derived from Bedlam, the common version of St Mary of Bethlehem, the name of the hospital for lunatics.
**Onopoly**: Sowernam's note says 'pamphlet maker' (it is an allusion to monopoly and, through Greek, to donkeys).
**general issue**: *OED* gives 'an issue raised by simply traversing the allegations in the declaration, as in the pleas "not guilty", "not indebted"'.
**sus[pected]**: the original has 'suspelled' which is a misprint, occasioned by breaking the world su-spelled – the compositor probably treated 'spelled' as a complete word, forgetting what was left on the line above.


PAGE 106
**scurril**: scurrilous.
**his book**: Swetnam's work was reprinted many times.
**current**: currency or drift of opinion.
**seely**: simple, silly.
**objecteth**: adduces, presents as argument.
**Euphues**: (1578) very influential and stylish prose work by John Lyly, loosely woven around a love story with moral reflections.
**Palace of Pleasure**: (1566) a collection of short stories, mainly translated from Italian, by William Painter.
**Euripides, etc.**: remarks denigrating women can be found in most of these writers, although such remarks cannot always be said to reflect the author's opinion (e.g., Ismene in Sophocles' *Antigone*: 'we are women; it is not for us to fight against men').
**Menander** (342–291 BC), follower of Euripides, dramatist specialising in love plots.
**Simonides**: (556–468 BC), lyric poet.
**Sophocles**: (496–406 BC), dramatist.
**Juvenal**: (?65–?130), satiric poet – *Satire* vi is against women.
**Plautus**: (?254–184 BC), comic dramatist (his *Amphytrio*, for example, contains apparent abuse of women).


PAGE 107
**colour**: excuse.
**sithence**: since.

PAGE 107 CONTINUED
**cample**: quarrel, wrangle.

PAGE 108
**object**: attribute, put forward; accuse.
**Incidit ... Charibdim**: he falls into Scylla who wishes to avoid Charybdis; Scylla is the name of a female sea-monster with six heads opposite the whirlpool Charybdis; between them is a narrow and dangerous channel; this is like an adage of Erasmus, which derives from Homer.
**Wild asses, etc.**: all names for fools and idiots.
**A cause**: the ideas here are Aristotelian; the Latin phrase means an essential or necessary cause, a necessity; a 'remote cause' is one that has no close or immediate bearing.

PAGE 109
**Asotos**: profligate (a word used in Luke xv.13).
**curiously**: elaborately, conscious of detail.
**Adiaphora**: a theological term for things on which the church has given no decision or guideline.
**babies**: dolls.
**counter**: debtors' prison.

PAGE 110
**colours**: dress; the general idea here is one familiar from contemporary satirists, of extravagance consuming inheritance.
**Diogenes**: (400–325 BC) founder of the Cynic philosophers, living in great personal poverty in Athens.
**(time)**: Sowernam quotes in Greek, which she translates in the margin.
**Joseph**: Gen. xxxix.12: Joseph flees from the approaches of his master's wife.
**Sauromatians**: Sarmatians, from an area now in Poland (mentioned in Plato's *Laws* ii.63).
**English verse**: *The Moral Fables of Aesop the Phrygian* appeared in 1570 in a verse translation by Henryson (this tale is number 5).

PAGE 111
**usage**: that a woman is made what she is by usage is a move away from the theory that character is dependent on the balance of the four humours. It is a more radical, social approach.

PAGE 112
**conditions**: circumstances, mode of being or mental disposition, character.
**learn**: teach.
**Sertorius**: Quintus S., successful Roman commander, praetor of Spain in 83 BC.
**kind**: natural behaviour.

PAGE 113
**distemperature**: disorder of mind or body.
**humorous**: moody, capricious.
**stall**: here seems to mean target (it can mean decoy or pickpocket's stooge).
**which they ... if she**: 'they' and 'she' both referring to the women.
**want**: lack.

PAGE 114
**Cassian**: this is attributed by Cicero to Lucius Cassius; the Latin means 'to whose benefit?' 'who has profited?'.
**next term**: i.e., when she is next in London (the continuation is never supplied).

PAGE 115

**Chapter VIII**: this may not be by Sowernam; it is more or less a summary stuck on at the end to finish off the work (the printer perhaps not having the promised last part, or in a rush to get it published).

**scaled**: scabby, skin diseased.

**ruff**: this image from Swetnam is continually repeated.

**mettle**: temperament.


PAGE 116

**stakes**: what bears are tied to in order to be baited.

**wrack**: this has a sense of creating damage, wrecking, if not of revenge; it could also imply 'reck': think; and that men are wrecked.

**giglots**: wanton women.


PAGE 117

**A good Jack**: this proverb means that a good husband makes a good wife.

**piece**: derogatory slang for woman; Turberville's translation of Ovid's *Epistles* (1567) has 'Fair Helena, that passing piece'.

**Medea**: see earlier note; she fell in love with Jason and escaped with him.

**Cressid**: she supposedly betrayed Troilus by willingly having sex with Diomedes, but Shakespeare's play, for example, illustrates to some extent the effect on the isolated woman of the alien environment of the male enemy camp.

**free**: noble, magnanimous.

**next**: this repeats what was said earlier, but there was no next time; it may be that the printer was hoping for a lucrative controversy.

# THE
# WORMING
## of a mad Dogge:

### OR,

## A SOPPE FOR
## *CERBERUS THE*

## Jaylor of Hell.

   †

## NO CONFUTATION BUT A
### sharpe Redargution of the
### bayter of Women.

   †

## By CONSTANTIA MUNDA
*——dux foemina facti.*

   †

Virg: Æn: I.
*Sigenus humanum & mortalia temnitis arma,*
*At sperate Deos memores fandi atque nefandi.*

   †

---

LONDON
Printed for LAURENCE HAYES, and are to be
sold at his shop neere Fleet-bridge, over
against St. Brides Lane.
1617

['Constantia Munda' is not the most witty of pseudonyms: in English 'Moral Constancy' hardly passes for a name. Rachel Speght, however, assumes her to be a woman when, in her *Dream*, she describes how Sowernam's attacks on Swetnam had to be continued by Munda:

> And yet her enterprise had some defect,
> The monster surely was not hanged quite:
> For as the child of Prudence did conceive,
> His throat not stopped, he still had power to bite.
> She therefore gave to Cerberus a sop
> Which is of force his beastly breath to stop.
>
> But yet if he do swallow down that bit,
> She other-ways hath bound him to the peace:
> And like an artist takes away the cause
> That the effect, by consequence, may cease.
> This frantic dog, whose rage did women wrong,
> Hath Constance wormed to make him hold his
>     tongue.

By 1621 Swetnam was silent; in fact, he had never written a riposte. His second book, published in 1617, was an instruction manual on fencing. If, as might be, he really was a resident of Bristol, it could be that he was just unaware of what the London printers were up to.

Again, as with Sowernam, there is the suspicion of a printer's manoeuvre. Munda's printer was Purslowe, one of the 1615 printers of Swetnam, for Thomas Archer. Purslowe printed Munda for a different distributor. The pamphlet seems a rushed job: the syntax and structure are a mess, and there is no paragraphing. Nevertheless, the author's mind seems learned and astute, albeit sometimes plagiarising. (The mind seems almost too learned for a woman – Juvenal is an unlikely author in a woman's education.) Munda complains of Sowernam as Sowernam complained of Speght, that she had been beaten to the job of replying. But whereas Sowernam had new things to say, Munda seems to depend on the traditional method of pamphlet satire and patches together bits of other authors. She also uses Speght quite heavily, which presumably she had time to do since her work was not registered until 29 April 1617. All of this makes the piece look very much like an attempt to cash in on current controversy.

Nevertheless, there are some very interesting ideas in this text – and if it is a man who has written it (which I half suspect) he is thinking some quite original thoughts. The problem is that they are buried deep in a hyperclever jumble of literary bits and pieces without many proper full-stops. Hence there is a greater proportion of my punctuation than usual in this text. Beware of the early sentences, they are very long.]

To the Right Worshipful Lady her Most
Dear Mother, the Lady Prudentia Munda, the true
pattern of piety and virtue, C.M. wisheth
increase of Happiness.

As, first, your pains in bearing me was such
A benefit beyond requital that 'twere much
To think what pangs of sorrow you sustained
In child-birth (when mine infancy obtained
The vital drawing-in of air); so your love,
Mingled with care, hath shown itself above
The ordinary course of nature. Seeing you still
Are in perpetual labour with me, even until
The second birth of education perfect me:
You travail still, though churched oft you be.                    †
    In recompense whereof what can I give,
But what I take? – even that I live,
Next to the heavens, 'tis yours. Thus I pay
My debt by taking up at interest, and lay                         †
To pawn that which I borrow of you: so
The more I give, I take; I pay, I owe.
Yet lest you think I forfeit shall my bond,                        †
I here present you with my writing hand:
Some trifling minutes I vainly did bestow
In penning of these lines that all might know
The scandals of our adversary; and
I had gone forward had not *Hester hanged
Haman* before (yet what here I wrote
Might serve to stop the cur's wide throat
Until the halter came). Since which I ceased                       †
To prosecute what I intended, lest
I should be censured that I undertook
A work that's done already. So his book
Hath 'scaped my fingers – but in like case
As a malefactor changeth place
From Newgate unto Tyburn, whose good hope                          †
Is but to change his shackles for a rope.
    Although this be a toy scarce worth your view,
Yet deign to read it and accept in lieu
Of greater duty: for your gracious look
Is a sufficient patron to my book.
    This is the worst disgrace that can be had:
A Lady's daughter 'wormed a dog that's mad'.
                            Your loving daughter
                            CONSTANTIA MUNDA

## To Joseph Swetnam

What? is thy shameless muse so fledged in sin,
† So cockered up in mischief? or hast been
Trained up by Furies in the school of vice? –
† Where the licentious devils hoist the price
Of uncaught mischief, and make a set reward
For hell-hound slanderers that naught regard
Their reputation or the wholesome laws
Of Virtue's commonwealth; but seek applause
By railing and reviling to deprave
The mirror of creation, to out-brave
Even heaven itself with folly. Could the strain
Of that your barren, idle, dunghill brain,
† As from a chemic limbeck, so distil
Your poisoned drops of hemlock: and so fill
† The itching ears of silly swains and rude
Truth-not-discerning rustic multitude
With sottish lies, with bald and ribald lines
Patched out of English writers, that combines
Their highest reach of emulation but to please
The giddy-headed vulgar (whose disease,
Like to a swelling dropsy, thirsts to drink
† And swill the puddles of this nasty sink).
Whence through the channels of your muddy wit
Your hotch-potched work is drawn, and the slimy
pit
Of your invective pamphlet filled to the brim
With all defiled streams; yet many swim
And bathe themselves (oh madness!) in that flood
Of mischief with delight, and deem that good
Which spoils their reason, being not understood.
When people view not well your devilish book,
Like nibbling fish they swallow bait and hook
† To their destruction: when they not descry
Your base and most unreverent blasphemy.
† How in the ruff of fury you disgrace
(As much as in you lies) and do deface
Nature's best ornament – and thinkst th'ast done
An act deserving commendation;
Whereas thy merits being brought in sight,
Exclaim thus on thee: 'Gallows claim thy right'.
    Woman the crown, perfection and the means
Of all men's being, and their well-being: whence
Is the propagation of all human-kind;
Wherein the body's frame, the intellect and mind
With all their operations do first find

Their essence and beginning; where doth lie
The mortal means of our eternity;
Whose virtues, worthiness, resplendent rays
Of perfect beauty have always had the praise
And admiration of such glorious wits,
Which fame, the world's great herald, fits –                    †
Crowning with laurel wreaths and myrtle boughs,
The tribute and reward of learned brows:
And that this goodly piece of nature be
Thus shamefully detested and thus wronged by
                                                    thee!
How could your vile untutored muse enfold
And wrap itself in envious, cruel, bold,
Nay impudent, detraction: and then throw
And hurl without regard your venomed darts
Of scandalous reviling at the hearts
Of all our female sex promiscuously,                            †
Of commons, gentry and nobility?
Without exceptions hath your spongey pate
(Void in itself of all things but of hate)
Sucked up the dregs of folly and the lees
Of mercenary pasquils, which do squeeze                         †
The glanders of abuses in the face                              †
Of them that are the cause that human race
Keeps his continuance. Could you be so mad
As to deprave, nay to call that bad,
Which God calls good? Can your filthy claws
Scratch out the image that the Almighty draws
In us his pictures? No! things simply good
Keep still their essence, though they be withstood
By all the 'complices of hell. You cannot daunt,
Nor yet diminish (howe'er you basely vaunt
With bitter terms) the glory of our sex;
Nor, as you michingly surmise, you vex                          †
Us with your dogged railing. Why, we know
Virtue opposed is stronger: and the foe
That's quelled and foiled addeth but more
Triumph to the conquest than there was before.
  Wherefore be advised: cease to rail
  On them that with advantage can you quail.

# THE
# WORMING
## of a mad Dogge

The itching desire of oppressing the press with many sottish and illiterate libels stuffed with all manner of ribaldry and sordid inventions – when every foul-mouthed malcontent may disgorge his
† Licambean poison in the face of all the world – hath broken out into such a dismal contagion in these our days, that every scandalous
† tongue and opprobrious wit, like the Italian mountebanks, will
† advance their peddling wares of detracting virulence in the public
† piazza of every stationer's shop. And printing, that was invented to be the storehouse of famous wits, the treasure of divine literature,
† the pandect and maintainer of all sciences, is become the receptacle of every dissolute pamphlet – the nursery and hospital of every
† spurious and penurious brat which proceeds from base, phrenetical,
† brain-sick babblers. When *scribimus indocti* must be the motto of every one that fools himself in print – 'tis ridiculous! But when
† *scribimus insani* should be the signature of every page – 'tis lamentable our time's so stupidly possessed and benumbed with
† folly that we shall verify the proverb 'L'usanza commune non è
† peccato' sin's custom house hath, *non sine privilegio*, writ upon his doors: as though community in offence could make an immunity.
† No! use of sin is the soul's extortion, a biting fenory that eats out
† the principal. Yet woeful experience makes it too true, *consuetudo peccandi tollit sensum peccati*: as may be seen by the works of divers
† men that make their pens their pencils to limn out vice, that it may seem delicious and amiable; so to detract from virtue and honesty as though their essence were only in outward appearance of goodness – as if mortality were only circumscribed within the conditions of
† our sex. *Coelum ipsum petimus stultitia*: foolish man will reprehend his creator in the admirable work of his generation and conserva-
† tion. Woman, the second edition of the epitome of the whole world, the second tome of that goodly volume compiled by the great God of heaven and earth, is most shamefully blurred and
† derogatively razed by scribbling pens of savage and uncaught monsters. To what an irregular strain is the daring impudence of
† blind-fold bayards aspired unto? – that they will presume to call in question even the most absolute work composed by the world's great architect. A strange blasphemy: to find fault with that which the Privy Council of the high and mighty Parliament of the
† inscrutable Tri-unity in heaven determined to be very good. To call that imperfect, froward, crooked and perverse, to make an arraign-
† ment and bear-baiting of that which the Pantocrator would, in his omniscient wisdom, have to be the consummation of his blessed week's work – the end, crown and perfection of the never-

sufficiently glorified creation: what is it but an exorbitant frenzy and woeful taxation of the supreme deity!

Yet woman, the greatest part of the lesser world, is generally † become the subject of every pedantical goose-quill. Every fantastic poetaster, which thinks he hath licked the vomit of his Coryphaeus † and can but patch a hobbling verse together, will strive to represent unseemly figments imputed to our sex (as a pleasing theme to the vulgar) on the public theatre: teaching the worser sort, that are † more prone to luxury, a compendious way to learn to be sinful. † These foul-mouthed railers *qui non vident ut corrigant, sed quaerunt quid reprehendant* (that reprove not that they might reform, but pry into actions that they might carp and cavil): so that this infamous profession they far exceed the vilest kind of Pharisaical ostentation, and so surmounting, beyond all comparison, railing † Anaxarchus (who for his detracting and biting tongue was pestled to † death in a brazen mortar). Who, as a learned Tuscan speaketh: 'gli † miseri vanno a tentone altrevolte a carpone per facer mercantantia dell'altrui da lor inventata è seminata vergogna, impudicamente cercano l'altrui deshonor erger la meretricia fronte e malzar la impudiche corna' (these wretched miscreants go groping, and sometimes on all four, to traffic with other folk's credits by their own divulged and dispersed ignominy: that impudently seek by others' dishonour to set a shameless face on the matter, and thus to put out their immodest horns) to butt at and gore the name and reputation of the innocent. Being so besotted with a base and miserable condition, and blind in themselves, they blush not in their tongues to carry the gall of Rabilius, and in their chaps the poison of † Callimachus, in their mouths the flame of mount Etna, in their eyes † Jupiter's lightning which he darted at the centaurs, in their thoughts Bellona's arrows, in their serpentine words the bitterness of Sulmo † against Orbecca: blending and commixing all their discourse with epatic aloes and unsavoury simples, deriving all their ingredients of † their venomed recipes from the apothecary's shop of the devil.

Notwithstanding, as the same learned man metaphorically speaks: 'Cotesti usei scangerati, città senza muro, navi senza governo, vasi senza coperto, cavalli indomiti senza freno non considerano' (These wide open doors, these unwalled towns, these rudderless ships, these uncovered vessels, these unbridled horses do not consider) that the tongue, being a very little member, should never go out of that same ivory gate in which (not without a great † mystery) divine wisdom and nature together hath enclosed it: signifying that a man should give himself either to virtuous speech or prudent silence, and not let tongue and pen run up and down, like a weaponed mad-man, to strike and wound any without partiality – everyone without exception – to make such an universal massacre (for so I may term it, seeing words make worse wounds † than swords). Yet lest villainy domineer and triumph in fury, we

will manacle your dissolute fist that you deal not your blows so unadvisedly. Though feminine modesty hath confined our rarest and ripest wits to silence, we acknowledge it our greatest ornament; but when necessity compels us, 'tis as great a fault and folly
† *loquenda tacere, ut contra gravis est culpa tacenda loqui.* Being too much provoked by arraignments, baitings and rancorous impeach-
† ments of the reputation of our whole sex, *stulta est clementia ... periturae parcere cartae*: opportunity of speaking slipped by silence
† is as bad as importunity upheld by babbling – (*loqui quae decet est melius quam tacere*). Know therefore that we will cancel your
† accusations, traverse your bills, and come upon you for a false indictment – and think not 'tis our waspishness that shall sting you.
† No, sir; until we see your malapert sauciness reformed, which will
† not be till you do 'make a long letter to us', we will continue Juno's

†     Non sic abibunt odia vivaces aget violentus iras animus
      Saevusque dolor aeterna bella pace sublata geret.

† Notwithstanding, for all your injuries, as Gelo Siracusanus answered Syagrus the Spartan: 'You shall not induce me, though stirred with anger, to demean myself unreverently in the retribution of your injuries'.

Your idle muse, and 'musing being idle' (as your learned epistle beginneth), shall be no plea to make your viperous scandals seem
† pleasing, *ipsa excusatio culpa est.* (Where, by the way, I note your untoward nature contrary to all men: for whereas in all others of your sex – by your confession – idleness engendereth love, in you hate.) You say, in the dedication of your book to your mistresses the common sort of women, that you had little ease to pass the time withal; but now, seeing you have basely wronged our wearied and worried patience with your insolent invective madness, you shall make a simple conversion of your proposition – and take your
† pastime in *little ease*. Why? – if you delight to sow thorns, is it not fit you should go on them barefoot and bare-legged? Your idle
† muse shall be franked up, for while it is at liberty most impiously it
† throws dirt in the face of half human-kind. Coriolanus when he saw his mother and his wife weeping (Livy ii), natural love compelled
† him to leave sacking the city for their sakes (*ab hoc exemplum cape*): but your barbarous hand will not cease to ruin the senses and
† beleaguer the forces of Gynaecia, not sparing the mother that brought forth such an untoward whelp into the world as thyself, playing at blindman-buff with all, scattering thy dissolute language at whomsoever comes next.
† You never heard of a boy, an unlucky gallows, that threw stones in the market-place he knew not whither? The wisely cynic philosopher bade him take heed lest he hit his father. *Nomine*
† *mutato narretur fabula de te*: you might easily, if you had had the

grace, perceive what use to make of it. But you go forward, pretending you were in great 'choler' against some women and in †
the 'ruff' of your fury. Grant one absurdity, a thousand follow. Alas, good sir, we may easily gather you were mightily transported with passion: anger and madness differ but in time. 'Twere a pleasant sight to see you in your 'great' standing 'choler' and 'furious ruff' together. Your choler, no doubt, was too great for a Spanish peccadillo, and your shag 'ruff' seemed so greasily to set †
forth your ill-looking visage that none of your she-adversaries durst attempt to confront your folly.

But now let us talk with you in your cold blood. Now the lees of your fury are settled to the bottom and your turbulent mind is defecated and clearer, let's have a parle with you. What if you had †
cause to be offended with some (as I cannot excuse all), must you needs shoot your paper-pellets out of your potgun-pate at all †
women? Remember, sweet sir, the counsel of Nestor to Achilles: †
[keep your great soul within your breast: temperance is better].

It had been the part of humanity to have smothered your anger, |†
hoping amends and reconcilement, and not presently to wreak your †
spleen. Architas in Tully would have taught you another lesson: †
'Quo te inquit modo accepissem nisi iratus essem?' But you (like a hare-brained scold) set your claws in the face of the whole world. But this argues your levity joined with degenerate cowardice. For had you but considered with mature deliberation that (as Virgil speaks)

– nullum memorabile nomen
Foeminea in poena est, nec habet victoria laudem          †
(*Aeneid* ii.[583–84])

('tis a poor achievement to overcome a woman), you would never have been so grievously troubled with the over-flowing of the gall, neither would the relish of your furred palate have been so bitter as †
what delicates soever you tasted should become unpleasing.

I read of a mad fellow which had lost his goods by sea, that whatsoever ships had come into the port at Athens he would take a catalogue of them; and very busy would he be in making an inventory of the goods they brought in and received, thinking all to be his. So you, having peradventure had some cursed wife that hath given you as good as you brought, whatsoever faults you espy in others you take that to heart. You run a-madding up and down to make a scroll of female frailties and an inventory of meretricial †
behaviours, ascribing them to those that are joined in the sacred bands of matrimony. Because you have been gulled with brass money, will you think no coin current? Because you have suffered †
shipwreck, will you dissuade any from venturing to traffic beyond seas?

Besides, you show yourself unjust in not observing a symmetry
† and proportion of revenge and the offence: for a pelting injury
should not provoke an opprobrious calumny. A private abuse of
† your own familiar doxies should not break out into open slanders of
the religious matron together with the prostitute strumpet; of the
nobly descended ladies as the obscure base vermin that have bitten
you; of the chaste and modest virgins as well as the dissolute and
impudent harlot. Because women are women, you will do that in an
hour which you will repent you of all your life-time after. Nay
†  rather, if the ruff of your fury would have let you look over it, you
would have diverted the floodgates of your poisoned streams that
way where you perceived the common shore to run, and not have
polluted and stained the clear and crystalline waters. Because
women are not women rather might be a fit subject of an ingenious
† satirist – *Cum alterius sexus imitata figuram est*: the reason is,

> Quem praestare potest mulier galeata pudorem,
† Quae fugit a sexu? (Juvenal, *Satire* vi.[252–53])

But when women are women, when we sail by the true compass of
honest and religious conversation, why should you be so doggedly
incensed to bark in general? Why should you employ your invention to lay open new fashions of lewdness which the worst of
women scarce ever were acquainted with? Imitating the vice of that
† pagan poet, whose indignation made verses; whose filthy reprehen-
sion opened the doors of unbridled luxury, and gave a precedent of
all admired wickedness and brutish sensuality to succeeding ages;
† whom great Scaliger indeed censureth not worthy to be read of a
pious and ingenuous man (*Poet.*, iii.9): that satyr brands all his
countrywomen with the same mark:

> Iamque eadem summis pariter minimisque libido est,
> Nec melior pedibus silicem quae conterit atrum,
† Quam quae longorum vehitur cervice Syrorum.

But he lived in a nation earthly, devilish, sensual: given over to a
reprobate sense, that wrought all filthiness with greediness. But
you, sir, were whelped in a better age, at least in a better climate,
where the gospel is preached and 'the voice of the turtle is heard in
† our land': where you might see (if you could perfectly distinguish) –
if you were not in the gall of bitterness – matchless beauties and
glorious virtues shining together. You might behold (if outrageous
rage had not drawn a film over your eyesight) the goodly habili-
ments of the mind combined with the perfection of outward
comeliness and ornaments of the body. Is there not as many
monuments erected to the famous eternising of charitable deeds of
women renowned in their generations as trophies to the most

courageous potentates? In the commemorations of founders and benefactors, how many women have emulated your sex in bountiful exhibitions to religious uses and furtherance of piety? I might produce infinite examples, if need were. But bray a fool in a mortar † (said the wise man) yet he will not leave his foolery: neither if whole volumes were compiled against your manifest calumnies would you ever be brought to a palinody and recantation. †

We have your confession under your own hand, where you say you 'might have employed yourself to better use than in such an idle business'. True: (A fool speaks sometimes to the purpose). If you † must needs be digiting your pen, the time had been far better spent † if you had related to the world some stories of your travels with a gentleman learneder and wiser than yourself. So you might have beguiled the time and exposed your ridiculous wit to laughter. You might have told how hardly such an unconstant 'bella curtizana de Venetiis' entertained you, how your teeth watered – and after, your † affections were poisoned with their heinous evils; how in the beginning of your thirty years' travel and odd, your constitution † inclined and you were addicted to pry into the various actions of † loose, strange, lewd, idle, froward and inconstant women; how you happened (in some stews or brothel-houses) to be acquainted with † their cheats and evasions; how you came to be so expert in their subtle qualities; how politicly you caught the daughter in the oven, † yet never was there yourself; how in your voyages your stomach was cloyed with these surfeits: and therefore, being a traveller, you had reason to censure hardly of women. Have you travelled half as long again as that famous pilgrim 'which knew the fashions of many † men and saw their cities'? Have you outstripped him in time and come so short of him in knowledge? Is this all the manners you have learned abroad these thirty and odd years? Is this the benefit of your observations? Is this all the profit your country shall reap by your foreign endeavours? – to bring home a company of idle humours of light huswives which you have noted and divulge them in print, to † your own disgrace and perpetual obloquy? Have you travelled three † times as long as an elephant, and is this the first fruit, nay all the † fruit, of your idle, addle coxcomb? Certainly you mis-spent your † time in your travels: for it had been more profitable for you if you had brought dogs from Iceland; – better for your country if you had † kept a dog there still.

But 'tis easy to give a reason of your exasperate virulence from your being a traveller. For it is very likely, when you first went abroad to see fashions, 'twas your fortune to light amongst ill company; who, trying what mettle you were made of, quickly matriculated you in the school of vice, where you proved a most apt non-proficient; and, being gulled of your patrimony, your purse † was turned into a pass, and that by women. Like a dog that bites the † stone which had almost beat out his brains, you come home swaggering:

†        Prodiga non sentit pereuntem foemina censum,
       At velut exhausta redivivus pullulet arca
       Nummus, et e pleno semper tollatur acervo,
       Non unquam reputant quantum sibi gaudia constant.

Which, if you cannot understand, is to this sense:

       A lavish woman thinks there is no stint
       Unto her purse: as though thou hadst a mint,
       She casts no count what money she'll bestow,
       As if her coin, as fast as 't ebbed, did flow.

    Such it may be (I speak but upon suspicion) were the conditions
† of those minions your minority had experience of in your voyages.
Wherefore none – either good or bad, fair or foul, of what estate
soever, of what parentage or royal descent and lineage soever, how
† well soever nurtured and qualified – shall 'scape the convicious
† violence of your preposterous procacity. Why did you not snarl at
† them directly that wronged you? Why did not you collimate your
infectious javelins at the right mark? If a thief take your purse from
you, will you malign and swagger with everyone you meet? If you
be beaten in an ale-house, will you set the whole town afire? If some
courtesans that you have met with in your travels (or rather, that
have met with you) have ill entreated you, must honest and
religious people be the scope of your malicious speeches and
reproachful terms?
    Yet it may be you have a further drift, to make the world believe
you have an extraordinary gift of continency: soothing yourself
with this supposition, that this open reviling is some token and
evidence you never were affected with delicate and effeminate
† sensuality; thinking this pamphlet should assoil thee from all
manner of levy and taxation of a lascivious life. As if, because you
cynically rail at all, both good and bad, you had been hatched up
† without concupiscence; as if nature had bestowed on you all (*ira*)
† and no (*concupiscentia*). 'Twas spoken of Euripides that he hated
women in *choro* but not in *thoro*, in *calamo* but not in *thalamo*: and
why cannot you be liable to the same objection? I would make this
excuse for you; but that the crabbedness of your style, the
unsavoury periods of your broken-winded sentences, persuade
† your body to be of the same temper as your mind. Your ill-
favoured countenance, your wayward conditions, your peevish and
pettish nature is such that none of our sex, with whom you have
obtained some partial conference, could ever brook your dogged
† frompard frowardness. Upon which malcontented desperation you
hanged out your flag of defiance against the whole world, as a
prodigious monstrous rebel against nature.
    Besides, if your currish disposition had dealt with men, you were

afraid that *lex talionis* would meet with you. Wherefore you †
surmised that, inveighing against poor illiterate women, we might †
fret and bite the lip at you; we might repine to see ourselves baited †
and tossed in a blanket, but never durst in open view of the vulgar †
either disclose your blasphemous and derogative slanders or maintain the untainted purity of our glorious sex. Nay, you'll put gags in
our mouths and conjure us all to silence; you will first abuse us,
then bind us to the peace. We must be tongue-tied, lest in starting
up to find fault we prove ourselves guilty of those horrible
accusations. The sincerity of our lives, and quietness of conscience,
is a wall of brass to beat back the bullets of your vituperious †
scandals in your own face. 'Tis the resolved aphorism of a religious
soul to answer: *ego sic vivam ut nemo tibi fidem adhibeat*; by our †
well-doings to put in silence the reports of foolish men. As the poet †
speaks:

> Vivendum recte tum propter plurima, tum de his
> Praecipue causis ut linguas mancipiorum contemnas
> (Live well for many causes, chiefly this,
> To scorn the tongue of slaves that speak amiss.)

Indeed I write not in hope of reclaiming thee from thy profligate
absurdities, for I see what a 'pitch' of disgrace and shame thy †
self-pining envy hath carried thee to, for thy greater vexation and †
more perplexed ruin. You see your black grinning mouth hath been †
muzzled by a modest and powerful hand, who hath judiciously
bewrayed and wisely laid open your singular ignorance couched
under incredible impudence; who hath most gravely (to speak in
your own language) 'unfolded every pleat, and showed every
wrinkle' of a profane and brutish disposition: so that 'tis a doubt
whether she hath showed more modesty or gravity, more learning
or prudence, in the religious confutation of your undecent railings.
But as she hath been the first champion of our sex that would
encounter with the barbarous bloodhound – and wisely dammed up
your mouth and sealed up your jaws, lest your venomed teeth like
mad dogs should damage the credit of many, nay all, innocent
damosels; so no doubt, if your scurrilous and depraving tongue
break prison and falls to licking up your vomited poison (to the end †
you may squirt out the same with more pernicious hurt), assure
yourself there shall not be wanting store of hellebore to scour the †
sink of your tumultuous gorge. At least we will cram you with †
antidotes and catapotions that, if you swell not till you burst, yet †
your digested poison shall not be contagious. I hear you foam at
mouth and growl against the author with another head like the †
triple dog of hell; wherefore I have provided this sop for Cerberus, †
indifferent well steeped in vinegar (I know not how your palate will
be pleased with it), to make you secure hereafter. I'll take the pains

† to worm the tongue of your madness and dash your rankling teeth
† down your throat. 'Tis not holding up a wisp nor threatening a
† cucking-stool shall charm us out of the compass of your chain: our
† pens shall throttle you, or, like Archilochus, with our tart iambics
† make you Lopez his godson. We will thrust thee like Phalaris into
thine own brazen bull, and bait thee at thy own stake, and beat thee
at thine own weapon.

†          *Quippe minuti*
          *Semper et infirmi est animi exiguique voluptas*
          *Ultio: continuo sic collige quod vindicta*
          *Nemo magis gaudet quam foemina:*

† 'tis your poet's own assertion that ultion, being the delight of a
weak and feeble mind, belongs to us.

†     Thou that in thyself feelest the lash of folly; thou that confessest
thyself to be in a fault, nay, that thou hast offended beyond
satisfaction (for 'tis hard to give a recompense for a slander); thou
that acknowledgest thyself to be mad, in a rough fury, your wits
† gone a-woolgathering that you had forgot yourself – (as I think –
† Nero-like, in ripping up the bowels of thine own mother). For I
have learnt so much logic to know *quicquid dicitur de specie, dicitur
de unoquoque individuo eiusdem speciei* (whatsoever is spoken or
predicated of the kind is spoken of everyone in the same kind): first
† therefore to bring you to an impious [absurdity] or inconvenience.
Is it not a comely thing to hear a son speak thus of his mother: 'My
† mother in her fury was worse than a lion being bitten with hunger,
·han a bear being robbed of her young ones, the viper being trod
on. No spur would make my mother go, nor no bridle would hold
her back. Tell her of her fault, she will not believe she is in any fault;
give her good counsel, but she will not take it. If my father did but
look after another woman, then she would be jealous. The more he
loved her, the more she would disdain him; if he threatened her, she
would be angry; when he flattered her, then she would be proud; if
he forbore her, it made her bold; if he chastened her, she would
turn to a serpent. At a word, my mother would never forget an
injury nor give thanks for a good turn. What an ass then was my
father to exchange gold for dross, pleasure for pain. 'Tis a wonderful thing to see the mad feats of my mother, for she would pick thy
pocket, empty thy purse, laugh in thy face and cut thy throat; she is
ungrateful, perjured, full of fraud, flouting and deceit, unconstant,
waspish, toyish, light, sullen, proud, discourteous and cruel. The
breast of my mother was the harbourer of an envious heart, her
heart the storehouse of poisoned hatred, her head devised villainy
and her hands were ready to put in practice what her heart desired.
Then who can but say but my mother a woman sprung from the

devil?' (p. 15) – you from your mother, and so Swetnam is the devil's grand-child.

Do you not blush to see what a halter you have purchased for your own neck? You thought, in your ruff of fury, like Augustus Caesar to make an edict that all the world should be taxed, when † yourself is tributary to the greatest infirmities. You blowed the fire † of sedition with the bellows of your anger, and the coals are burning in your own bosom: 'Periculoso plenum opus aleae, tractas et † incedis per ignes suppositos cineri doloso' (Horace, *Odes* II [i.6– 8]). Is there no reverence to be given to your mother because you are weaned from her teat and never more shall be fed with her pap? You are like the rogue in the fable, which was going to the gallows † for burglary, that bit off his mother's nose because she chastised him not in his infancy for his petty larcenies. Is this the requital of all her cost, charge, care and unspeakable pains she suffered in the producing of such a monster into the light? If she had crammed gravel down thy throat when she gave thee suck, or exposed thee to the mercy of the wild beasts in the wilderness when she fed thee with the pap, thou couldst not have shown thyself more ungrateful † than thou hast in belching out thy nefarious contempt of thy mother's sex.

Wherefore methinks it is a pleasing revenge that thy soul arraigns thee at the bar of conscience, and thy distracted mind cannot choose but haunt thee like a bumbaily to serve a *sub poena* on thee; the † style and penning of your pamphlet hath brought you within the compass of a *praemunire*, and every sentence, being stolen out of † other books, accuseth you of robbery. So that thou carriest in thyself a walking Newgate up and down with thee; thy own perplexed suspicions like Prometheus' vulture is always gnawing on † thy liver. Besides, these books which are of late come out (the latter † whereof hath prevented me in the designs I purposed in running over your wicked handiwork) are like so many red-hot irons to stigmatise thy name with the brand of a hideous blasphemer and incarnate devil. Although thou art not apprehended and attached † for thy villainy – I might say felony – before a corporal judge, yet thine own conscience, if it be not seared up, tortures thee and racks † thy tempestuous mind with a dissolution and whirring to and fro of thy scandalous name, which without blemish my pen can scarce deign to write. You find it true which the poet speaks:

Exemplo quodcunque malo committitur, ipsi
Displicet authori, prima est haec ultio quod se
Judice nemo nocens absolvitur, improba quamvis
Gratia fallacis praetoris vicerit urnam.
             (Juvenal, *Satire* xiii[.1–4])
(What sin is wrought by ill example, soon

The displeased author wisheth it undone.
† And 'tis revenge when, if the nocent wight
Umpires his cause himself, in his own sight
He finds no absolution: though the eyes
Of judgement wink, his soul still guilty cries.)

'Tis often observed that the affections of auditors (and readers too) are more offended with the foul-mouthed reproof of the brawling accuser than with the fault of the delinquent. If you had kept yourself within your pretended limits and not meddled with
† the blameless and innocent, yet your prejudicate railing would rather argue an unreverent and lascivious inclination of a depraved nature than any love or zeal to virtue and honesty. You ought to have considered that, in the vituperation of the misdemeanours and
† disorders in others' lives, this cautelous proviso should direct you: that in seeking to reform others, you deform not yourself – especially by moving a suspicion that your mind is troubled and
† festered with the imposthume of inbred malice and corrupt hatred.
† For 'tis always the badge and cognizance of a degenerous and illiberal disposition to be ambitious of that base and ignoble applause, proceeding from the giddy-headed plebeians, that is
† acquired by the miserable oppressing and pilling of virtue. But
† every wrongful contumely and reproach hath such a sharp sting in it that, if it fasten once on the mind of a good and ingenuous nature, 'tis never drawn forth without anxiety and perpetual recordation of dolour; which, if you had known, your hornet brains would not have buzzed abroad with a resolution to sting some, though you lost your sting and died for it. You would not, like the cuttle-fish, [have] spewed out your inky gall with hope to turn the purest
† waters to your own sable hue: *ut non odio inimicitiarum ad vituperandum sed studio calumniandi ad inimicitias descenderes* (that you would arm yourself not with the hate of enmity to dispraise vice, but with the study of calumny to make enmity with virtue).

Yet 'tis remarkable that ignorance and impudence were partners in your work. For as you have, of all things under the sun, selected
† the baiting, or (as you make a silly solecism) the bear-baiting, of
† women to be the tenter-hooks whereon to stretch your shallow
† inventions on the trivial subject of every shackrag that can but set pen to paper; so, in the handling of your base discourse, you lay
† open your imperfections *arripiendo maledicta ex trivio*: by heaping together the scraps, fragments and reversions of divers English
† phrases, by scraping together the glanders and offals of abusive terms, and the refuse of idle-headed authors, and making a mingle-
† mangle gallimaufry of them. Lord! how you have cudgelled your brains in gleaning multitudes of similes, as 'twere, in the field of many writers, and threshed them together in the flour of your own

devisor – and all to make a poor confused mescelline: whereas thine †
own barren soiled soil is not able to yield the least congruity of †
speech. 'Tis worthy laughter what pains you have taken in turning
over Parismus, what use you make of the *Knight of the Sun*, what †
collections out of *Euphues*, *Amadis a Gaul*, and the rest of Don †
Quixote's library, sometimes exact tracing of Aesopical fables and †
Valerius Maximus, with the like school-boys' books. So that if these †
pamphleteers would severally pluck a crow with you, *furtivis* †
*nudata coloribus moveat cornicula risum*: let every bird take his own
feather and you would be as naked as Aesop's jay. Indeed, you have †
shown as much foolery as robbery in feathering your nest, which is
a cage of unclean birds and a storehouse for the off-scourings of
other writers. Your indiscretion is as great in the laying together
and compiling of your stolen ware as your blockishness in stealing,
for your sentences hang together like sand without lime. You bring
a great heap of stony rubbish comparisons one upon the neck of
another, but they concur no more to sense than a company of
stones to a building without mortar: and 'tis a familiar Italian
proverb, *duro e duro non fa muro* (hard and hard makes no wall). †
So your hard dull pate hath collected nothing that can stand
together with common sense, or be pleasing to any refined disposition – rough and unhewn morsels digged out of others' quarries,
potsherds picked out of sundry dunghills. Your mouth indeed is †
full of stones (*lapides loqueris*), but not so wisely nor so warily †
crammed in as the geese that fly over the mountains in Cilicia:
which carry stones in their beaks lest their cackling should make
them a prey to the eagles (– where you might learn wit of a goose).

[Say something worth saying or keep silent]; either speak peace †
or hold your peace. Is it not irksome to a wise and discreet
judgement to hear a book stuffed with such-like sense as this: 'The
world is not made of oatmeal'? I have heard of some that have
thought the world to have been composed of atoms, never any that
thought it made of oatmeal. 'Nor all is not gold that glisters, nor the
way to heaven is strewed with rushes; for a dram of pleasure an
ounce of pain; for a pint of honey a gallon of gall; for an inch of
mirth an ell of moan, etc.' None above the scum of the world could †
endure with patience to read such a medley composed of discords.
Sometimes your doggerel rhymes make me smile, as when you †
come:

'Man must be at all the cost,
And yet live by the loss;
A man must take all the pains
And women spend all the gains;
Their catching in jest
    And keeping in earnest.
And yet she thinks she keeps herself blameless,

And in all ill vices she would go nameless.
  But if she carry it never so clean,
† Yet in the end she will be counted for a cony-catching quean.
    And yet she will swear that she will thrive
    As long as she can find one man alive.'


†    I stand not to descant on your plain-song, but surely, if you can make ballads no better, you must be fain to give over that profession. For your muse is wonderfully defective in the ban-
† dileers, and you may safely swear with the poet:

> Nec fonte labra prolui caballino,
> Nec in bicipiti somniasse Parnasso
> Memini.

Sometimes you make me burst out with laughter when I see your contradictions of yourself (I will not speak of those which others have espied, although I had a fling at them, lest I should *actum*
† *agere*). Methinks, when you wrote your second epistle 'neither to the wisest clerk nor yet to the starkest fool', the giddiness of your head bewrays you to be both a silly clerk and a stark fool (or else the
† young men you write to must be much troubled with the megrim and the dizziness of the brain), for you begin as if you were wont to run up and down the country with bears at your tail: 'If you mean to see the bear-baiting of women, then trudge to this bear-garden apace and get in betimes, and view every room where thou mayst best sit,' etc.

Now you suppose to yourself the giddy-headed young men are flocked together and placed to their own pleasure, profit and heart's ease. Let but your second cogitations observe the method you take in your supposed sport. Instead of bringing your bears to the stake, you say 'I think it were not amiss to drive all women out of my
† hearing, for doubt lest this little spark kindle into such a flame and raise so many stinging hornets humming about mine ears that all the wit I have' (which is but little) 'will not quench the one nor quiet the
† other.' Do ye not see your apparent contradiction? *Spectatum admissi risum teneatis, amici?* You promise your spectators the bear-baiting of women, and yet you think it not amiss to drive all women out of your hearing: so that none but yourself, the
† ill-favoured hunks, is left in the bear-garden to make your invited guests merry. Whereupon, it may very likely be, the eager young men, being not willing to be gulled and cheated of their money they paid for their room, set their dogs at you. Amongst whom Cerberus, that hell-hound, appeared, and you bit off one of his heads: for presently after you call him the 'two-headed dog' – whom all the poets would fain to have three heads. You therefore, having snapped off that same head, were by the secret operation of

that infernal substance converted into the same essence. And that may serve as one reason that I term you Cerberus the Jailer of hell: for certainly *quicquid dicitur de toto, dicitur de singulis partibus* (that which is spoke of the whole is spoken of every part); and every limb of the devil is an homogeneal part. †

Do ye not see, goodman woodcock, what a springe you make for † your own self? Whereas you say 'tis a great discredit for a man to be accounted a scold; and that you deal after the manner of a shrew which cannot ease her cursed heart but by her unhappy tongue: observe but what conclusion demonstratively follows these premises.

> A man that is accounted a scold hath great discredit;
> Joseph Swetnam is accounted a scold;
> *Ergo*, Joseph hath great discredit.

If you deny the *minor*, 'tis proved out of your own assertion, † because you deal 'after the manner of a shrew', etc. Where we may note, first, a corrupt fountain, whence the polluted puddles of your accustomed actions are derived – 'a cursed heart'; then, the cursedness of your book (which, if you might be your own judge, deserves no more the name of a book than a collier's jade to be a † king's steed) to be the fruit of an unhappy tongue; thirdly, your commodity you reap by it – discredit. Nay, if you were but a † masculine scold, 'twere tolerable; but to be a profane railing Rabsheka, 'tis odious. †

Neither is this all your contrariety you have included. For, presently after, you profess you wrote this book with your hand but not with your heart; whereas, but just now, you confessed yourself to deal after the manner of a shrew 'which cannot otherwise ease your cursed heart but by your unhappy tongue': so your hand hath proved your unhappy tongue a liar. This unsavoury nonsense argueth you to be at that time possessed with the fault you say commonly is in men – to wit, drunkenness – when you wrote these jarring and incongruous speeches – whose absurdities accrue to such a tedious and infinite sum that, if any would exactly trace them out, they should find them like a mathematical line, *divisibilis* † *in semper divisibilia*. ('Twould put down the most absolute arithmetician to make a catalogue of them.) Wherefore I could wish thee to make a petition that you might have your books called in and burnt. For were it not better that the fire should befriend thee in purifying the trash and eating out the canker of thy defamation, † than thy execrable designs and inexcusable impudence should blazon abroad thy drunken temerity and temulent foolhardiness to † future ages? than thy book should peremptorily witness thy open † and atheistical blasphemy against thy creator, even in the very threshold and entrance? – but above all, where thou dost put a lie on

God himself, with this supposition: 'If God had not made them only to be a plague to man, he would never have called them † necessary evils' (p. 31). Which I thus anticipate: But God never called them necessary evils; therefore God made them not to be a † plague to man. Or else, turning the conclusion to the mean, thus: But God did not make them to be a plague, but a helper and procurer of all felicity; therefore God never called them necessary evils.

Were it not, I say, far better for you that your laborious idle work should be abolished in the flames than it should publicly set † forth the apert violation of holy writ in sundry places? One in the beginning (as I remember) where you falsely aver that the blessed patriarch David exclaimed bitterly against women: and like the tempting devil you allege half scripture – whereas the whole makes against yourself. For thus you affirm he saith: 'It is better to be a door-keeper than to be in the house with a froward woman'. In the whole volume of the book of God, much less in the *Psalms*, is there any such bitter exclamation? But this is the ditty of the sweet singer of Israel: whereby he did intimate his love unto the house of God, and his detestation of the pavilions of the unrighteous, by this antithesis: 'It is better to be a door-keeper in the house of the Lord than to dwell in the tabernacles of the ungodly'. Now, if you have a † private spirit that may interpret by enthusiasms, you may confine the tabernacles of the ungodly only to froward women: which how absurd and gross it is, let the reader judge. Dost thou not blush, † graceless, to pervert (with Elymas) the straight ways of God by prophaning the scriptures, and wreathing their proper and genuine † interpretations to by-senses, for the bolstering and upholding of your damnable opinion? – besides thy pitifully wronging of the philosophers, as Socrates, Plato and Aristotle, etc., whom your illiterate and clownish muse never was so happy to know whether † they wrote anything or no. Your ethnic histories: although they rather make against men than women, yet in your relation you most † palpably mistake and tell one thing for another, as of Holofernes, † Antiochus, Hannibal, Socrates and the rest; which the poor deluded † Corydons and silly swains account for oracles and maintain as † axioms. The quirks and crotchets of your own pragmatical pate you father on those ancient philosophers that most extremely oppose † your conceit of marriage. For Plato made this one of his laws: that whosoever was not married at thirty-five years of age should be punished with a fine. Further, he implies a necessity of marriage, even in regard of the adoration of God himself: (' 'Tis necessary that there should be a lawful generation and education of children that life as a lamp may continue to posterity, that so there might always be some to worship God.') What more divinely or religious- † ly could be spoken by a paynim? How then durst you say that the philosophers that lived in the old time had so hard an opinion of

marriage that they took no delight therein – seeing the chief of them were married themselves? I could be infinite to produce examples and symbols to make you a liar in print: ('Nothing is more sweet than a good wife.') (Theognis [l.1225]) ('He that hath a good wife †
hath a merry life'.) (Protagoras) Most famous is that retortion of Pittacus, one of the seven wise men of Greece, when he demanded a †
fellow wherefore he would not take to him a wife and the fellow answered: ('If I take a fair wife, I shall have her common; if a foul, a torment'). The wise man replied: ('If thou getst a foul wife, thou shalt not have her common; if a fair, no torments.') There is as much reason for the one as the other. But 'tis but wasting paper to reckon up these obvious sayings. Let that same acclamation of Horace stand for a thousand others: †

> Faelices ter et amplius,
> Quos irrupta tenet copula, nec malis
> Divulsus querimoniis,
>   Suprema citius solvet amor die.
> (Thrice and more times are they blest,
> That in wedlock's bands do rest,
> Whose faithful loves are knit so sure,
> That blameless endless they endure.)

But you that will traduce the holy scriptures, what hope is there but you will deprave human authors. You tax Plato and Aristotle of a lascivious life, that, by the light of natural reason, were chiefest establishers of matrimony both in regard of economic and politic affairs (Plato, *De Legibus*, i[vi]; Aristotle, *Oeconomics* I.viii).

Do these things deserve commendations of any? – but rather the scorn and reproof of all. What a silly thing it is, let Monsieur Swetnam judge, when Valerius Maximus relates in his 4[th] book a history of one Tiberius Gracchus: that found two serpents in his †
bed-chamber and killed the male, which, by the prediction of soothsayers, designed himself to death because he dearly loved his wife Cornelia: and you, like an ass, tell this tale of Valerius Maximus. As if, because Joseph tells a tale of one Bias that bought †
the best and worst meat, which was tongues, in the market, he that reads it should say that one lying ass Swetnam bought the best and worst tongues. (But certainly, if that Bias had met with your tongue in the market, he would have taken it for the worst and most unprofitable meat – because from nothing can come worse venom than from it.)

What should I speak of the figments of your dull pate: how absurdly you tell of one Theodora, a strumpet in Socrates' time, †
that could entice away all the philosopher's scholars from him. Is not the vain and inconstant nature of men more culpable by this example than of women? – when they should be so luxuriously bent †

that one silly light woman should draw a multitude of learned
† scholars from the right way? Yet neither Laertius nor any that write
† the lives of philosophers make mention of this Theodora. But I have
read of a glorious martyr of this name, a virgin of Antiochia in the
time of Diocletian the emperor, who, being in prison, a certain
† barbarous soldier, moved with lust in himself and the lustre of her
beauty, would have ravished her by violence; whom she not only
deterred from this cursed act by her persuasive oratory, but, by her
powerful entreaties, by changing vestments wrought her delivery
by him.

I would run through all your silly discourse and anatomise your
† basery, but as some have partly been bolted out already, and are
promised to be prosecuted, so I leave them as not worthy rehearsal
† or refutation. I would give a *supersedeas* to my quill: but there is a
most pregnant place in your book, which is worthy laughter, that
comes to my mind, where you most graphically describe the
difference and antipathy of man and woman. Which being considered, you think it strange there should be any reciprocation of
love; for a man, say you, delights in arms and hearing the rattling
† drum, but a woman loves to hear sweet music on the lute, cittern or
† bandora. I prithee, who but the long-eared animal had rather hear
the cuckoo than the nightingale? Whose ears are not more delighted
with the melodious tunes of sweet music than with the harsh-
sounding drum? Did not Achilles delight himself with his harp as
well as with the trumpet? Nay, is there not more men that rather
affect the laudable use of the cittern, and bandora, and lute for the
recreation of their minds than the clamorous noise of drums?
† Whether is it more agreeable to human nature to march amongst
murdered carcasses – which you say man rejoiceth in – than to
enjoy the fruition of peace and plenty, even to dance on silken
carpets – as you say is our pleasure? What man soever maketh wars,
is it not to this end – that he might enjoy peace? Who marcheth
among murdered carcasses but to this end – that his enemies being
subdued and slain, he may securely enjoy peace? 'Man loves to hear
the threatening of his prince's enemies, but woman weeps when she
hears of wars.' What man that is a true and loyal subject loves to
hear his prince's enemies threaten? – is not this a sweet commendation, think you? Is it not more humane to bewail the wars and loss
of our countrymen than to rejoice in the threats of an adversary?
But you go forward in your paralleling a man's love to lie on the
cold grass but a woman must be wrapped in warm mantles. I never
heard of any that had rather lie in the cold grass than in a feather
bed, if he might have his choice. Yet you make it a proper attribute
to all your sex.

Thus you see your chiefest elegancy to be but miserable patches
and botches. This antithesis you have found in some author betwixt
a warrior and a lover, and you stretch it to show the difference

betwixt a man and a woman. *Sed nos has a scabie teneamus ungues*: †
I love not to scratch a mangy rascal, there is neither credit nor
pleasure in it.

You threaten your second volley of powder and shot: wherein
you will make us snakes, venomous adders and scorpions (Second
Epistle), and I know not what. Are these terms beseeming the
mouth of a Christian, or a man which is *ovo prognatus eodem*? Did †
not your mother hatch the same cockatrice egg, to make you in the †
number of the generation of vipers? And I take you to be of that
brood which Homer calls, *tanuglossoi*, (always lolling out the †
tongue); and all the historiographers term *scopes*, that give a most †
unpleasing and harsh note, quasi *periskoptousai*, (cavilling and
taunting); and, as Caelius wittily notes them to be so called, *quasi* †
*sciopas en skia ekhontes tēn opa* (having their face obscured in †
darkness). So this your book, being but the howling of a night bird,
shall circumscribe thy name in the dungeon of perpetual infamy.
Thou that art extolled amongst clowns and fools shalt be a hissing,
and a by-word to the learned and judicious (insomuch as thine
unlucky shrieking shall affect thee with ghastly terrors and amaze-
ments). Never think to set forth more [a]larums of your brutish-
ness, but as Labienus, who was surnamed Rabies (madness) – †
because he used such liberty of his detracting tongue that he would,
without regard or discretion, rail upon all men in his exasperate
mood – when all his books and writings were made a bonfire of
(which in those days was a new-found way of punishing untoward
wits), 'Eam contumeliam', saith mine author, 'Labienus non tulit
neque superstes ingenio suo esse voluit': Labienus took snuff at this
contumelious destruction of his despised labours. He was unwilling
to be the surviving executor of his own wit, whereupon, in a
melancholy and desperate mood, he caused himself to be coffined
up and carried into the vault where his ancestors were entombed.
Thinking (it may be) that the fire which had burned his fame should
be denied him, he died and buried himself together.

I do not wish you the same death (though you have the same
conditions and surname as he had) – but live still to bark at virtue.
Yet these our writings shall be worse than fires to torture both thy
book and thee. Wherefore, transcribing some verses that a gentleman wrote to such an one as yourself, in this manner I conclude:

> Thy death I wish not, but would have thee live
> To rail at virtue's acts, and so to give
> Good virtues lustre (seeing envy still
> Waits on the best deserts, to her own ill).
> But for yourself learn this: let not your hand
> Strike at the flint again – which can withstand
> Your malice without harm and to your face
> Return contempt, the brand of your disgrace;

Whilst women sit unmoved, whose constant minds
(Armed against obloquy) with those weak winds                †
Cannot be shaken. For who doth not mark                      †
That dogs for custom, not for fierceness, bark.
These any foot-boy kicks, and therefore we
Passing them by, with scorn do pity thee.
For being of their nature mute at noon,
Thou darest at midnight bark against the moon:
Where mayst thou ever bark, that none shall hear
But to return the like. And mayst thou bear
With grief more slanders than thou canst invent,
Or e'er did practise yet, or canst prevent.
Mayst thou be matched with envy, and defend
Scorn toward that which all besides commend.
And may that scorn so work upon thy sense
That neither suffering nor impudence
May teach thee cure: or, being overworn
With hope of cure, may merit greater scorn.
If not too late, let all thy labours be
Condemned by upright judgements, and thy fee,
So hardly earned, not paid. May thy rude quill
Be always mercenary, and write still
That which no man will read, unless to see
Thine ignorance, and then to laugh at thee.
And mayst thou live to feel this, and then groan
Because 'tis so, yet cannot help; and none
May rescue thee till your checked conscience cry
'This, this, I have deserved', then pine and die.
    *Et cum fateri furia iusserit verum,*                    †
    *Prodente clames conscientia 'Scripsi'.*

                                        FINIS


                          NOTES

**Cerberus**: the dog with many heads (usually three) that guarded the entrance to the
    Greek underworld.
**Redargution**: confutation; refutation.
**Constantia Munda**: moral constancy.
**Sigenus ... nefandi**: Virgil, *Aeneid* i, 542–43: If ye think light of human kinship and
    mortal arms, yet look unto gods who will remember right and wrong.


PAGE 127
**churched**: the ceremony of thanksgiving after childbirth.
**taking up**: borrowing; the financial images here elaborate the basic paradox that she
    has borrowed her life from her mother and when she tries to pay back her mother
    through the activities of her life she realizes how much she has borrowed.
**forfeit ... bond**: be unable to pay back.

PAGE 127 CONTINUED

**halter**: she may mean Sowernam's pamphlet (where the word halter is used).

**Newgate ... Tyburn**: from prison to hanging (recalls Swetnam, p. 13).

PAGE 128

**cockered up**: coddled, indulged.

**hoist ... price**: raise the price, value more.

**chemic limbeck**: alchemical alembic – used in distilling.

**silly**: ignorant, rustic (this, like much here, anticipates phrases used in the text later on).

**sink**: sewer, cesspool.

**descry**: perceive, discover.

**ruff of fury**: the Swetnam phrase again.

PAGE 129

**fits**: provides with what is fit.

**promiscuously**: indiscriminately.

**pasquils**: lampoons.

**glanders**: horse disease involving swelling and mucous discharge.

**michingly**: surreptitiously.

PAGE 130

**Licambean**: Munda quotes a line from Ovid: 'Tincta licambaeo sanguine tela dabet' (*Ibis* l. 54) The poem was translated into English in 1569 and a note on this line tells us that Lycambus had promised his daughter Niobe in marriage to the poet Archilocus but then fell in love with her himself. Archilocus attacked them so savagely that 'for shame they hanged themselves'.

**opprobrious**: vituperative.

**mountebanks**: itinerant quacks.

**detracting**: disparaging.

**stationer's shop**: where books were sold.

**pandect**: complete body of a nation's laws, a complete treatise.

**phrenetical**: deranged.

**scribimus indocti**: we write untaught (or ignorant).

**scribimus insani**: we write insane.

**L'usanza ... peccato**: common usage is not a sin.

**non sine privilegio**: refers to the phrase *cum privilegio* which denoted the sole right of printing (usually under royal privilege).

**use**: usury, using money lent at a premium.

**fenory**: interest on money.

**principal**: capital, main sum lent.

**consuetudo ... peccati**: the habit of sinning takes away the sense of sin; close to the proverb 'consuetudo peccandi multitudinem facit peccantium'.

**limn out**: portray (adorn).

**Coelum ... stultitia**: mainly translated by Munda (in foolishness we attack – or outbrave – heaven itself).

**epitome**: summary, compendium.

**razed**: scratched, wounded, erased.

**bayards**: proverbial type of blind or ignorant recklessness (orig. horse).

**Tri-unity**: Munda's note says Genesis i.

**Pantocrator**: Almighty.

PAGE 131

**lesser world**: as opposed to heaven.

**poetaster**: inferior poet, rhymester.

**Coryphaeus**: leader of chorus in Greek drama.

PAGE 131 CONTINUED

**public theatre**: we are aware of some Puritan attacks on the immorality of the stage; here is a critique from a woman's view.

**compendious**: profitable, succinct.

**Pharisaical ostentation**: taken from Luke xviii.11 (the story of the Pharisee and publican praying); more directly, lifted from Benvenuto (see **learned Tuscan** below): 'the worse kind of Pharisaical ostentation' (A3r).

**Anaxarchus**: Munda quotes a line from Ovid, *Ibis* l. 571, and she has taken everything in the brackets from Benvenuto (A3r); Anaxarchus (4th C. BC) was highly thought of by Alexander the Great and killed by Nicocreon of Cyprus, in a stone mortar.

**learned Tuscan**: Munda's note: Benvenuto Italiano; she quotes from *Il passagiere* (*The passenger*) (1612), trs. by King and printed as a parallel text. Benvenuto is described as 'Professor of his native tongue for these nine years in London'. The quotation comes from the introductory epistle where he is talking of critics and revilers of worthy writers. Everything down to the words 'or prudent silence' comes from this source.

**Rabilius**: presumably Rabirius, a poet mentioned by Ovid; there was also a Rabirius defended by Cicero.

**chaps**: jaws, chops.

**Callimachus**: (305–240 BC) writer of lyrics and epigrams, famous for his bitter controversy with Apollonius; Ovid mentions him in *Ibis*.

**Etna**: the flames are mentioned in Ovid, *Ibis* l. 598; the lightning at l. 328.

**Bellona**: early Roman war goddess.

**Sulmo, Orbecca**: in Giraldi Cintio's play *Orbecche* (perf. 1541), King Sulmone punishes his daughter Orbecche for secretly marrying Oronte – he has the husband's head and hands, and the corpses of their two sons, served to her on salvers.

**epatic**: hepatic; dark, reddish aloes. Munda quotes in the margin from Juvenal vi.180 (talking of pride).

**simples**: ingredients.

**ivory gate**: i.e., teeth.

**words make worse wounds**: Munda notes this is a French proverb.

PAGE 132

**loquenda ... loqui**: Munda quotes in the margin from Sophocles, *Ajax* l. 293, to the effect that 'for women silence is respectable'. (Also quoted in Aristotle's *Politics*.)

**stulta ... cartae**: Juvenal, *Satire* i.17–18: it is a foolish clemency ... to spare the paper that will be wasted anyway.

**Loqui ... tacere**: To say what is proper is better than to keep silent. Munda quotes this in Greek.

**traverse your bills**: in law, formally to deny the indictment or statement of the case.

**malapert**: impudent.

**make a long letter to us**: Munda quotes this in Latin from Plautus, *Aulularia* II.iv.46; it is a metaphor for hanging oneself (the body hanging perpendicularly looks like a long letter, an *I*).

**Non sic ... geret**: Seneca, *Hercules Furens* ll. 27–9: My feelings of hatred will not thus go away. My violent mind will hold long-lasting anger, and savage anguish, with peace removed, will wage eternal war.

**Gelo Siracusanus**: Gelon (540–478 BC), a cavalry commander under Hippocrates who captured Syracuse and became its ruler. Munda quotes in Greek, from Herodotus vii.160.

**ipsa ... est**: in his translation of Ovid, Drayton has: fault itself is the fault's excuse.

**little ease**: originally a specific prison in the Tower, any confined cell.

**to sow thorns**: from Benvenuto, A5r.

**franked up**: shut up (a frank was a place for feeding up hogs).

PAGE 132 CONTINUED

**Coriolanus**: Livy, *Ab Urbe Condita* II.xl.9; compare with the scene in Shakespeare's play.

**ab hoc exemplum cape**: take example from this.

**Gynaecia**: womanhood.

**an unlucky gallows**: a similar story of Diogenes, where the boy throws stones at a gibbet, is told in Diogenes Laertius vi.45.

**Nomine ... de te**: Horace, *Satires* I.i.69–70: by a change of name the story can be told of you.


PAGE 133

**choler**: anger; Munda quotes from Swetnam, then puns on collar and ruff (standing collars were fashionable at this time).

**peccadillo**: Munda's gloss: a little sin.

**shag**: either rough material or cloth with a velvet nap on one side.

**defecated**: purified.

**parle**: discussion.

**potgun**: popgun, hence braggart.

**Nestor**: in fact Odysseus, from *Iliad* ix.256; Munda quotes in Greek.

**it had been ... anger**: in the margin: 'Animum tu pectore fortem contineas, sibi qui bene temperat optimus esto.' (May you keep a brave spirit in your breast: let him who restrains himself well be the best.)

**wreak**: give vent to.

**Tully**: Cicero, *Tusculan Disputations* IV.xxxvi.78: What a visitation you would have got if I had not been angry! (Architas, a Greek philosopher in Plato's time, is addressing his bailiff.)

**nullum ... laudem**: slightly incorrect quotation: There is no glorious renown in a woman's punishment and such victory wins no honour.

**furred**: as in deposits on tongue.

**meretricial**: whorish.

**brass money**: this is reminiscent of the *Iliad* vi.236, where Glaucus exchanges with Diomedes his gold armour for bronze, and Zeus takes away his wits.


PAGE 134

**pelting**: paltry.

**doxies**: whores.

**look**: printed 'looked'.

**cum ... est**: misquotation from Juvenal, *Satire* vi.341 (*Satire* vi is about women): he is talking of the strength of female passion and a house 'in which every picture of the male form must be veiled'.

**Quem praestare ... sexu**: What modesty can you expect in a woman who wears a helmet, abjures her own sex? (I have corrected orig. *Quam*).

**pagan poet**: Juvenal.

**Scaliger**: J.C. Scaliger, Italian philologist and scholar (1484–1558). The work referred to seems to be *Poetices libri septem*, but Juvenal is commented on at vi.6 (p. 325) in the edition of 1561 that I consulted.

**Iamque ... Syrorum**: from Juvenal, *Satire* vi.349–51: High or low their passions are all the same. She who wears out the black cobblestones with her bare feet is no better than she who rides upon the necks of eight stalwart Syrians.

**the voice ... land**: Cant. ii.12 ('turtle': turtle dove).


PAGE 135

**bray ... mortar**: see Coverdale translation of the Bible (1537): 'Though thou shouldst bray a fool with a pestle in a mortar like oatmeal, yet will not his foolishness go from him' (Prov. xxvii.22); 'bray': pound.

**palinody**: verse recantation.

PAGE 135 CONTINUED

**A fool ... purpose:** Munda quotes this in Greek (compare Aulus Gellius, *Noctes Atticae* II.vi.5).

**digiting:** here meaning 'fingering' (digit: point out)?

**bella ... Venetiis:** Munda's note says 'Mr. Th. Coriat': the reference is to Coryate's travel book, *Coriat's Crudities* (1611), where on p. 261 he begins a description of Venetian courtesans and there is a picture of a famous courtesan, Margarita Emiliana 'bella cortesana di Venetia'. Coryate writes a defence of the courtesans (unlike Swetnam) and says how he visited a courtesan 'yet was nothing contaminated therewith, nor corrupted in manner' (p. 271). Munda may have recognised Swetnam's borrowing from Coryate.

**teeth watered:** as in 'mouth watered'.

**thirty years' travel:** Munda refers to Swetnam's first Epistle.

**inclined:** either 'was disposed' or 'decayed'.

**stews:** brothels.

**politicly:** craftily.

**daughter in the oven:** proverb – you don't find someone in an unlikely place unless you've been there yourself.

**famous pilgrim:** Odysseus; the quotation is *Odyssey* i.3 (Munda quotes the Greek in the margin).

**huswives:** housewives/hussies (this development of the Jacobean word is very interesting in the sexism it reveals).

**obloquy:** shaming, disgrace.

**three times as long:** Swetnam says he travelled 'thirty and odd years'.

**addle:** muddled.

**dogs from Iceland:** fashionable lap-dogs (picking up Swetnam's remark that if he had brought dogs from Iceland women would have been interested in seeing them).

**non-proficient:** one who fails to make progress.

**patrimony:** inheritance.

**pass:** the most likely meaning here is the order that passes a pauper back to her/his parish, though *OED* records first usage in 1647.

**a dog that bites:** close to the proverb: 'A dog bites the stone, not him who throws it.'


PAGE 136

**Prodiga ... constant:** Juvenal, *Satire* vi.362–65 (*At* should be *ac*, *quantum* should be *quanti*).

**minions:** lovers.

**convicious:** abusive.

**procacity:** insolence.

**collimate:** collineate – bring into a straight line, aim at.

**sensuality:** this is an interesting analysis of the deliberate cultivation of a role of 'masculine' hardness, and the part that styles of writing play in this.

**assoil:** absolve.

**(ira), (concupiscentia):** anger, desire: these are Munda's marginal glosses to the Greek words she uses in the text ('spleen' rather than 'anger' is better for the first word).

**Euripides:** I cannot trace this; *thoro*: bed, *calamo*: a pen (for animals); *thalamo*: bed chamber. Aulus Gellius, *Noctes Atticae* XV.xx talks of his dislike of women.

**persuade your body:** persuade me that your body is ...

**frompard:** frampold – peevish.


PAGE 137

**lex talionis:** talion law – an eye for an eye; Munda glosses 'like for like'.

**poor illiterate women:** the connection of illiteracy with supposed female modesty is

PAGE 137 CONTINUED

an important one: it suggests that modesty is created by the material circumstances of education, that the male domination of literacy deliberately silences women. There is a definite sense here of the woman needing to speak out 'in the open view' in order to prevent the continued operation of male oppressiveness.

**repine**: fret, complain.

**baited**: harassed.

**tossed in a blanket**: humiliating punishment.

**vituperious**: vituperative.

**ego sic ... adhibeat**: I shall live in such a way that no one will believe you.

**the poet**: Juvenal, *Satire* ix.119–20 (*tum* should read *cum*; *de* should read *est.*)

**a pitch**: Munda quotes in the margin from Juvenal's *Satire* x.106–7 (referring to the crash following Sejanus' huge ambition); she is also punning on 'pitch' from Swetnam's 'he that toucheth pitch may be defiled therewith' (p. 34), which is also in Lyly.

**self-pining**: self-tormenting.

**black mouth**: literal translation of Melastomus.

**licking ... poison**: compare Speght, p. 59.

**hellebore**: medicinal plant, drug.

**sink**: sewer, cesspool.

**catapotions**: Munda's word – antidotes (literally, potions that 'answer' or neutralise).

**growl ... author**: does this mean Swetnam was preparing a riposte to Speght? Note how in this passage Munda only refers to Speght: it confirms what she says at the start, that she was writing a pamphlet at the same time as Sowernam was and that Sowernam was printed first.

**triple dog of hell**: Cerberus had three heads.

PAGE 138

**worm**: to extract from the tongue of a dog the 'worm' (a small tendon) as a safeguard against rabies.

**rankling**: Speght uses the same adjective (p. 60).

**wisp**: straw figure for a scold to rail at.

**cucking-stool**: scolds were fastened to a chair and sometimes ducked on it as a public humiliation (Swetnam refers to the scolds' cucking-stool in his Epistle: he says he is going to answer his female critics with silence because he does not want to be a scold).

**compass ... chain**: the reach of his dog chain? Or the compassing, the inventing, of a dog chain for him.

**Archilocus**: one of the earliest Greek poets (714–676 BC), most famous for his very bitter satires; Munda's phrase 'tart iambics' may recall Horace: 'Archilocum proprio rabies armavit iambo.' (Rage armed Archilocus with his own *iambus*) (*Ars Poetica* l. 79).

**Lopez**: the notorious Dr Lopez was involved in an assassination attempt on Elizabeth I.

**Phalaris**: his claim to historical celebrity is for tyranny and cruelty, ruled in Sicily (date uncertain – but early); he shut up his victims in a bull made of brass and lit a fire underneath it; the cries of those inside sounded like the animal's lowing.

**Quippe ... foemina**: Juvenal, *Satire* xiii. 189–92: For vengeance is always the delight of a little, weak and petty mind; of which you may straightaway draw proof from this – that no one so rejoices in vengeance as a woman.

**ultion**: vengeance.

**Thou that ... satisfaction**: Munda quotes in the margin from Juvenal, *Satire* xiii. 193–5: Juvenal is asking why 'you should suppose a man escapes punishment' ... 'whose mind is ever kept in terror by the consciousness of an evil deed which lashes him with unheard blows, his own soul ever shaking over him the unseen whip of torture'.

PAGE 138 CONTINUED

**a-woolgathering**: based on Swetnam: 'my wits were gone a-woolgathering, in so much that in a manner forgetting myself, and so in the rough of my fury' (A3r).

**Nero-like**: Nero had his mother killed.

**[absurdity]**: Munda quotes here in Greek; 'inconvenience' also has the (obsolete) meaning: absurdity.

**My mother, etc.**: Swetnam, p. 15.


PAGE 139

**Augustus Caesar**: familiar as the Caesar Augustus of the New Testament nativity stories.

**tributary**: one who pays tribute (the joke under here is that 'tax' can mean accuse).

**Periculoso ... doloso**: a task full of dangerous hazard – walking, as it were, over fires hidden beneath treacherous ashes.

**rogue in the fable**: Aesop, tale 351 (Halm edn).

**more ungrateful**: the margin has: 'Ingratum si dixero omnia dixero'. (If I say ungrateful, I shall have said everything.) This has almost proverbial status, and perhaps originates with Cicero.

**bumbaily**: bailiff employed in arrests.

**sub poena**: writ commanding a defendant to answer a charge.

**praemunire**: writ as above, but especially of charges connected with asserting the supremacy of the Pope.

**Prometheus' vulture**: for teaching men about various sciences and the use of fire Prometheus was chained to a mountain and an eagle or vulture spent each day eating out his liver (it grew again in the night).

**the latter**: again Munda is conscious of her task – much has already been said by Sowernam.

**apprehended, attached**: both words mean arrested ('attached' also means 'indicted').

**seared**: cauterised.


PAGE 140

**nocent**: guilty.

**prejudicate**: prejudiced.

**cautelous**: cautious.

**imposthume**: abscess, sore.

**cognizance**: emblem, crest.

**degenerous**: degenerate.

**pilling**: plundering, spoliation.

**contumely**: abuse.

**ut non ... descenderes**: inaccurate quotation from Cicero, *Oratio pro L. Murena* xxvii.56.

**solecism**: impropriety in speech, grammar or society.

**tenter-hooks**: used to stretch drying cloth.

**shackrag**: ragged, 'low' person.

**arripiendo ... trivio**: Cicero, *Oratio ... Murena* vi.13: by collecting together curses out of the street.

**glanders**: horse disease.

**offals**: refuse, dregs.

**mingle-mangle gallimaufry**: confused jumble ('mingle-mangle' is a Speght word).


PAGE 141

**devisor**: contriver, here 'brain'?

**mescelline**: maslin – mixed grain (rye with wheat) or bread of mixed corn.

**soiled**: polluted.

**Parismus**: see the romance by Emanuel Forde, *The renowned history of Parismus, Prince of Bohemia* (1598).

PAGE 141 CONTINUED

**Knight of the Sun**: Spanish romance by Ortunez de Calahorra, translated into English by Margaret Tyler (1578).

**Euphues**: John Lyly's famous mixture of love and moralising (1578).

**Amadis a Gaul**: more correctly, Amadis de Gaul: 15th C. Spanish romances, translated into English by Anthony Munday (Book I, 1590?, Book II, 1595).

**Don Quixote**: Cervantes' story appeared in English translated by Thomas Shelton in 1612 (the hero is an archetype of folly).

**Valerius Maximus**: Renaissance folk culled many of their accounts of the sayings and doings of ancient Romans from Maximus' *De dictis factisque memorabilibus*, or *Factorum et dictorum memorabilium*.

**pluck a crow**: proverbial: find faults.

**furtivis ... risum**: back-to-front quotation from Horace, *Epistles* I.iii.19–20: the poor crow, stripped of his stolen colours, awakes laughter.

**Aesop's jay**: wore a peacock's plumage (tales 200, 201 in Halm edn).

**Italian proverb**: originally medieval Latin, later English proverb.

**potsherds**: fragments of pot.

**lapides loqueris**: Plautus, *Aulularia* II.i.29: you speak hard words.

**say something ... silence**: Munda quotes in (inaccurate) Greek, which she more or less translates.

**ell**: 45 inches.

**doggerel**: what Munda has done is to spot rhymes within what is printed as prose, e.g., Swetnam (p. 15): 'Man must be at all the cost and yet live by the loss, a man must take all the pains and women will spend all the gains'. (The next couplet comes from p. 29.) By herself printing it as doggerel, she has used typography to make us look afresh at the silliness of what Swetnam is saying: the unthinking acceptance of familiar ideas in prose is replaced by an awareness of the nursery rhyme stupidity of the same ideas.

PAGE 142

**cony-catching**: cheating (cony: rabbit).

**quean**: in Henry Cecil Wyld's immortal phrase: 'a flaunting, brazen woman'.

**descant**: sing an ornamental variation on the plainsong.

**bandileers**: seemingly a misprint, split ba/ndileers. A 'bandileer' is a sash or broad belt – the closest word to it is perhaps 'banderol': an inscription of honour.

**the poet**: Persius, *Satires*, prologue 1–3: I never soused my lips in the nag's spring [the hoof of Pegasus struck out the stream Hippocrene]; never, that I remember, did I dream on the two-topped Parnassus.

**actum agere**: to plead a case already finished – act to no purpose.

**megrim**: migraine.

**little spark**: compare Speght, p. 59.

**Spectatum ... amici**: Horace, *Ars Poetica* l. 5: could you, my friends, if favoured with a private view, refrain from laughing?

**ill-favoured**: ugly.

**hunks**: bearish, surly person.

PAGE 143

**homogeneal**: similar.

**woodcock**: fool.

**springe**: snare.

**minor**: technical term in logic – term which forms the subject of the conclusion of a syllogism.

**jade**: worn-out horse (Munda is quoting here from Swetnam's second Epistle).

**commodity**: profit.

**Rabsheka**: title of Assyrian official sent to demand surrender of Jerusalem.

**divisibilis ... divisibilia**: what is divisible in parts can always be divided into smaller parts.

PAGE 143 CONTINUED
**canker**: ulcerous sore.
**blazon**: proclaim.
**temulent**: drunken.
**peremptorily**: decisively.


PAGE 144
**anticipate**: forestall, foresee and try to prevent.
**mean**: in logic, the middle term.
**apert**: manifest.
**enthusiasms**: supernatural inspiration.
**Elymas**: or Bar Jesus, a false prophet in Acts xiii.6.
**straight**: honest.
**by-senses**: perverse interpretations.
**ethnic**: pagan, gentile.
**Holofernes, etc.**: Swetnam tells how all these men were undone or ruined by their
    love of certain women. Munda suggests that, apart from the stories reflecting
    badly on the men, they are actually mistaken: Swetnam says Socrates 'most
    dearly loved Aspasy an old and overworn strumpet' (p. 23) – in fact this is
    Aspasia, distinguished and learned wife of Pericles whose salon Socrates may
    have attended (the strumpet's name was Theodote: Swetnam gets it wrong again
    later). So too he says Hannibal was fatally delayed at Capua through love: this is a
    common story but historically incorrect since Hannibal's army retained its
    strength.
**Antiochus**: may be Antiochus I, King of Syria, who fell in love with his father's wife
    Stratonice.
**Corydons**: typical rustic name.
**crotchets**: cranky, perverse idiosyncracies.
**Plato**: in *Laws* iv.721 B. Munda goes on to quote in Greek from *Laws*.
**paynim**: pagan.


PAGE 145
**Theognis, etc.**: Munda quotes from Theognis, Protagoras and the Pittacus story in
    Greek, which she translates.
**seven wise men**: the others were Bias of Priene, Chilo of Sparta, Cleobulus of
    Lindos, Periander of Corinth, Solon of Athens, Thales of Miletus.
**Horace**: from *Odes* I.xiii.17–20.
**Tiberius Gracchus**: to have killed the female snake would have meant the death of
    his wife – that was his choice (Valerius Maximus IV.vi.1).
**Bias**: Swetnam tells the story of Lyas, a servant of Amasis, King of Egypt.
**Theodora**: another of Swetnam's mistakes spotted by Munda; she knows he means
    Theodote.
**luxuriously**: lustfully.


PAGE 146
**Laertius**: Diogenes Laertius, author of a collection of lives of the philosophers.
**Theodora**: also known as St Dorothea, see Philip Massinger's play *The Virgin
    Martyr* (1622).
**lust ... lustre**: a nice play on words that neatly asserts what makes men tick, the lust
    preceding lustre.
**bolted out**: sifted out; Speght and Sowernam have already taken apart Swetnam.
    Possibly the 'promise' to prosecute refers to the promised third part of *Ester hath
    hang'd*.
**supersedeas**: writ to command a stay of legal proceedings.
**cittern, bandora**: the cittern was similar to the guitar, the bandora a bass version of
    the same.

**PAGE 146 CONTINUED**

**long-eared animal**: ass.

**human nature**: Munda finally makes the separation of socialised gender from biology; all this stuff about marching and sweet music that Swetnam trots out is simply the attempt to make social difference out of biological, to cultivate maleness of role, to stereotype gender.


**PAGE 147**

**sed nos ... ungues**: Martial, *Epigrams* V.lx.11: I keep my nails from such an itch (Martial saying that he refuses to grant fame to the person who has attacked him by answering back).

**ovo ... eodem**: Horace, *Satires* II.i.26: born from the same egg.

**cockatrice**: basilisk (its glance destroyed).

**always ... tongue**: *Odyssey* v.66: Munda quotes in Greek here. I have transliterated the Greek because this is a display of etymology.

**scopes**: owl (mentioned in the same line of the *Odyssey* as above: there seems to be confusion between owls and crows).

**Caelius**: possibly Marcus Caelius Rufus, a correspondent of Cicero.

**sciopas**: shadowed faces (from *opa scia*); Munda again quotes in Greek.

**Labienus**: famous orator, very critical of the regime of Augustus, hence his nickname 'Rabienus' (Munda has missed the jokey rhyme with Labienus). All that follows to the end of the paragraph is taken from Seneca the Elder, *Controversiae* x.Preface 5–7. The Latin means: Labienus did not take this insult lying down, nor did he wish to outlive his own genius.

**surnamed**: i.e. Rabies (appropriate to the 'dog' Swetnam).


**PAGE 148**

**obloquy**: slander.

**weak**: original spells 'weate'; we could read 'wet'.

**For who ... bark**: this story is mentioned by Speght.

**Et cum ... Scripsi**: Martial, *Epigrams* X.v.18–19: And when the Fury has ordered you to confess the truth, with your conscience betraying you, may you cry out 'I have written'.

# THE
# Women's Sharpe Revenge:

OR

## An answer to Sir Seldom Sober

that writ those railing Pamphlets
called the Juniper and Crabtree
lectures, etc.

Being a sound Reply and a full confutation
of those books: with an Apology in this
case for the defence of us women

*Performed by*
*Mary Tattle-well and Joan Hit-him-home, spinsters*          †

Imprinted at London by I.O. and are to be sold by Ia. Becket at
his shop in the inner Temple-gate
1 6 4 0

[The publication of *The Women's Sharp Revenge* (hereafter *WSR*) followed the familiar pattern. In 1639 John Taylor, whom *WSR* calls Sir Seldom Sober, wrote a pamphlet attacking female scolds titled *A Juniper Lecture* which was a collection of stories about sharp-tongued women. Its sequel, *Divers Crabtree Lectures*, was followed closely by a reply, *WSR*. Indeed, in the *Juniper Lecture*, Taylor tells us that he had thought of writing a sequel attacking men but has been prevented 'for I do hear that there are divers women set their helping hands to publish such a book themselves, in their own praise, with an answer to this book: called by the name of *Sir Seldom Sober*, or *The woman's sharp revenge against the Author*' (p. 96). Taylor has given the game away: the women would have had to have moved pretty sharply to have penned an answer, in detail, to a book that had not yet been fully written. The whole classic gender controversy set-up collapses – Taylor is the author of everything.

Taylor's authorship is established by the links between style, language and subject matter in *WSR* and Taylor's other works (see my notes). (Taylor also claims to write as a woman – Mary Makepeace – in the Epistle to *Divers Crabtree Lectures*.) What is perhaps more interesting is why he wrote the pamphlet, although this in itself is becoming a familiar story. By 1640, Taylor had been churning out books, pamphlets and trivia for well over twenty years. He could turn his hand to most topics of the moment: from fashions to royalty, from economic abuses to sectarian groups – nothing too daring, all self-consciously popular. Taylor cultivated the image of his soubriquet 'the Water Poet'; he was the commonsensical Londoner with stories of street life (after all, such things sold). And in the 1630s he appears to have teamed up with a printer, John Okes. Okes apparently specialised in Taylor's sort of product; he tended to lose interest in any more serious works that came his way.

What may have given the cue for a new gender controversy was the reprinting in 1637 of Swetnam's pamphlet. On 4 August 1638 Okes registered Taylor's *Juniper Lecture*, then on 24 April 1639 he registered together 'A Book called *A Crabtree Lecture* with *the womans sharp revenge* etc.'. It was to be some months before *WSR* appeared, so that it seems Okes was making a move to copyright the title that Taylor had already advertised in *Juniper* (I am advised by Maureen Bell that this sort of use of the Stationers' Register was not uncommon). When *WSR* did appear all sorts of hints in the language proved that Taylor had read at least some of the texts from the Swetnam controversy (see notes).

In my opinion, therefore, Taylor and Okes set up a custom-made gender controversy, with a view to making money out of the current interest in sex roles. This exploitation effectively trivialises what can otherwise be a serious discussion. Women are thus reduced simply to objects for entertainment. The fabricated gender controversy contributes to a tradition that sees women as jokes or monsters or fairground curios. It is worth recalling that in these months Okes joined in a rush of ballads to cash in on some new grotesque: on 4 and 5 December appeared 'The Woman Monster', 'A Maiden Monster', 'A Strange Relation of a female Monster', 'The hog-faced gentlewoman' (Okes's contribution). The names Taylor chooses for his fake authors are advertisements: Mary Tattlewell (formed on the basis of a name Taylor invented for *Crabtree* – Mary Makepeace) and Joan Hit-him-home are both labels for aggressive women.

A woman did not have to be pig-faced to be a monster. The scold was seen by male writers as a grotesque: 'she will be melancholy, malicious, and her most study shall be to be ill-conditioned: she will mump, hang the lip, swell (like a toad that hath lain a year under a wood-pile), pout, lour, be sullen, sad and dogged. She will knit the brows, frown, be wayward, froward, cross and untoward on purpose to torment her husband. Her delight is chiefly to make debate abroad and to be unquiet at home' (*Juniper*, p. 75). Taylor may have taken the idea of an attack on scolds from Swetnam: 'a woman's chief strength is in her tongue: the serpent hath not so much venom in his tail as she hath in her tongue' (Swetnam, p. 41). The technique of *Juniper* is to demonstrate how the woman rails at the man in each 'lecture' and at the end of each lecture there is a summing up. For example, the 'scold rampant' accuses her husband of being a drunken slob and an oaf; at the end is the husband's speech to one of his neighbours '*out of his wife's hearing*': 'My wife sure, good neighbour, was born at Billingsgate and was certainly nursed up there, she hath such a vile tongue' (*Juniper*, p. 66). Male faults are ignored, a 'normal' community of male neighbours is established, and the woman is consigned to joke status.

The supposed answer to *Juniper* and *Crabtree*, produced as it was out of cynicism, dwindles into a shapeless rant about various social 'abuses', especially drunkenness (Taylor's favourite topic). But one point about it is worth making. If Taylor and Okes thought this pamphlet would sell well, that implies that they thought there was an audience who wanted to read it. And the text of *WSR* is not, as we might expect, entirely trivial: there are some interesting attacks on the moral double-standards of men and what is perhaps the best statement of the inequality of education that I have come across in this period. If Taylor was writing this for a particular audience, it perhaps suggests something about what that silent audience was thinking.]

# The Epistle of the Female Frailty to the Male Gender in General

Reader,

If thou be'st of the masculine sex, we mean thee and thee only; and therefore greet thee with these attributes following: affable, loving, kind and courteous. Affable we call thee because so apt – I will not say to prate – but to prattle with us; loving, in regard that, the least † grace being from us granted, you not only vow to love us but are loath to leave us; kind, that you will not meet with us without congees, not part from us without kisses; and courteous, because so † willing to bring yourselves upon your knees before us: more prone to bow unto beauty than to Baal, and to idolatrize to us rather than † unto any other idol. And therefore our hope is, that what you use to protest in private you will not now blush to profess in public. Otherwise, in clearing our cause and vindicating our own virtues, we shall not doubt to divulge you for the only dissemblers.

And in this case we appeal unto your own consciences, even to the most crabbed and censorious, the most sour and supercilious – which of you all hath not solicited our sex? petitioned to our persons? praised our perfections? etc. Which of you hath not met us coming, followed us flying, guarded us going, stayed for us standing, waited on us walking, and ambushed us lying? Use women to court men? Or have we at any time complained of their coyness? Have we bribed them with our bounties? troubled them with our tokens, poetized in their praises, prayed and protested, sued and solicited, voted and vowed to them? Or rather they to us? † Would you apprehend a new antipodes, to make all things to be carried by a contrary course and run retrograde?

Then let the radish root pluck the gardener up by the heels, and the shoulder of mutton put the cook upon the spit: for you as well may prove the one as produce the other.

Yet suffer you us to be reviled and railed at, taunted and terrified, undervalued and even vilified; when among you all we cannot find one champion to oppose so obstinate a challenger but that we are compelled to call a ghost from her grave, to stand up in the defence of so proud a defiance. Since, then, you will not be combatants for us in so just a cause, we entreat you to become competent judges, to censure indifferently betwixt the accuser and the accused: to punish his petulancy and not to favour us, if we be found the sole faulty.

So, if you shall give our defamer his due, and that we gain the honour of the day – if you be young men, we wish you modest maids in marriage; if bachelors, beautiful mistresses; if husbands, handsome wives and good huswives; if widowers, wise and wealthy widows; if young, those that may delight you; if old, such as may comfort you. And so we women bequeath unto you all our best wishes.

† *From our Manor of Make-peace. Dated the third day of Gander-* † *month, in the year of Jubilee, not of Juniper.*

Mary Tattlewell.<br>Joan Hit-him-home.<br>Spinsters.

## The Epistle to the Reader

† Long Meg of Westminster, hearing the abuse offered to women, riseth out of her grave, and thus speaketh:

> Why raise you quiet souls out of the grave,
> To trouble their long sleep? What peevish knave
> Hath wakened my dead ashes, and breathed fire
> Into cold embers? – never to respire
> Till a new resurrection. So forced now
> (Through innocent women's clamours) that I vow

Th' earth could not hold me, but I was compelled
To look on what 'tis long since I beheld,
The sun and day. What have we women done,
That any one who was a mother's son
Should thus affront our sex? Hath he forgot
From whence he came, or doth he seek to blot
His own conception? Is he not ashamed
Within the list of mankind to be named?
Or is there in that masculine sex another –
Saving this monster – will disgrace his mother?
I Margery, and for my upright stature
Surnamed Long Meg – of well disposed nature,
And rather for mine honour than least scorn
Titled from Westminster, because there born –
And so Long Meg of Westminster: to hear
Our fame so branded could no way forbear
But, rather than digest so great a wrong,
Must to my ashes give both life and tongue.
And then, poor Poet, whatsoe'er thou be'st,
That in my now discovery thy fault seest.
Confess thine error, fall upon thy knees,
From us to beg thy pardon by degrees.
Else I, that with my sword and buckler durst
Front swaggering ruffians, put them to the worst.     †
Of whom the begging soldier, when he saw
My angry brow, trembled and stood in awe.
I, that have frighted fencers from the stage     †
(And was indeed the wonder of mine age),
For I have often, to abate their prides,
Cudgeled their coats and lammed their legs and sides.
Cross me no tapster durst at any rate,
Lest I should break his jugs about his pate.
'Tis known the service that I did at Boulogne,
Beating their French arms close unto their woollen:
They can report that with my blows and knocks
I made their bones ache worse than did the pox.
Of which King Henry did take notice then,
And said: 'Amongst my brave and valiant men
I know not one more resolute, or bolder',
And would have laid his sword upon my shoulder,
But that I was a woman. And shall I,
Who durst so proud an enemy defy,
So famed in field, so noted in the Frenchies,
A precedent to all our British wenches,
Fear to affront him? – or his soul to vex,
Who dares in any terms thus taunt our sex?
Therefore relent thine error I advise thee,

Else in what shape soe'er thou shalt disguise thee
I shall inquire thee out; nay, if thou should
† Take on thee all those figures Proteus could,
It were in vain; nay, which the more may daunt thee,
Even to the grave I vow my ghost shall haunt thee.
Therefore, what's yet amiss strive to amend:
† Thou knowest thy doom, if farther thou offend.

[Here follows a contents list covering only the first few pages.]

# THE
# Women's Sharp Revenge

As from several causes proceed sundry effects, so from several actions arise sundry honours, with the addition of names and titles annexed unto them; neither need we stand to prove that by argument which we find by daily experience. As for example: some are raised for their wealth, others for their worth; some by the law, others by their learning; some by martial discipline, and (by your favour too) others for malicious detraction – as thinking to rise by others' ruins, and by supplanting others to support themselves. In which number we must rank you, Master Satirist, the passionate author of those most pitiful pamphlets called the *Juniper Lectures* and *Crab-tree Lectures*: who, by your mere knavery, ambitious to † purchase knighthood and to add a sir-reverence to your name, are now arrived to the height of your aim, and from plain Seldom Sober are now come to the title of Sir Seldom Sober. Who we term so, for he is ashamed to set his name to books – a name fitting his nature, and well complying with his condition.

And as there have been formerly, by your means, Sir Seldom Sober, many railing, bitter, invective pasquils and scurrilous libels, some written, some printed, and all dispersed and scattered abroad, all of them made and forged on purpose to calumniate, revile, despite, jeer and flout women: and now lately, one or two of the sons of ignorance have penned three several, sweet, filthy, fine, ill-favoured pamphlets, which are printed and (out of the most deep shallowness of the authors' abundant want of wisdom) they are called *Lectures* – as, the *Juniper Lecture*, the *Crab-tree Lecture* and † the *Wormwood Lecture* – wherein they have laid most false aspersions upon all women generally. Some they have taxed with incontinency, some with uncivility, some with scolding, some with drinking, some with backbiting and slandering their neighbours, some with a continual delight in lying, some with an extraordinary

desire of perpetual gossipping. In a word, we are each of us accused
and blazed to be addicted and frequently delighted with one †
grievous enormity or other, wherein, although it be true that we are
all the daughters of Eve in frailty, yet they might have remembered
that they likewise are all the sons of Adam in failing, falling and
offending. We are not so partial in the defence of all women's
virtues that we thereby do hold none to be vicious. Some are
incontinent by nature, or inheritance from their mothers; some
through extreme want and poverty have been forced to make more
bold with that which is their own, than to beg, steal or borrow from
others. Some, by the harsh usage of their too unkind husbands,
have been driven to their shifts hardly; some, having had the hard †
fortune to match with such coxcombs as were jealous without a
cause, have by their suspicious, dogged and crabbed dealing
towards their wives given too often, and too much, cause to make
their jealousy true. And whereas a woman's reputation is so poor †
that, if it be but so much as suspected, it will be long before the
suspicion will be cleared; but, if it be once blemished or tainted, the
stains and spots are of such a tincture that the dye of the blemishes
will stick to her all her lifetime, and to her children after her. But for
the man, he takes or assumes to himself such a loose liberty, or
liberty of licentious looseness, that though he be (as they call it) a
common town bull, or a runner at sheep, though he pass the †
censures of spiritual courses or high commissions, yet, by custom, †
his disgrace will be quickly worn out, and say it was but a trick of
youth. For the shame or scandal of a whore-master is like a nine †
days' wonder or a record written in sand, or like a suit of tiffany or †
cobweb lawn, soon worn out. But the faults of a weak woman are a †
continual alarum against her; they are engraven in brass, and like a
suit of buff: it may be turned, and scoured, and scraped, and made a †
little cleanly, but it lasts the whole life-time of the wearer. But to
come to the work in hand, as, you have a title bestowed upon you †
by your back-friends – and we think deservedly. †

So, we have known some who have arrived to that worshipful
title through favour also, rather than desert, and more by voices
than their virtues, merely by the mad suffrage of the many-headed
monster, Multitude which consisteth of Man. Yet upon better
advice and more mature consideration, when their merits and
misdemeanours have been more narrowly sifted and looked into
(being well compared together), they have not only been disgraced
but degraded. So that now that worshipful work for which you
have been so much magnified by the masculines, being now called
into question by a feminine jury of women, it is thought after a true
and just examination thereof to be merely vilified and that it is
nothing but a mere scandalous report; and therefore most justly
condemned by the unanimous assent of all our sex. Before whom
your Bartholomew Fair book and most lying lectures hath not only †

† been convented, but arraigned, lawfully convicted, and most justly condemned.

Now because no equal and indifferent censure shall any way justly except at the jury that went upon the cause, they were these: twelve good women and true, which will give you, in order:

The fore-woman who had the first and prime voice, who gave up the verdict, was Sisley set-him-out; Sarah set-on-his-skirts; Kate call-him-to-account; Thomasin tickle-him; Prudence pinch-him,
† Frank firk-him; Bess bind-him; Christian commit-him; Parnel punish-him; Moll make-him-yield; Beatrice banish-him; Helen hang-him.

Now if this be not a competent jury, not to be excepted at, and a legal trial, no way to be revoked, we appeal unto you men, our greatest adversaries and most violent abaters of our injuries.

And yet, further to make the cause more plain and evident of our sides, we thought it good in our better consideration not only to publish unto the world the calumnies and slanders aspersed upon
† us, but our just articles objected against him; and, by comparing them together, to distinguish so betwixt them that the truth may grow apparent.

But first, touching the person who put these foul and calumnious aspersions upon us: if he were a Tailor, most sure he was a woman's
† tailor, or, if so, no good artist; because, not being able to take the measure of a woman's body, much less was he powerful to make a true dimension of her mind – and therein you are gone, Master Taylor. Nay, what artist soever you were (for in one I include all), most of you have wives and children, and love them and are indulgent over them, and wherefore then do you encourage such invectives against us? If you being of yourselves lewd, we be loving;
† we well tutored, you untoward; we familiar, you froward; we doting, and you dogged; and what we get by spinning in the day, you spend in the night and come reeling from the tavern or the ale-house: is the fault ours? or are we worthy any to be blamed for this?

Next in our curious inquisition and search we find him moreover to be no scholar at all, as neither understanding us in our gender, number, nor case, etc.

Not in one gender, for in all the creatures that were ever made
† there is a mutual love and an alternate affection betwixt the male and the female: for otherwise there would be no generation at all. But this most approved consociety by all his industry and endeavour he striveth to annihilate and disannul, forgetting that even he himself
† by the same unity and unanimity had his first original and being.

† Then he faileth in number, by making all of us, in general, not only to be wayward but wicked, tedious but troublesome, lazy but loathsome, with many of the like enormities (and indeed, we know not what his inveterate malice or madness would stretch unto): when, if perchance there may be found a singular number of such

delinquents, yet there may be a plural – and that stretcheth beyond all limit and account – who never transgressed or fell into those gross errors, of which he so satirically accuseth our sex.

But in our cases he is most horrible out, and directly opposeth all the rules of grammar. For instance:

In the nominative, by calling us out of our names; and in the stead of 'maidenly' 'modest' 'matron-like', etc., to brand us with the characters of scolds, vixens, praters, prattlers, and all the abusive epithets that spleen or malice can invent or devise.

In the genitive, by making us to be loose, lascivious, wanton, wilful, inconstant, incontinent, and the mothers of misbegotten children; by which he unadvisedly bringeth himself within the doubtful suspicion of spuriousness and bastardy.                                     †

In the dative, by giving and conferring upon our general sex such strange and almost unheard of aspersions; which, as we have little desired, forgetting that he includeth his mother, sisters, and nieces, daughters – nay, his own bosom wife (if he have any in the same catalogue).

In the accusative, by false calumnies and injust accusation contrary to all scholarship; as ignorant that *Faemineo generi tribuuntur – Propria quae maribus.*                                              †

In the vocative, because it is like to the nominative.

In the ablative, because he striveth to take away our credits, reputations, fame, good name, etc. All which argue and approve that he was in a bad mood, and worse tense, at the writing of those  †
malicious lectures.

A poet sure he could not be: for not one of them but with all his industry strived to celebrate the praises of some mistress or other. As for example: amongst the Greeks, Aristophanes, Menander,  †
etc.; amongst the Romans, Catullus his Lesbia, Gallus his Licoris,  †
and Ovid his Corinna; amongst the Spaniards, George de Monte-  †
mayor his Diana, and Aulius March his Teresa; amongst the  †
Italians, Petrarch his Laura, etc.; and of our own nation, learned  †
Master Spenser his Rosalind, and Sam Daniel his Delia, etc.          †

Now, to make the case more plain and evident of our sides, we have thought it good to publish unto the world those matters of which he was arraigned and now justly convicted. The first was scoffing and taunting at our sex in general. Now who knows not but that quips and scoffs are nothing else but the depraving of the actions of others, the overflowing of wits and the superfluous scums of conceit, and, for the most part, asking others of those errors of  †
which themselves stand most guilty: and he that playeth the scoffing fool best, though it may be in him a sign of some wit, yet it is an argument of no wisdom at all. Adders keep their venom in their tails, but the poison of a buffoon lieth in his tongue; and faults wilfully committed by mocking cannot be satisfied or recompensed by repentance. But better it is for a man to be born foolish than to

employ his wit unwisely: for mockery is nothing else but an artificial injury; and we find by proof that there be more mockers than well-meaners, and more that delight in foolish prating than that practise themselves in wholesome precepts. We must confess that to jest is tolerable but to do harm by jesting is insufferable: so it is too late to prevent ill after ill committed, or to amend wrong after injury received. Many things that are sweet in the mouth may prove bitter in the stomach, and scoffs pleasant to the ear may be harsh to the better understanding. But whosoever shall undertake in his curiosity of wit to deride an innocent, either with flattery or foolery, shall but delude himself in his own insufficiency and folly: for as the fairest beauty may prove faulty so even the wittiest scoff may prove ridiculous. And notwithstanding all those fools' bolts so fondly aimed and so suddenly shot, we have this sentence from one of the wise men to comfort us: that loss which is sustained with modesty is much better than the gain purchased by impudence. Nay, to be accounted a prince's jester is to be esteemed no better than a mere mercenary fool. And this railer being in a lower rank, as having dependence upon none but his own defamatory pen, what epithet bad enough may we devise to confer upon him? But we † remember thus much since we first read our accidence:

Quae vult, quae non vult audiet
Thus Englished:
He that to speak will not forbear,
More than he would have spoke shall hear.

The second thing of which he standeth convicted is detraction † and slander; which is the superfluity of a cankered heart overcome with choler, and, wanting means and opportunity of desired revenge, grows into scandalous and reproachful speeches: the testates of Hate and Malice; whose condition is to call Innocence into question, though not able to prove aught against it. And such are worse to us than vipers, for those when we spy we kill them, but these when we cherish they kill us. It is observed that the corrupt heart discovereth itself by the lewd tongue, and those that speak evil of women are held no better than monsters amongst good men: but such for the most part who seek to bring others into hatred have in process of time grown odious even to themselves. But such may be compared to him which bloweth the powder that flusheth into his own face and troubleth his seeing. Nay, such are said to murder three at once: first, himself; next, him that gives ear to his scandals and reports them after him; and lastly, him whose good name he seeketh to take away; not considering that nature hath bestowed upon us two ears and two eyes yet but one tongue, which is emblem unto us, that though we hear and see much yet ought we to speak but little. They that keep their tongues, keep their friends: for few words cover much wisdom, and even fools being silent have passed for wise men. But the proverb is: that even those that but listen or give encouragement to scandal or mis-report deserve to lose their hearing, if not their ears.

And therefore, gentle reader, believe not every smooth tale that is told, neither give too much credit to the plaintiff before you hear the defendant['s] apology for himself; lest through light trust thou be deceived, and by thy too easy belief manifestly deluded.

But it is the fashion of all these calumniating coxcombs to bite those by the back whom they know not how to catch by the bellies.

The third thing objected, and proved, upon him is palpable lying: against which the Egyptians made a law, that whoso used it should not live; the like did the Scythians, the Garamantes, the Persians † and the Indians. Now, how much he hath belied the worthiness of our sex – I appeal to any understanding reader, who hath perused his books, if he have not branded us with many a false and palpable untruth, as shall be made more apparent hereafter when we come to the enrolling of his books and anatomizing his *Lectures*. But it is an † old said saw, and a true: we cannot better reward a liar than in not † believing anything he speaketh. So odious is the very name that, in the opinion of many, a thief may be preferred before him. For it is his property to take upon him the habit and countenance of honesty, that he may the more secretly insinuate and more subtlely deceive by his knavery.

He was indicted also of heresy and false opinion, which hath power to make men arm themselves one against another and all of them against us. It is born of wind and fed by imagination; never judging rightly of anything as it is indeed but as it seems to be; making what is probable improvable, and impossibilities possibilities. Nay, it is of such force that it overthroweth the love betwixt man and wife, father and child, friend and friend, master and servant. Nay more, it is as the spring and fountain of sedition: and who knows not but all sedition is evil, how honest soever the ground be pretended.

And last of perjury, in making breach of that oath which he made when he was first married. For in the stead of taking his wife to have and to hold, for better and worse, 'with my body I thee worship, with all my worldly goods I thee endow,' etc., he hath run a course clean contrary to all this in taunting and scoffing, baiting and abusing, railing and reviling at all our sex in general; from which number even his wife to whom he vowed all the former and who nightly sleepeth, or ought to sleep, in his bosom is not excluded. Or say that she was of a perverse and turbulent spirit, a crabbed or cursed condition, or a dissolute and devilish disposition; say that she was given to gadding and gossipping, to revelling or rioting (so that he might very well sing 'I cannot keep my wife at home'); or say that, not without just cause, she might make him jealous: what

is this to the generality of the female gender? One swallow makes
not a summer: nor for the delinquency of one are all to be delivered
† up to censure. As there was a Lais, so there was a Lucrece; and a
† wise Cornelia as there was a wanton Corinna. And the same sex that
hath bred malefactors hath brought forth martyrs.

And this is an argument which we might amplify even from the
original of all history; nay, and would not spare to do it, had we but
the benefit of your breeding.

† But it hath been the policy of all parents, even from the
beginning, to curb us of that benefit, by striving to keep us under
and to make us men's mere vassals even unto all posterity. How else
comes it to pass that, when a father hath a numerous issue of sons
and daughters, the sons forsooth they must be first put to the
grammar school, and after perchance sent to the university, and
trained up in the liberal arts and sciences, and there (if they prove
not block-heads) they may in time be book-learned. And what do
they then? Read the poets perhaps, out of which, if they can pick
out anything maliciously devised or malignantly divulged by some
mad muse, discontented with his coy or disdainful mistress, then in
imitation of them he must devise some passionate elegy and pitiful
† 'ay-me'. And, in the stead of picking out the best poets who have
strived to right us, follow the other who do nothing but rail at us:
thinking he hath done his mistress praise, when it may be he hath no
† mistress at all but only feigns to himself some counterfeit Phyllis or
† Amaryllis – such as had never any person, but a mere airy name.
And against them he must volley out his vain enthusiasms and
raptures to the disgrace and prejudice of our whole sex.

When we, whom they style by the name of 'weaker vessels',
though of a more delicate, fine, soft and more pliant flesh, and
therefore of a temper most capable of the best impression, have not
† that generous and liberal education lest we should be made able to
† vindicate our own injuries: we are set only to the needle, to prick
our fingers; or else to the wheel to spin a fair thread for our own
undoings; or perchance to some more dirty and debased drudgery.
If we be taught to read, they then confine us within the compass of
† our mother's tongue, and that limit we are not suffered to pass; or if
(which sometimes happeneth) we be brought up to music, to
singing and to dancing, it is not for any benefit that thereby we can
† engross unto ourselves, but for their own particular ends – the
better to please and content their licentious appetites when we come
to our maturity and ripeness. And thus, if we be weak by nature,
they strive to make us more weak by our nurture: and, if in degree
of place low, they strive by their policy to keep us more under.

Now, to show we are no such despised matter as you would seem
to make us, come to our first creation: when man was made of the
mere dust of the earth, the woman had her being from the best part
of his body, the rib next to his heart; which difference even in our
complexions may be easily decided. Man is of a dull, earthy and

melancholy aspect, having fallows in his face and a very forest upon †
his chin, when our soft and smooth cheeks are a true representation
of a delectable garden of intermixed roses and lilies.

We grant it for a truth, that as there is no sword made of steel but
it hath iron; no fire made of the sweetest wood but it hath smoke;
nor any wine made of the choicest grapes but it hath lees: so there is
no woman made of flesh but she hath some faults. And I pray you,
are there any men who are not subject to the like frailties?

Others have said that closets of women's thoughts are always
open, and the depth of their hearts hath a string that reacheth to
their tongues. And say this be granted, may we not also say of
men's breasts, that lie unveiled to entertain all vices? And whatsoever they cannot sufficiently twattle with their tongues, they cannot
contain themselves there but they must publish it with their pens:
(one of the grand faults of which our arch adversary at this present
standeth convicted).

I have heard from the mouth of the learned that a fair, beautiful
and chaste woman was the perfect image of her creator, the true
glory of angels, the rare miracle of earth and the sole wonder of the
world. And moreover that the man who is married to a peaceable
and virtuous wife, being on earth hath attained heaven, being in
want hath arrived to wealth, being in woe is possessed of weal, and
being in care enjoyeth comfort. But contrarily of man, whoever
gave such a noble character?

But I will not insist too long upon this argument, though it might
be strong there by the authority both of precedent and history, lest
we might be critically taxed of self-love and flattery. And yet, that
we may make a safe fortification and bulwark against our adversary's so violent assault and battery, give us leave to proceed a little
further.

If we be so contemptible grown either in quality and condition,
in conversation or deportment, in name or nature, how comes it
that so many elaborate pens have been employed in our praise, and
there have been such witty encomiums writ in our commendation?
– such as have swelled volumes and enricheth libraries. What odes,
hymns, love-songs and laudatories, in all kind of sweet measure and †
number, have not been by poets devised to extol the beauties and
virtues of their mistresses? What power have they not called upon?
And what muse not invoked, that they might give them their full
meed and merit? By which only, divers have attained to the honour †
of the laurel amongst all nations, tongues and language, in all
frequency from antiquity. Were it a thing new or rare, or of late
birth, it perhaps might be called into some suspicion and question:
but carrying with it the reverence of age, antiquity and custom,
what can we hold him but some novice in knowledge and child in
understanding, that shall presume or dare any kind of way to
contradict it?

But there are many malevolent and ill-disposed persons who,

having by all crafty and subtle trains insidiated the chastities as well of maids as matrons – making no distinction betwixt wives and matrons; who, being disappointed in their ill purpose by the virtues of those good women whom they thought to vitiate, have presently grown into such a passionate fury and melancholy madness that, having no other means to revenge themselves, they have studied
† how by their tongues to trouble them or by their pens to traduce them. And so, whose bodies they could not compass, their good names they would corrupt; and of such this age affords too many, which, alas the while, makes a great sort of us much to suffer in our
† reputations. But we again comfort ourselves with this poor cordial: that, of sufferance cometh ease; and, though truth may be blamed, yet can never be shamed.

Others there are who of their ill fortune hath been to light upon a bad match, a shrew, a wanton, or the like (as there are of all sorts in all sexes). They set down their rest there and seek no farther, but measure all other men's corn by their own bushel, as thinking none can be rich because he himself is a bankrupt: which is just as if a man that by chance shall cut his finger should ever after refuse the use of a knife; or, having scorched his hand, swear never to warm him at the fire; or, having been pinched with a strait shoe, vow all his life-time to go barefoot.

Further, if we were such toys and trifles, or so vile and vicious, as our adversary striveth to make the world believe we are, how comes
† this seeking, this suing; this courting, this cogging; this prating, this protesting; this vowing, this swearing – but only to compass a smile, a kind look, a favour or a good word from one of us? Can any be so simple to seek his affliction? Or so sottish to sue for his own ruin? What fool would trouble himself to find his own torment? Or what coxcomb pursue his own confusion? Is he not worse than frantic that desires his own fall? And more than a mad man that hunteth after his own misery? Then, by consequence, if
† we be apish and waggish, wilful and wanton, such cares, such burdens, such troubles, such torments, such vexation, such ser-
† pents, such sirens, or such may-games, or rather monsters, as you would make of us – why cannot you let us alone and leave us to our own weakness and imperfections? If, then, seeing such palpable danger before your eyes, and you wilfully run into it; if you see hell gates open, and you violently enter them: are you not more simple
† than babes and children? – nay, than fools, coxcombs, frantics and mad men: epithets, attributes not without your own guilt most justly and deservedly thrown upon you.

And much good may they do you: I pray you wear them for our sakes as the best favours you have merited from us. Whilst we in the interim strive to vindicate our sex from all vainly supposed, but voluntary suggested, calumnies.

We have heard of a Gunpowder Treason plotted by men, but

never heard since the beginning of the world such a devilish and damned stratagem devised by women. And yet you are the masculine milk-sops that dare do nothing, and we the feminine undertakers that dare to enterprise all things! Can you read of any female guilty of the like inhuman acts? Or was anyone of our sex ever nominated to be conscious of traitorous conspiracy against their †
king and country? Nay, rather, women have been sorry that through the lusts and importunity of men they have been forced to be the mothers of such monsters. And therefore, Sir Seldom Sober, it may be presupposed that, when you writ this bitter invective, you were either in your holiday and hiccup healths, in your boozing cups and bouncing cans, and had got a politic pot in your pate, or †
you were else in your deadly dumps and drowsy dreams, which †
were so violent at that time upon you that they made you destitute of knowledge and quite void of understanding.

It is further known that, when men, out of their vain ambitious fooleries, have commenced war one against the other, when a city hath been besieged and the faint-hearted men have been ready to give it up to spoil and ransack, the women have stood up, manned and maintained the walls, and stopped and defended the breaches (whilst your brave male martialists have been ready to beray *their* †
breeches) – beat the enemy out of their trenches, saved their selves from prostitution, their city from desolation and their husbands and children from captivity and bondage.

Nay more, it is authentically recorded that when two provinces of Greece fought together, and the one party fled and gave way to the enemy, the wives and mothers of these which were distressed stopped them in their flight: and showing themselves naked above the navel, called unto them and rated them for their cowardice, demanding of them whether they went to cover themselves in the places from whence they first came and were first conceived, and to be buried where they were born. At which sight they were so abashed and ashamed that they took fresh courage; and, turning their faces from them upon the enemy, they gained thereby a great and glorious victory.

Some do accuse us to be much given to lying; indeed, I must confess it to be a fault in the most of the best wives. Yet I would have our detractor to know that every excuse is not a lie, or, if it be, then are most husbands beholding to their wives for excusing them too often in lying to save their credits. For alas, poor wretches, we are fain to hide and cover their faults and imperfections with our poor excuses; as for example: if one of them be cruel, crabbed, and currish that he will snap, snarl and bite with his dogged language and conditions, then the poor woman (like a fool) reports him to be a kind, loving and affectionate husband; *ergo*, she lies. Another knows her husband to be a wicked whore-hunter and that he doth, in a manner, keep a trull or two under her nose; yet she will say her † husband is a very honest man: *ergo*, she lies too. A third spends most of his time in drinking or gaming, and his poor wife is so kind as to acknowledge him for a good, painful, sober and civil husband: and I am sure she lies abominable. I could insist further into such particulars, but these are sufficient to show that the most part of women being liars is only out of their goodness to cover the faults and abuses of wicked men.

Whereas they tax us of incivility, I would have any indifferent man or woman to take notice that it is a very hard winter when one † wolf doth eat another, or when the kill doth upbraid the oven for being burnt. For though we do not brag or prate (like the boasting † vain-glorious Pharisee) that we are not like other folks in condi- † tions, or, in a word, not worthy to compare with men for their unknown invisible good parts and qualities, yet surely we neither can, or do, run head-long into such impious enormities, with such uncontrollable violence, as they do: as if they were created for no other use or purpose than to swear, blaspheme, quarrel, be drunk, † game, roar, whore, murder, steal, cheat – and, in brief, to be daily practisers and proficients in the most liberal seven deadly sins. And these are the excellent civil behaviours of those man-like monsters that do tax women generally with incivility.

If women be proud, or addicted to pride, it is ten to one to be laid that it is the men that makes them so. For like enchanters they do never leave or cease to bewitch and charm poor women with their flatteries, persuading us that our beauty is incomparable: our † complexion of white and red like strawberries and cream; our cheeks like damask roses covered with a veil of lawn; our lips are coral, our teeth ivory, our hairs gold, our eyes crystal, or suns or loadstars or love's darts; our glances lances; our voices, our breaths perfumed music; our virtues immortal; and our whole frame, feature and composure celestial.

When I was a young maid of the age of fifteen, there came to me † in the wooing way very many of those fly-blown, puff-paste suitors. Amongst the rest, one of them was as brave a gentleman as any tailor could make him. He underwent the noble title of a captain, etc. If I had made trial of him, I doubt not but I might have found him a most desperate chamber champion, for he did scent of the musk-cat instead of the musket; he was an ambergris gallant that † once was a valiant tilting rush-breaker at the marriage of the Lady † Josinqua, daughter to the Duke of Calabria. Verily, he was a dainty † perfumed carpet captain, a powdered potentate, a painted periwig- † frizzled, frounced, geometrical curious glass-gazer, a combed, † curled and curried commander, a resolute professed chaser or † hunter of fashions, and a most stiff, printed, bristled beard- starcher.

† This Captain Compliment, with his Page Implement, laid hard siege to the weak fortress of my frail carcass: he would swear that

his life or death were either in my accepting or rejecting his suit; he would lie and flatter in prose, and cog and foist in verse most † shamefully. He would sometimes salute me with most delicious sentences, which he always kept in syrup, and he never came to me empty-mouthed or handed. For he was never unprovided of stewed anagrams, baked epigrams, soused madrigals, pickled roundelays, † broiled sonnets, parboiled elegies, perfumed posies for rings, and a † thousand other such foolish flatteries and knavish devices – which I suspected; and the more he strived to overcome me or win me with oaths, promises and protestations, still the less I believed him: so that at last he grew faint at the siege, gave over to make any more assaults and, vanquished with despair, made a final retreat. In like manner I wish all women and maids in general to beware of their gilded glosses: an enamoured toad lurks under the sweet grass, and a fair tongue hath been too often the varnish or embroidery of a false heart. What are they but lime-twigs of lust and school-masters † of folly? Let not their foolish fancy prove to be your brain-sick frenzy. For if you note them, in all their speech or writings, you shall seldom or never have any word or syllable in the praise of goodness or true virtue to come from them. Their talk shall consist either of wealth, strength, wit, beauty, lands, fashions, horses, hawks, hounds, and many other trivial and transitory toys; which, as they may be used, are blessings of the left hand, wherewith they † entice and entrap poor silly, young, tender-hearted females to be enamoured of their good parts (if they had any). But if men would lay by their tricks, sleights, falsehoods and dissimulations, and, contrarily, in their conversing with us use their tongues and pens in the praise of meekness, modesty, chastity, temperance, constancy and piety, then surely women would strive to be such as their discourses did tend unto. For we do live in such an age of pollution † that many a rich wicked man will spend willingly and give more to corrupt and make spoil of the chastity and honour of one beautiful untainted virgin, than they will bestow, in charity, towards the saving of an hundred poor people from perishing by famine here or from perdition in a worser place. And because they say women will † always lie I do wish that, in this last point I touched upon, they would make or prove me a liar.

Who but men have been the authors of all mischiefs? Had that fire-brand of Troy, Paris, not stolen Helen from her husband King Menelaus, surely she had remained a wife in Sparta and never been strumpeted in Phrygia: the ten years' siege and sacking of Ilion was † never sought by women but wrought by men. Who but men are traitors, apostates, irreligious sectaries and schismatics? Alas, alas – these are vessels of vices and villainies which the weak hands or brains of women could never broach. Who but men are extortioners, usurers, oppressors, thieves, perjured persons and knights of the post? Who but men do write, print, divulge and scatter libels, †

† rhymes, songs and pasquils against the known truth, against sovereign authority, against all law, equity and conformity to loyalty? Who but men have and do set forth pestiferous pamphlets, emblems and pictures of scurrility and nasty obsceneness? I am sure
† that Ovid and Aretine were no women, nor was there ever any woman found to be the authoress of such base and vile inventions.

In one of their late, wise, ridiculous lectures, they do cast an
† aspersion upon us that we are mighty gossips and exceeding scolds. To the first, I answer that the most part of our meetings at gossippings are long of the men rather than to be imputed to us: for when children are born into the world, although men feel none of the wifery, yet women have a more known sympathy and feeling of one another's pains and perils: and therefore, in Christianity and neighbourly love and charity, women do meet to visit and comfort the weakness of such as in these dangerous times do want it. And whereas they say that we tipple and tittle-tattle more than our shares, I shall, before this discourse is ended, cast that ball back
† again in their teeth, and emblaze them truly to be most vain and idle talkers – and that no living thing created is so sottish, senseless, brutish and beastly, as most of them have been, and are, daily, nightly and hourly in their drink: for their much talk (to no
† purpose) doth show that there is a running issue or fistula in their minds.

Men might consider that women were not created to be their slaves or vassals: for as they had not their original out of his head (thereby to command him), so it was not out of his foot to be trod upon, but out of a *medium* – out of his side to be his fellow-feeler, his equal and companion. But as the devil can be, at one time, both the Prince of Darkness and an Angel of Light, so can these double-hearted men bear fire in one hand and water in the other: so that one knows not where to have them nor how to find them,
† being neither hot or cold but like luke-warm Laodiceans.

For many of them are like the cinnamon tree: their rind better than the trunk. They are – too many of them – rare Doctors of Devility, crafty merchants, whose wares are flatteries, congees,
† cringes, compliments, legs, faces, and mimic marmosetical gestures, and are fitter by half for stamps to coin any current wickedness than any women can be.

Everything – but man – doth naturally incline to be in his proper place, as for example: lead, stones, or any ponderous or weighty matter or metal will sink down, fire doth mount upwards, rivers run to the sea, trees to the earth and fowls to the air. Everything doth seek to be in his natural place constantly; only men are inconstant, and seldom or never doth keep his constant course. Nay, the very beasts and unreasonable creatures are his school-masters and go beyond him in goodness. He may learn meekness of the lamb, simplicity of the dove, diligence of the ants, kindness of

the stork, memory of the ox and ass, fidelity of the dog, watchfulness of the cock, subtlety of the serpent, magnanimity of the lion: the eagle, or vulture, doth go beyond him in sight or seeing; the dog surpasseth him in the sense of smelling; stags, hares and birds do outgo him in swiftness; horses and elephants in strength; and crows or ravens in length of life. Besides, everything – except man – hath the wit to shun and avoid danger – as sheep will run from the wolf, the cat from the dog, the hare from the hound, the rat from the cat, the chick from the kite and the dove from the hawk: but man will not avoid wickedness nor run from the devil. He is also so voracious and insatiate that though a park will satisfy an herd of deer, a meadow will suffice many cows and a bull, a field will serve horses, a forest will feed wild beasts and fowls, the earth doth content worms and vermin, the sea contains fishes: and man – only man – is never contented. His ingurgitating maw is the sepulchre of †
fishes, fowls, beasts, herbs, fruits, roots, and all things else, whatsoever that his rapine can prey upon. Besides, he hath in him the pride of the horse, the lion's fierceness, the wolf's ravening, the dog's biting: more addicted to truculency than the bear, more obstinate than the ox, more beastly rash than the boar, more various than the leopard, more mutable than the chameleon, as deceitful as the fox, as desperate as the elephant, fearful as a hare, revengeful as the camel, as lascivious as the goat, as full of scoffing and jeering as an ape, as uncleanly as a sow, as silly as a sheep, and as foolish as an ass. This land hath robbed and cheated almost all other nations of their vices, for we have gotten gluttony from Greece, wantonness from Italy, pride from Spain, compliment from France, drunken- †
ness from Germany, infidelity from the Jews, blasphemy from the Turks, idolatry from the Indians, superstition from Rome, sects †
from Amsterdam: errors from all places makes schisms and divisions at home. And these are the rare virtues and admirable qualities of the most part of such men as have, and do daily inveigh and rail against women with their scandalous tongues and infamous abusive libels. And, in a word, to conclude this point: if any man be great in office or dignity, and that he hath uncontrollable power to do what he will, it is a hard matter for him to restrain himself from doing much hurt and little good.

Dogs do naturally bark and snarl at strangers and such as they do not know: and so those men that are ignorant in their malice (or malicious in their ignorance) do reprehend and abuse women, and in their railing they have the uncharitable art to make the small mole-hills of our frailty appear like mountains; and with their inveterate spleen they metamorphose our pigmy faults into huge giants. But let me be so bold, with leave, as to ask them if ever any women were such monsters as Nero, Heliogabalus, Caligula, †
Haman, Julian, Cain, Iscariot, Ahab, Achitophel, Rabsheka, †
Nebuchadnezzar, Holofernes, Jeroboam, Pharoah, Nimrod, †

† Cham, Belshazzar (or Balthaser), Goliath, Esau, Achan, Gehazi,
† Absalom, Manasseh, Sisera, Shimei, Amon, Nabal, Herod,
† Caiaphas, Ananias, Pilate, Elymas, Domitian, Catiline, Sulla,
† Marius, Sardanapalus, and thousands more such commanders,
inventors, maintainers and defenders of mischiefs and all sorts of
wickedness and villainies; of which the stories of their detestable
lives, with their deserved deaths, do make most horrible and
loathed mentions. Nor hath these kingdoms of England and
Scotland been always clear from the tyranny of such – as the
chronicles will witness of Macbeth and Richard the third; and I am
sure that women were not the complotters or contrivers of the
Powder Treason; nor ever did any woman devise projects and
† monopolies.

Thus anyone, that hath but common sense or reason in him, may
perceive that those who so bitterly rail against women do forget that
women were their mothers, or that they had their birth, or
† secondary original being, from women. I will not be so lavishly or
unmannerly invective against men, but that amongst them there
hath been – and are, and I am not out of hope there will always be –
many of that noble sex that do scorn and despise those scurrilous,
† sordid libels: who are no better than the devil's pen-posts; that have
the art to write by rote and rail at random, without regard of truth
or equity (for a just and wise man deems nothing to be reasonable
that hath not equity in it); whose sweet, stinking, poetical verses
runs all manner of feet without measure, rhyme or reason – and
Satan's cloven foot withal into the bargain. I touch not any way
† upon good poets, for to them Fortune is blind and, in her blind
† bounty, she returns a small share for Minerva; and vicious great-
ness, golden foppery and silken ignorance are most deadly enemies
to the Muses – as eminent persons do not always carry scales about
them to weigh the merits of deserving men. But I speak of our
† mongrel rhymesters that, with an affectate overweening conceit of
themselves, do imagine that they can cough logic, speak rhetoric,
sneeze grammar, belch poetry, piss geometry, groan music, vomit
† apothegms and squirt oratory. These – and such as these – are the
† most furious and fierce pendragonists; these are the most pestifer-
† ous jacksquitterers that, if they could, would blow and blast the
fame of women. These can change the shapes of their inventions
according as the times and purpose best befits their servile inclina-
tions. For they have all got the theory of well-speaking (when they
please), but if ever they busy themselves with the practice of
well-doing, I will be at the charge to pay for their hanging. For it is
more easy to make a good nimble footman of the running gout than
it is to make one of these an honest man.

Although some few – and those few too many – women do
profess goodness in hypocrisy, yet that is not a general disparagement to such as are truly virtuous in sincerity. For if I may be so

bold as to speak that which is recorded in holy writ, I shall prove presently out of the best authors that ever lived that women have been, and are, and will be, must be and shall be, either men's betters or their equals; or – at the least – not to be so much undervalued as not to be abused, vilified and traduced by every idle and paltry pot-companion.                                                              †

As for the first man, he was made of earth, clay – yea, of the very slime of the earth; also, he was created in the open wide field – as all the rest of earthly creatures were. And being made, I must confess he was perfect, and full of perfection: yet doth his very name demonstrate that he was of a mean and pure substance. For the word, or name, Adam doth signify clay or red earth. But when that earth and slime was purified and made perfect, with being fully possessed with a reasonable soul, then man being in paradise (a most pleasant and delectable place), there in that choicest and principal garden of delight – many being refined from his dross – was woman created. There was she named Eve, or Hevah, which is as much as to say Life, because she was the mother of all men and women that should ever live or have living. She was made out of the side of the man, near to his heart, because he should heartily love her. And as all the rest of the creatures were created before man, to show that he was not brought into a bare and naked world (although himself was so), but it was gloriously and magnificently adorned and beautified with all things fitting for the entertainment of so glorious an image, or deputy to the Greatest, yet in that great state he was alone, without anyone to have a participation or joyful fellow sympathetical feeling of his felicity. Then did it please the great creator to create the noble creature – woman – to be his helper, associate and companion. Therefore I conclude that, as man was made of pollution, earth and slime, and woman was formed out of that earth when it was first refined; as man had his original in the rude wide field, and woman had her frame and composure in †
paradise: so much is the woman's honour to be regarded and to be held in estimation amongst men.

To these few I could add infinite, but I study to avoid prolixity; only I desire of you, Sir Seldom Sober, and the rest of your most pitiful partisans, to be resolved in this one question: how cometh the world to be thus peopled? And whence groweth this goodly generation upon the earth, which from the first creation hath continued to this present, and shall last to all posterity? We are not like these swift Spanish jennets which, some write, engender only †
by the wind, purperated without man. Do we, the despised, sue to †
you, the well-disposed? or, being the vessels, petition to you, the proditors of your fames and honours? When was it known in any †
age that our sex have groaned at your gates and sat waking whole cold winter's nights at your windows? When sonneted to your signiorships or love-lettered to your lordships? when haunted you

in your houses and waylaid you in your walks? These you have
done, and daily and hourly do, to us. And if we have been either
wayward in our words or but counterfeited a coyness in our
countenances, your brave high spirits have been ready to homage
yourselves, nay some have done it really – as thinking to enter the
† strict way by a string. Nay, many times when you are denied the
† game you have offered fees, and by rape to hazard the gallows.

If the husbandman till, plough, sow and harrow his ground, etc.,
it is in hope of an harvest; or if he labour and take pains, it is in hope
of his hire. If the merchant hazard his purse and person by sea, it is
in the expectation of some great gain and profit. And can you wise
men take toil and travail; wake and watch, rise early and go to bed
late; spend your time, wits and money; vow and protest, swear and
forswear; engage your fortunes and endanger your lives; and all
these for wily, wanton, wayward, wicked women? By gaining
whom you can but lose yourselves, and to purchase them cannot be
without your so great prejudice. Most sure, if this cause shall come
before a just judge and have the benefit of a considerate censure, but
we, so much reproved and reviled, shall be acquit by proclamation;
and you, Sir Seldom Sober, with the rest of your railing society, be
found sole guilty of calumny, scandal and most palpable contradiction – your intimations and intents, your proposition and your
purpose, your method and your meaning having no coherence or
correspondence the one to the other.

And therefore we weak women stand up against you mighty men
(for so you think yourselves): when alas we know by proof that
when you brave masculines are at any time encountered by our
feminine sex, even in the first assault, you are as soon tamed as
talked with; and can scarce really tell us you love us but you are as
ready to turn tail and leave us. And yet are not ashamed to animate
yourselves in your own assemblies, and would make the world to
believe that you, the first cowards, are the sole conquerors.

But, forsooth, when you fail in your prowess you think to fit us
in your proverbs (which you privilege by their antiquity); but
indeed they are so stale in their very names that they stink in our
† noses. For example, when the mistress calls up her apprentice, she
saith, if she be crossed, she will make him 'leap at a crust': as if
citizens kept such penurious houses that they were ready upon the
least occasions to starve their servants. Nay, that she, taking her
husband's authority out of his hands, will beat her boy the rogue
and baste the kitchen-maid who rules the roast, till she make their
bones rattle in their skins: and when she hath gotten her will, then
† rattle-baby rattle.

Then, in your lecture of the wife to her husband: 'is the house a
† wild-cat to you?' And why a wild-cat, you tame fool? – unless you
study to set odds betwixt man and wife, and to make them agree in a
house like dogs and cats together.

Then comes in the country farmer's wife, with her couple of capons, when all her she-neighbours dare take their oaths that her husband is a cock of the game. Yet she must call him Francis Furmity-pot, Bernard Bag-pudding or Bacon-face, William Wood- †
cock, Dirty Dotterill or Dunstable, Harry Horse-head, Simon †
Sup-broth, Ralph Roast-a-crow, Tom Turd-in-thy-teeth, and the like beastly and bastardly names, merely of your own dirty devising: as knowing what belongs to yourselves, when we cannot find in our hearts to foul our mouths with any such filthy language.

But sure, Sir Seldom (or never) Sober, your father was some jakes-farmer and your mother a midwife, or he some rake-shame or †
rag-gatherer and she the daughter of a dung-hill, that their son is forced to patch out his poetry with such pitiful proverbs. And cannot we come upon you with the like? and, in tasking of your rudeness, tell you you should have talked 'under the rose'; to †
punish your too much prating, tell you 'little said, soon amended'. In terrifying you from the like troubling of yourself, that 'there is a day to come that shall pay for all'; and to restrain you within some regularity, 'a man may bring his horse to the water but he cannot make him drink'. In not sparing of your spouse-breach, 'there is falsehood of fellowship'. When we shall bury one untoward husband and take another, 'seldom comes the better'. When you fool us with your flatteries, you play with us at 'wily beguile you'. And to conclude with that most learned ballad, sung about the streets and composed by your fellow-poet M.P., 'O such a rogue †
would be hanged'. This we could do, nay this we much care not to do: unless you moderate your flying Muse and mend your manners.

Nay, we could anatomize you into atoms and dissect you into diminutives, to make you less than nothing; but it is the modesty of our madam-ships and the patience that our sex professes to parley before we punish, and to hang up a flag of truce before we offer to tyrannize. But if you take heart and hold out, and seem not sorry at this our first summons, we will not only beat you but batter you, bombast and baffle you, canvass and cudgel you, brave you and †
bastinado you: but leave you to the terrible trophies of our †
victorious triumph and the remarkable memory of your most miserable and unpitied massacre. Yet in all this we do not menace the men but their minds, not their persons but their pens, the horridness of their humours and the madness of their muses – which indeed towards us have been insupportable and intolerable. There-fore be advised, and let us hear either of your public acknowledge-ment or at the least your private recantation, either to us all in general or some in particular, etc.; or we will make thy own pen thy poniard, thy ink thy baneful potion, thy paper thy winding sheet, †
thy standish thy coffin, thy sand-dust thy grave-dust to bury thy †
shallow wit in, with thy face downward: which if we do not, let us forever bear the burden with our faces upwards. †

Now concerning your very passionate but most pitiful poetry, a question may be made: whether you be a land laureate or a marine
† muse; a land poet or a water poet; a scholar or a sculler; of
† Parnassus or Puddle Dock; of Ionia or Ivy Bridge. But howsoever,
† it is not in the compass of our reading that Mnemosyne ever lived at
† Milford Lane, or Terpsichore at Trig Stairs, where they say the devil once took water.

Nay, more than all this – a little further to magnify our sex – are not the four parts of the world, Asia, Africa, Europe and America, deciphered and described under the persons of women and their
† gender? The nine muses, the twelve sibyls, were they not all women? The four cardinal virtues, Justice, Fortitude, Prudence, Temperance, women? The three graces, the handmaids to Venus, women? The three theological virtues, Faith, Hope and Charity, women? Nay, Wisdom itself, is it not Sapientia and figured in the form of a woman? Are not all the arts, sciences and virtues, of whatever quality or condition soever, portrayed in the persons of women? Whither then, I pray you Sir Seldom Sober, were your
† wits wandering, or went a-woolgathering, when you beat your brains about this poor and most pitiful pamphlet? Have we claimed this to ourselves? Nay, rather hath it not been meritoriously conferred upon us by you men? Had you thought yourselves worthy of these noble and brave attributes you would have sequestered them from our sex and celebrated them to yourselves. But those who thought themselves more wiser than you have
† showed yourself in this witty [tale] of these honours (to support and maintain which they thought themselves too weak), have both by their words and writings thought us worthy.

Now, whether is the greater approbation for any cause in
† question, or for any person convented to be acquitted: by one single man or by a whole senate? by a private, censorious and supercilious cynic than by a full, free and general assembly?

Besides, we claim a further privilege, that is, to be tried by our peers; and grant us but that and then, besides kaisers and kings, princes and potentates, sovereigns and subjects, court, city, camp and country, we have the graces and the goddesses, the nymphs and
† the meriads, the virgins, the vestals, the wives, the widows, the country wench, the countess, the laundress, the lady, the maid-
† marian, the matron, even from the shepherdess to the sceptre: all ready to give up their voices of our sides – that his *Crab-tree* cudgel
† oil and his *Juniper* sauce lecture is false, foolish, sottish, superfluous, railing, ridiculous, absurd, nay more, abominable.

All sentences and condemnations go by a jury of twelve, and they too ought not only to be of understanding but good men and true: and shall the generality of our sex be convented and convicted by one poor ignorant silly sot? Then we may say (and not to our small
† grief) that the woman called Astraea, otherwise called Justa, hath

flown up to heaven and left no justice abiding upon the earth. Had
she been still our judgess she would, no doubt, have censured: that
as men have heretofore had the liberty to take many wives, so
women might have now the privilege every one to take two
husbands at least; till they could find any one woman who could
meet with two men of the same mind with this Gregory, who †
would make himself a grand juryman. (But read the wise woman's
*Juniper*, and she will jerk him for this.) †

But were there now surviving to vindicate our virtues any of the
ancient Greek poetesses, a Nicostrate or Caripena, a Mucia or a †
Meroe, a Sosipatra or a Cleitagora, an Aspasia Milesia or Praxilla †
Syconia, a Myro Byzantia or Corinna Thebana; or amongst the †
Romans, an Hortensia or Hipparchia, a Claudia or a Cornelia, †
Apollo Argentaria or Proba Valeria, a Vittoria Collumna or Marcel- †
la Romana, etc.: if, I say, any of these were now surviving, what a †
pitiful thing would they make of this petulant poet. And with one
of their invective iambics, to despair and hang himself; and in the
stead of a Juniper, read unto him a gibbet lecture.

How have you stuffed your store-house with a catalogue of
common prostitutes and courtesans, which made me think when I
first saw your book it had been the register of Bridewell. And I pray †
you, who vitiated them but you that would seem the virtuous? and
who corrupted them, but you the male crocodiles? Was there ever †
Gill without her Jack, or Flirts without her Franion? As parents †
lose the names of father and mother when their issue fails them, and †
children are no more sons and daughters when they have no parents
to protect them, so it is not possible that the world could yield
anyone branded with the name of a whore but there must be a
whore-master to make her so. Moreover, there was never strumpet
but had her pimp to usher her, nor any madam mackerel without a †
pander to man her.

You tell us a great many stories, and to small purpose, of Helen
an harlot, who had no doubt lived in honest life with Menelaus her
husband had there not been a bold-faced Paris to betray her; of a
Lais, a famous courtesan in Corinth, who valued every night's
lodging at a thousand drachmas. And why did she set so high a price
upon her prostitution? but the better to conserve her chastity and
fright away libidinous fools from hunting her habitation. And so of
the rest, by which any indifferent reader may perceive that all things
make with us which you maliciously have suggested against us.

I will not meddle with your pitiful poetry and rhyme dotterel,
borrowed out of ballads: and yet why should I say borrowed, when
I can answer them in this one distich: †

Though borrowing now be into fashion grown,
Yet I dare swear, what thou writ'st was thy own.

For indeed, I know not who else will challenge them.

In your lecture of an old rich widow to a young gallant, where you think to task her of her wit, what do you else but approve her wisdom? – who will not suffer her modest gravity to be fooled by his youthful prodigality. And so what you strive to condemn as a vice, in effect you crown for a virtue.

† You make your country farmer's wife to call wiseacres her husband wittol, Mopus and mooncalf, Hobbinot and hobnails, lourden and looby, Francis Fill-gut and Furmity-pot, booby and blockhead, dunce and dotard, bull-beef, barley-pudding, Sim Slobber-chops, and the like. And like enough he may be all these, and
† she in this gives but the devil his due and the clownish Corydon his own true character. And what disparagement can this be to us? Or what great honour to you of the male sex, that amongst men there can be found such a monster?

Can you blame the jealous woman for having such care over her husband's health, purse and person? For what is jealousy but a too much indulgence and over-love? And I fear ten, at this time, of twenty are not much troubled with it.

Your lecture of your kind loving wife to her husband we allow, and none so shameless in their slanders but sometimes or other are constrained to tell truth and shame the devil: and if you had only followed the same theme you might have escaped from being thus threatened. But many who have strived to make have marred, and
† in shunning Scylla have fallen into Charybdis; and this our impudent poet hath imitated such ignorant pilots: where, if he had had the skill to steer his vessel in the mild channel, he might have arrived at an happy harbour and so escaped that shame and ship-wreck
† which his silliness hath made him to suffer. Had Icarus in his flight kept an equal distance betwixt the sea and the sun, the one had not melted his wax nor the other moistened his wings, nor he been made a wretched prey to the waters.

In your widow's lecture to your widower, what terms doth she use but of your teaching? and what dirty language but of your own devising? I thought you would have told us a tale wherein you might have made them equal sharers in their own simplicity, which was to this effect:

A widower and his widow sitting at supper with a good joint of meat together, and falling into some cross words (before they had
† tasted a bit of it – and having both good stomachs), a poor man came to the door to beg an alms for God's sake. The man, not knowing which way more to vex his wife, called to his servant and,
† cutting the meat in the middle, laid one half upon his trencher and said: 'Here take this and carry it to the poor man, and bid him pray for the soul of my former wife'. Which seeing, she said nothing; but when the servant was returned she took the other half that was in the dish and gave it unto him, saying 'And I pray thee carry this to

the poor man, and desire him to pray for the soul of my first husband'. By which means both themselves and their servants were forced to go to bed supperless. Now here the blame nor burden could be great, because it was borne upon equal shoulders. But you, as in all the rest, make the woman only to rail and the man, like so many silly sots, to make no reply at all: as if we were all mad, they milk-sops and meacocks; we froward, they foolish; we either †
sheepish or shrewish, and they only simple and sottish; which how false it is, and far from any probability of truth, common experience can testify. For whosoever shall observe his style and method shall find that what he so much boasts of he hath borrowed from the basest of our sex, as being in all his tinkerly terms more foul-tongued than a fish-wife and more open-mouthed than any oyster- †
wench.

A word or two more concerning the virtue and chastity of women: there was never any man could generally compare with women. To speak of the best and most blest – the one and only Virgin Mother, she that was at one time maid, mother, wife, child and sister to her son; she that most happily was elected from all eternity to be the blessed bringer forth of a saviour for all repenting and true believing sinners: she was so fully filled and replenished with grace that she is justly styled 'blessed amongst women', and for a further proclaiming of her happiness, 'All generations shall call her blessed'. She was the world's only wonder and most rare and sovereign mirror of chastity. Many thousands more are mentioned for that only famous virtue of continency in divine and profane histories, whose honourable and venerable memories shall outlive time and flourish in glorious eternity. Besides, as there have been, and are, innumerable of our noble sex that have lived and died virgins, so likewise millions of them who have been married, and after marriage became widows, they have been so inclined to the love of chastity that they would never be won to accept of a second marriage. And for an inimitable example of a worthy matron, it is recorded that Anna the prophetess was but seven years a married †
wife, but that after her husband was dead she lived a widow fourscore and four years: an example above any you men can show.

Moreover women were so chaste that, though they did marry and were married, it was more for propagation of children than for any carnal delight or pleasure they had to accompany with men. They were content to be joined in matrimony with a greater desire of children than of husbands; they had more joy in being wives: for in the old law it was a curse upon women to be barren. And surely, if †
there had been any lawful way for them to have had children without husbands, there hath been, and are, and will be, a †
numberless number of women that would or will never be troubled with wedlock nor the knowledge of man. Thus good and modest women have been content to have none, or one man, at the most, all

their whole life-time, but men have been so addicted to incontinency that no bounds of law or reason could restrain them. For if we
read the story of the Kings of Judah there we may find the wisest
that ever reigned (Solomon) had no fewer than three hundred wives
and seven hundred concubines; and that his son, Rehoboam, had
eighteen wives and sixty concubines, by whom he begat twenty-
eight sons and threescore daughters. There have been some good
women that, when they could have no children, they have been
contented that their husbands should make use of their maid-
† servants – as Sarah and Rachel and Leah did – but I never heard or
read of any man that, though he were old, diseased, decrepit,
gouty, or many and every way defective and past ability to be the
father of any child, that hath been so loving to his wife as to suffer
her to [be] made a teeming mother by another man …

[It seems an unnecessary compliment to reprint *The Women's Sharp
Revenge* in full. The work declines into a ragbag of anecdotes. Taylor
seems to exhaust himself on the subject of women and to return to his
constant satirical attacks on drunkenness. There is plenty of further
evidence for Taylor's authorship here, with words and phrases that can be
paralleled in his other works. He is particularly given away by his lists of
drinking slang which find close echoes in, for example, *The Water-
Cormorant His Complaint* and the *Arrant Thief*.

Only some notion of scholarly completeness could justify reprinting the
whole of *WSR* (and even that may be impossible, since the Bodleian
Library copy is not complete). Frankly I think it is a waste of time and
space to print any more of it. Furthermore, it seems proper in a volume
devoted to women's writing to cut short a man's attempt spuriously to
insert his presence. The women should take *their* sharp revenge. (I will
gladly supply any interested reader with the edited text and notes of what
remains unpublished.)

## NOTES

PAGE 159
**Hit-him-home**: the name Hannah Hit-him-home is invented as part of a list of
   aggressive or troublesome female types in the Epistle to *Divers Crabtree
   Lectures*.

PAGE 161
**prate**: boast, chatter.
**congees**: bows (in greeting).
**Baal**: heathen god.

PAGE 162
**antipodes**: places on earth directly opposite each other; hence topsy-turvy.
**Make-peace**: the invented name of the woman who writes a prefatory poem to the
   *Juniper Lecture*. (Tattle-well is similarly formed.)
**Gander-month**: the month after the woman's confinement, when the man, at a
   'loose end', can play around.

PAGE 162 CONTINUED
**Long Meg of Westminster**: a legendary figure who ran a pub and beat up any men who were braggarts or bullies; this poem summarises the main features of her career; pamphlets (and a play) about her began appearing from the early 1580s.

PAGE 163
**Front**: confront.
**frighted fencers**: may be a reference to the lost play, more likely a reference to the *Swetnam* play which did not feature Meg but did have Swetnam humiliated as a fencer. Meg underlies or is referred to by a number of the portrayals of 'strong' women: her appearance here is appropriate and sets the tone.

PAGE 164
**Proteus**: a classical divinity who could change shape at will.
**doom**: fate, destiny.
**sir-reverence**: respect (from 'sir'); also shit.
**Wormwood lecture**: there is no record of this – it may have been invented on the basis of the names of the other two (juniper is medicinal but prickly, crab and wormwood both bitter). There is a marginal note here: 'And a new lecture, called the Bolster Lecture': this appeared in 1640, written by Philogenes Panedonius (Richard Brathwait), apparently to 'silence a Canopy Lecture'.

PAGE 165
**blazed**: proclaimed (usually of a bad reputation).
**shifts**: tricks, stratagems.
**woman's reputation**: this is quite close to Sowernam's analysis. If it is a custom-made pamphlet, that presupposes an audience for this sort of thinking.
**common town bull**: phrase used in *Juniper Lecture*, p. 63; see also Anger, p. 34.
**courses**: (religious) assemblies.
**high commissions**: an Elizabethan ecclesiastical court (abolished 1641).
**trick of youth**: a Sowernam phrase.
**tiffany**: fine woven silken gauze.
**lawn**: fine woven linen or cotton.
**buff**: leather; compare Taylor's phrase 'as tough as a buff jerkin' in *Wit and Mirth* (1635).
**as**: often used here for 'such as', 'for example'.
**back-friend**: false friend *or* backer.
**Bartholomew Fair**: fair held on 24 August; when used to describe anything it implies triviality.

PAGE 166
**arraigned**: compare the arraignments of Swetnam.
**Frank**: Frances.
**Parnel**: prostitute.
**articles**: the various charges of an accusation.
**woman's tailor**: a type of unmanliness (sounds odd coming from 'female' authors).
**froward**: perverse, refractory.
**alternate**: reciprocal.
**original**: beginning, derivation.
**in general**: the complaint against slander, talking against all women rather than particular cases, is common among women at this period.

PAGE 167
**spuriousness**: illegitimacy of birth.
**Faemineo ... maribus**: this phrase is used in the Epistle to *Divers Crabtree Lectures* where it is loosely translated as 'though the Feminine gender be troublesome, let

PAGE 167 CONTINUED

us seek to please proper men, lest they bring us down upon our Maribones'. (The phrase also appears in Taylor's *A Common Whore* (1622).)

**bad mood**: same joke in *Common Whore*.

**Aristophanes**: (*c.* 450–385 BC) comic dramatist.

**Menander**: (*c.* 342–289 BC) his plays often had love plots.

**Catullus**: (84–54 BC) erotic poet (**Lesbia**: real name Clodia).

**Gallus**: (born *c.* 69 BC) wrote four books of love elegies, friend of Augustus and Virgil (**Licoris**: real name Cytheris, an actress).

**Ovid**: (43–17 BC) one of the most influential of Roman satiric and love poets.

**de Montemayor**: (1519–61) his *Diana* is a pastoral prose romance.

**Aulius March**: Ausias March (?1397–1459) wrote poems reflecting on the death of his second wife Joana Scorna.

**Petrarch**: (1304–74) made very influential use of sonnet form.

**Spenser**: (?1552–99) Colin Clout, Spenser's spokesman in *The Shepheardes Calendar*, loves **Rosalind**.

**Daniel**: (1562–1619) *Delia* is the name of his sonnet sequence.

**asking**: examining, investigating.


PAGE 168

**accidence**: basic principles of grammar.

**cankered**: polluted, diseased.


PAGE 169

**Scythians**: Scythia could indicate an enormous area of central Asia or North Europe.

**Garamantes**: a nation of inner Africa.

**enrolling**: officially recording.

**saw**: saying, proverb.


PAGE 170

**Lais**: (fl. *c.* 360 BC), one of the most famous whores (from Corinth).

**Lucrece**: (d. 510 BC), killed herself to preserve her honour after being raped.

**Cornelia**: (fl. 180 BC), daughter of Scipio Africanus – as a widow managed her estate, educated her children and wrote a prose style admired by Cicero.

**Corinna**: the woman Ovid writes to (there was also a poet of this name).

**policy ... parents**: what follows is a useful critique of educational discrimination (one of the things the female authors had to overcome). Helpful also is the characterisation of a specifically male reading matter and cultural production – this theme runs through all the pamphlets.

**ay-me**: tag phrase denoting a sort of melancholic poetry.

**Phyllis, Amaryllis**: archetypal pastoral names.

**liberal**: cultivated, as against the 'mechanical' activities of women; the context virtually implies men have a higher-*class* education.

**needle**: the archetypal women's work, explicitly rejected by most independent-minded female characters in plays and poems.

**mothers' tongue**: mother tongue (women are not taught foreign languages); but also they are only taught to the level of their mothers' education.

**engross**: associated with 'monopoly', possess exclusively.


PAGE 171

**fallows**: ploughed land.

**laudatories**: eulogies.

**meed**: reward.


PAGE 172

**traduce**: slander (the reason for the attack on slander is that in that society a woman's

PAGE 172 CONTINUED

social place was supposed to depend on her reputation for virtue and chastity. It did not depend on what the woman could do or make. The happiness and well-being of her personal life thus rested only on what was said; she was a victim of language, and could be destroyed by slander).

**cordial**: what follow are proverbs.
**cogging**: fawning, wheedling.
**apish**: affected, foolish.
**may-games**: objects of ridicule (from May Day sports).
**frantics**: lunatics.


PAGE 173
**nominated**: named.
**politic**: prudent (ironic here).
**pot ... pate**: to be drunk.
**dumps**: fits of depression.
**beray**: dirty.
**trull**: prostitute.


PAGE 174
**one ... another**: a proverb denoting that times are bad.
**Pharisee**: from Luke xviii.11 (the story of the Pharisee and the publican praying).
**conditions**: characters or social circumstances.
**roar**: machismo playing (roaring boys were bullying young male show-offs).
**white and red, etc.**: highly conventional male descriptions of female beauty.
**puff-paste**: insubstantial.
**rush-breaker**: someone not man enough to hold a lance, only a rush.
**Josinqua**: I have no idea about this story, it may be invented.
**carpet captain**: another image of unmanliness – a captain of bedrooms not battlefields (the pamphlet becomes very interested in proper manliness).
**periwig-frizzled**: a wig in tight curls.
**frounced**: curled or pleated.
**geometrical**: of clothes, hanging stiffly.
**curious**: fastidious, pedantic.
**curried**: groomed, well combed.
**printed**: of a ruff, properly pleated.
**Implement**: a person acting as a tool to someone else's desires. With all this foregoing description compare Taylor again: 'A complimental courtier that in his French, Italian and Spanish cringes, congees and courtesies would bend his body' (*Wit and Mirth*) – alliteration is a feature of Taylor's style.


PAGE 175
**foist**: fraudulently allege (also 'cog').
**roundelays**: songs with refrains.
**posies**: short verse mottos (spelt poesies in original).
**lime-twigs**: used to trap birds.
**blessings ... hand**: disadvantageous 'blessings'.
**discourses**: again the idea that women are moulded by social treatment and by language.
**worser place**: hell.
**Phrygia**: where Troy was in Asia Minor.
**Ilion**: Ilium, Troy.
**knights ... post**: perjurers; those hired to give false evidence.


PAGE 176
**pasquils**: lampoons.

PAGE 176 CONTINUED

**Ovid and Aretine:** Pietro Aretino (1492–1556) had a special reputation for lewd writings and was attacked almost as regularly by women writers as the Roman poet Ovid.

**gossips:** female friends invited to be present at a birth; godparents.

**emblaze:** publicly declare (often of notoriety).

**issue or fistula:** bodily discharge/sewer; suppurating ulcer.

**Laodiceans:** famous for apathy and indifference.

**cringes:** creeping bows (compare this passage with that quoted above from *Wit and Mirth*).

**marmosetical:** apish, foolish.

PAGE 177

**ingurgitating maw:** guzzling stomach.

**compliment:** flattery.

**superstition:** false religion (Catholicism); this passage is a satirical commonplace and the pamphlet seems to be wandering far from its initial theme (Taylor wrote pamphlets about 'false' religions).

**Heliogabalus:** Roman emperor (b. 205) who encouraged sun worship – Taylor says: 'He in his court did cause a stews [brothel] be made,/ Whereas *cum privilegio* whores did trade' (*A Common Whore*).

**Caligula:** Roman ruler (37–41) notorious for autocracy and cruelty, had incest with his sister.

**Haman:** plotted to massacre the Jews and prevented by Esther.

**Julian:** (332–63) the atheist, an emperor who encouraged pagan worship.

**Cain:** the murderer of his brother.

**Iscariot:** betrayer of Christ.

**Ahab:** husband of Jezebel, influenced by her pagan beliefs.

**Achitophel:** conspired with **Absalom** against Absalom's father, King David.

**Rabsheka:** title of the Assyrian official sent to demand the surrender of Jerusalem.

**Nebuchadnezzar:** king of Babylon who captured Jerusalem.

**Holofernes:** enemy commander slain by Judith.

**Jeroboam:** rebelled against Solomon.

**Pharoah:** responsible for keeping the Jews in captivity.

**Nimrod:** founder of Nineveh.

PAGE 178

**Cham:** the son cursed by Noah.

**Belshazzar:** last king of Babylon.

**Goliath:** slain by David.

**Esau:** a symbol of those whom God rejects.

**Achan:** looted after the assault on Jericho.

**Gehazi:** Elisha's servant who took a gift his master had refused.

**Manasseh:** idolatrous elder son of Joseph who lost the right of the first born.

**Sisera:** Canaanite general opposed by Deborah.

**Shimei:** cursed David and approved Absalom's rebellion.

**Amon:** idolatrous son of Manasseh.

**Nabal:** refused hospitality to David's troops.

**Herod:** responsible for the Massacre of the Innocents.

**Caiaphas:** high priest before whom Jesus was tried.

**Ananias:** (Annus in original) president of Sanhedrin when Paul was brought before it.

**Pilate:** symbolically washed his hands of Jesus' blood, then delivered him to be crucified.

**Elymas:** or Bar Jesus, a false prophet in the *Acts of the Apostles*.

**Domitian:** (ruled 81–96) son of emperor Vespasian, initiated a reign of terror.

PAGE 178 CONTINUED

**Catiline**: (d. 62) conspirator against Rome, attacked by Cicero.

**Sulla**: (b. 138 BC) took Rome in war against **Marius** (b. 157 BC), both of them responsible for various massacres.

**Sardanapalus**: (1st half 9th C. BC) Taylor says: 'Was to his whores such a companion,/ That he in their attire did sew and sing' (*Common Whore*).

**projects and monopolies**: the great Jacobean economic abuses – projectors would set up wild financial schemes which frequently diddled people (*plus ça change*); favourite targets of Taylor, see e.g., *The Complaint of M. Tenter-hook the Projector and Sir Thomas Dodger the Patentee* (1641).

**secondary**: because the primary being comes from God.

**pen-posts**: messengers (carrying what has been penned).

**Fortune is blind**: thus traditionally represented.

**Minerva**: goddess associated with wisdom; the whole sentence means that good poets sometimes have skill, but their merits are often ignored by the wealthy.

**mongrel**: interesting word here – is it an attempt to retrieve the language of the Swetnam battles?

**affectate**: affected, stuck up.

**squirt**: as with diarrhoea.

**pendragonists**: tyrants.

**pestiferous**: pestilential, noxious.

**jacksquitterers**: those with diarrhoea.


PAGE 179

**pot-companion**: drinking companion ('companions' in original).

**composure**: composition.

**jennets**: small Spanish horses.

**purperated**: misprint for 'perpetuated'?

**proditors**: betrayers.


PAGE 180

**strict ... string**: Ariadne fell in love with Theseus and assisted him in finding his way out of the labyrinth by suggesting that he unravel string as he goes in.

**game**: sex.

**when the mistress ...**: all that follows is a fairly close résumé of the various lectures contained in *Juniper* (the mistress will make her apprentice so hungry he will leap at a crust).

**rattle-baby**: a young chattering child.

**rattle**: scold, censure; the phrase seems to mean that the scold will scold on unprevented.

**wild-cat**: the wife asks the husband if the house is a wild-cat because he seems not to want to stay in it.


PAGE 181

**Furmity**: frumenty (wheat boiled in milk).

**Bag-pudding**: a pudding boiled in a bag; also a clown.

**Woodcock ... Horsehead**: all more or less names for idiots.

**mother a midwife**: a very strange insult to find in a pamphlet genuinely by women (even at this period).

**rake-shame**: dissolute man.

**under the rose**: in strict confidence; all that follow are proverbs.

**M.P.**: presumably the famous ballad-writer Martin Parker, but I cannot trace the ballad.

**bombast**: inflated language – hence to hector?

**baffle**: disgrace, cheat.

**canvass**: from hawking, to entangle in a net.

PAGE 181 CONTINUED
**bastinado**: beat on the soles of the feet.
**baneful**: poisonous.
**standish**: ink pot.
**sand-dust**: used for blotting.
**faces upwards**: lying on their backs while copulating.

PAGE 182
**marine muse**: the jokes follow from Taylor's soubriquet 'the Water Poet'.
**Puddle Dock**: in Blackfriars.
**Ionia**: centre of ancient Greek culture.
**Ivy Bridge**: in Ivy Lane off the Strand.
**Mnemosyne**: mother of the muses.
**Milford Lane**: off the Strand.
**Terpsichore**: the muse of dance.
**Trig Stairs**: in Trig Lane, Upper Thames Street. It should be added that Taylor cultivated the image of the Water Poet with special knowledge of the river business.
**sibyls**: thought to have powers of prophecy (usually there are ten).
**a-woolgathering**: compare Swetnam: 'when I first began to write this book, my wits were gone a-woolgathering', p. A3ʳ; compare also Munda's mockery of the phrase, p. 138. These may be coincidence, but I doubt it: Swetnam was reprinted in 1637.
**in this witty**: the text is corrupt here; something is missing – I don't know how much.
**convented**: summoned for trial.
**meriads**: probably nereids, sea-nymphs.
**maid-marian**: a figure not confined to Robin Hood stories but present in morris dances and May games.
**cudgel oil … sauce**: elaborations of the idea of the bitter medicine.
**Astraea**: goddess of justice who left the world at the end of the golden age.

PAGE 183
**Gregory**: a gallant, a fool.
**wise woman's 'Juniper'**: probably a reference to the last of the Juniper lectures, by 'an ancient grand Gossip over a cup of sack and strong waters' – a story of a widow who humiliated her husbands. This seems to be a piece of self-advertisement by Taylor.
**jerk**: whip, scourge, satirise.
**Nicostrate**: Greek name for Carmenta, a prophetic divinity with a temple in Rome.
**Caripena**: I cannot trace this, may be misprint for Carmena (see **Nicostrate**).
**Mucia**: (fl. 60 BC) elder daughter of Q. Mucius Scaevola, renowned for her conversational excellence (spelt Musaea in original).
**Meroe**: either Merope, one of the Pleiades, or Myro, fable writer from Rhodes.
**Sosipatra**: Neoplatonic prophetess from the region of Ephesus, married to the philosopher Eustathios.
**Cleitagora**: lyric poet mentioned by Aristophanes in *The Wasps* (422 BC).
**Aspasia Milesia**: (fl. 445 BC) lover of Pericles, her house was a literary and intellectual centre in Athens.
**Praxilla Syconia**: (fl. 451 BC) poet of Sicyon, famous for her metrical variety.
**Myro Byzantia**: (fl. 300 BC?) mother of poet Homerus, wrote elegiac, epic and lyric poems.
**Corinna Thebana**: (fl. 500 BC?) lyric poet, contemporary of Pindar whom she defeated five times for the prize in the public games.

PAGE 183 CONTINUED

**Hortensia:** (fl. *c.* 55 BC) defended the wealthy women of Rome before the triumvirs (albeit against special taxation).

**Hipparchia:** (*c.* 328 BC) married, despite parental pressure, the Cynic Crates, wrote treatises.

**Claudia:** a famous vestal virgin.

**Cornelia:** (fl. 180 BC) Scipio's daughter, very learned, wrote fine letters.

**Apollo Argentaria:** Argentaria Polla, widow of the Roman poet Lucan (d. 65 BC); a patron of the poet Martial.

**Proba Valeria:** poet greatly admired in the Middle Ages, but little is known about her (may be Falconia Proba, fl. 379?).

**Vittoria Collumna:** a Latinised spelling of Vittoria Colonna (1490–1547), aristocrat and poet, associated with church reform, inspired some of Michelangelo's poems.

**Marcella Romana:** (end 4th C.) friend of Jerome; centre of a circle of religious and intellectual women.

**Bridewell:** a prison.

**crocodiles:** those who express false sorrow.

**Franion:** a reckless gallant or lover.

**lose:** printed 'loosed'.

**mackerel:** bawd, procuress.

**distich:** verse couplet.

PAGE 184

**wiseacres ... Slobber-chops:** all these names indicate foolishness, idiocy, half-wittedness, boorishness, lumpishness.

**Corydon:** typical pastoral name.

**Scylla:** a sea-monster opposite the whirlpool **Charybdis** (see Sowernam, p. 108 for a similar phrase).

**Icarus:** escaped from Crete by flying, but flew too near the sun and melted the wax holding his wings together.

**stomachs:** appetites.

**trencher:** wooden or metal plate.

PAGE 185

**meacocks:** weaklings, cowards (Swetnam uses a similar phrase, which in turn comes from Lyly).

**fish-wife:** fish-wives had a reputation for bad language.

**Anna:** prophetess mentioned in Luke ii.36.

**old law ... barren:** for barrenness as a curse from God, see e.g. Genesis xxx.2.

**children without husbands:** the shocking aspect of the quite widespread stories of Amazons derived partly from their supposed controlled mating with men once a year for the purpose only of reproduction not pleasure.

PAGE 186

**Sarah, Rachel, Leah:** Genesis xxx.4, Genesis xvi.3, Genesis xxx.9 (both Rachel and Leah were Jacob's women: thus the ways of patriarchy).

# Endpiece

When he writes a spoof female reply, Taylor takes from women their voice; and he mocks that voice by giving it the comic name of Mary Tattlewell. It is a further, and powerful, blow in the continuing male war against the women they described as 'scolds'. The scold was not just a hysterical and irrational railer. In a world where the ideal woman was quiet and submissive, any woman who criticised that male world and who asserted her authority in it was a scold. Taylor has a mother tell her daughter: 'if you can make such use of your tongue as the most part of wise women do nowadays you may awe the good man with his goods and family like an empress' (*Juniper*, p. 51). The attack on scolds is about power in the family and in society. The husband is advised to 'tame' his wife if he is not to be the laughing stock of his neighbours. Such taming, says Swetnam, justifies male violence against women:

> Is it not strange of what kind of mettle a woman's tongue is made of, that neither correction can chastise nor fair means quiet; for there is a kind of venom in it that neither by fair means nor foul they are to be ruled. All beasts by man are made tame, but a woman's tongue will never be tame ... Therefore as a sharp bit curbs a froward horse, even so a cursed woman must be roughly used; but if women could hold their tongues, then many times men would their hands. (Swetnam, p. 40)

'Unwomanly' aggressiveness is only one of the things wrong with the scold; another is that she associates with other women: 'every woman hath one especial gossip at the least which she doth love and affect above all the rest, and unto her she runneth with all the secrets she knoweth' (Swetnam, p. 41) – which justifies not telling a woman any secrets. ('Gossip' here means female companion; that it came to acquire derogatory overtones demonstrates the endemic sexism.) Taylor's 'mother' character complains to her gossip 'that I was restrained of that freedom and liberty which I had a mind to have,

195

and debarred of that predominance and command which women are ambitious to aspire to' (*Juniper*, p. 51). The scold's freedom of tongue is an emblem of social freedom. Both have to be curtailed: the good wife stays submissively at home. Swetnam advises the virtuous woman, if approached by any other man, to say:

> when I was a maid I was at the disposition of my parents, but now I am married I am at the pleasure of my husband; therefore you were best speak to him and to know his mind what I shall do. And if her husband be out of the way, let her always behave herself as if he were present. (Swetnam, p. 55)

It is a formula for complete psychological domination: the husband thinks for his wife, she is never allowed to act as if she were out of his presence.

Irrational as these ideas are they acquire a semblance of normality because they are repeated over the years (despite the gaps between them, Swetnam closely echoes Lyly, and Taylor echoes Swetnam). The works in which they recur are linked in a chain that imprisons women. There is no female tradition; male satirists attack female community. Swetnam employs the bogey of evil reputation to scare off women from associating together:

> let a woman avoid so much as may be the company of a woman which hath an ill name, for many of them endeavour by their evil fashions and dishonest speech to bring others to do as they do, and many of them wish in their hearts that all women were like unto themselves. (p. 54)

It is in the face of loss of reputation and being branded a scold that the women pamphleteers write. The male writers make the tradition and trot out the received ideas; the women have to intervene and break open their space.

And it is not just traditions of male writing they face. We have noticed how male printers play a major part in the publication of the women's pamphlets. These examples of women's writing are controlled by, and to a certain extent shaped or distorted by, the male-owned process that publishes them. Women's thoughts, men's books. The last pamphlet has shown that even the idea of argument between women and men can be taken over, and exploited, by men. Women's issues are allowed a niche in patriarchal society because they sell. Reader, you and I are perhaps having the same thought: am I, the male editor of these women's pamphlets, acting out yet again the role of John Okes?

I think I am, so I want to hand over to more women's voices. The first are two examples, chosen from several, of 'ordinary' wives trying to do something to redress the downright exploitation they have encountered at their husbands' hands by sending petitions to one of the most powerful men in the land. What follows are summaries taken from the *Calendar of State Papers Domestic*:

November 18, 1639. Petition of Honor, wife of George Cotton, to Archbishop Laud. Complains of the ill-treatment of her husband, who upon her marriage promised to settle on her for jointure £30 a year land; but now, having wasted and consumed his property all but £20 per annum, paid him by Nicholas Pledall, has left her and her children ready to perish. Prays order for her relief.

March 17, 1638. Petition of Mary Woely, wife of Richard Woely, of St Botolph without Bishopsgate, to Archbishop Laud. Petitioner brought unto her husband (to whom she has borne 12 children) £400 in marriage and £30 a year, which he still possesses, and has been his wife 28 years. For 2¾ years her husband has refused to live with her, having three times turned her out of his dwelling-house, she not knowing any just cause. He denies competent means, and would enforce her to take a chamber to live by herself, without any of her children, and upon such poor allowance as will not suffice, although he has £200 per annum coming in by reason of the premises. Prays order that two of her children may live with her, and that her husband may allow competent means for her and them.

These women were acting in isolation, pathetically pleading with a male-controlled state to alleviate their distress. Theirs are lost and silenced voices. When women spoke with sufficient force for their message to be public they spoke as a community of women, and as women who were no longer going to entrust what they had to say to men. They spoke as women together for women together: the Leveller women's petition to Parliament, 7 May, 1649, signed by ten thousand women:

Since we are assured of our creation in the image of God, of an interest in Christ equal unto men, as also of a proportionate share in the freedoms of the commonwealth, we cannot but wonder and grieve that we should appear so despicable in your eyes as to be thought unworthy to petition or represent our grievances to this honourable House. Have we not an equal interest with the men of this nation in those liberties and securities contained in the *Petition of Right*, and other the good laws of the land? Are any of our lives, limbs, liberties or goods to be taken from us, no more than from men, but by due process of law and conviction of twelve sworn men of the neighbourhood? And can you imagine us to be so sottish or stupid as not to perceive or not to be sensible when daily those strong defences of our peace and welfare are broken down and trod underfoot by force and arbitrary power?

# Select Bibliography and FurtherReading

Anger, Jane, *Jane Anger Her Protection for Women* (1589) facsimile in Bodleian Library; Huntington Library.

Lyly, John, *Euphues the Anatomy of Wit* in *Complete Works*, ed. R. Warwick Bond (Oxford, 1902).

Munda, Constantia (pseud.), *The Worming of a Mad Dogge* (1617) Bodleian Library, British Library, Huntington Library.

Sowernam, Ester (psued.), *Ester hath hang'd Haman* (1617) Bodleian Library, British Library, Huntington Library.

Speght, Rachel, *A Mouzell for Melastomus* (1617), Bodleian Library, British Library, Huntington Library.

Swetnam, Joseph, *The Arraignment of Lewd, idle, froward and unconstant women* (1615; frequent reprints) Bodleian Library, British Library, Huntington Library.

Tattle-well, Mary and Joan Hit-him-home (Taylor, John?) *The Women's Sharpe Revenge* (1640), Bodleian Library, incomplete.

There is very little on the pamphlets:

Dusinberre, Juliet, *Shakespeare and the Nature of Woman* (Macmillan, 1975), just touches the subject.

Kahin, Helen, 'Jane Anger and John Lyly' in *Modern Language Quarterly*, viii (1947), p. 31.

Shepherd, Simon, *Amazons and Warrior Women* (Harvester, 1981) fuller, but hideously expensive.

There is much more on women and society in general:

Oakly, Ann, 'Wisewoman and Medicine Man' in *The Rights and Wrongs of Women*, ed. Mitchell and Oakley (Penguin, 1976) on midwives and childbirth, but not confined to the period of the pamphlets.

Rowbotham, Sheila, *Hidden from History* (Pluto, 1973).

Thomas, Keith, 'The Double Standard' in *Journal of the History of Ideas*, xx (1959), p. 195, for the double standard of gender morality.

Wrightson, Keith, *English Society 1580–1680* (Hutchinson, 1982).

# Name Index

# Subject Index